MARK CHILD

The author is a young Southern writer who has been
Features Editor of *Southern Living* magazine and now
works for *Atlanta Constitution*. He is currently at
work on his second novel, also set in the Southern
states. He lives in Atlanta, Georgia.

Mark Childress

A WORLD MADE OF FIRE

Copyright © 1985 by Mark Childress

First published in Great Britain in 1985 by Hodder and Stoughton Ltd

Sceptre edition 1987

Sceptre is an imprint of Hodder and Stoughton Paperbacks, a division of Hodder and Stoughton Ltd

British Library C.I.P.

Childress, Mark
  A world made of fire.
  I. Title
813'.54[F]   PS3553.H486

ISBN 0-340-40315-2

Printed and bound in Great Britain for Hodder and Stoughton Paperbacks, a division of Hodder and Stoughton Ltd., Mill Road, Dunton Green, Sevenoaks, Kent (Editorial Office: 47 Bedford Square, London, WC1 3DP) by Richard Clay (The Chaucer Press) Ltd., Bungay, Suffolk. Photoset by Rowland Phototypesetting Ltd., Bury St Edmunds, Suffolk.

For Grandmother, Bill, all those who cared
Also for John Logue

Smoke came unexpected to the world.
— Charles McNair,
'The Creation of Smoke'

With relief, with humiliation, with terror,
he understood that he also was an illusion,
that someone else was dreaming him.
— Jorge Luis Borges,
'The Circular Ruins'

1909

ONE

All the children were up the hall in pairs and threes, asleep. Callie Bates tipped back her chair and set heels on the hearth, breathing in sweet spitting hickory, searching the fire for faces she knew she would find. Her right cheek was starting to parch, and she shifted, so she might wrinkle more evenly. One log stuck out a tongue of blue flame and she saw her eldest girl, Stella, there, laughing. Beyond, in the yellow fire dance, she saw William, and past him, the squabbling twins, and in twinkling explosions, the littlest girls . . . She pressed a hand to her side, feeling a fullness within the muslin.

Across her back a muscle spoke of stooping and churning, of lifting her children, of years when her back was the only strong one in the house. She had spent the last twenty years straining, and waiting – for Sundays, for him. For his face at the door.

She cracked a pecan on the bone in her hand. He was late. Every Sunday he tapped on the glass in the door, as faithful to Callie those nights as he was to his wife in the week. To Callie, he brought a fire. She yearned for his touch, soft as sifted white flour, the pulse of his heart in his fingers. Now it was midnight on Sunday, a nameless red road in a time before lights came that far to the country, and Callie was waiting.

Tonight she had news.

She felt it crumpled in her pocket, its plain hard message embossed in her mind for all time. A gangly boy brought it six miles from town on a bicycle with a bell, then waited to hear what it said, as if that was his job. She read it aloud. His eyes brightened with tears, but Callie's own eyes never changed. She found him a dime and he left, whistling.

She took some small comfort from huddled old things – the

Regulator clock slicing time into bits, the stern whitebeard faces in gray tarnished frames, the pie safe, the chair. She found herself drawn to the sideboard. Its warped drawer resisted, but she squeezed her hand in and found it – the crystal, concealed in its red velvet scarf. An old sphere of glass, colored green, with dye swirls and uneven bubbles inside, a gift from Brown Mary, who delivered her babies. She'd said it had power, and Callie had almost believed. She could hear Mary's hooo! bubble up from the glass. The thing had the magic of a window revealed in a room that has always been dark.

She carried it back to her chair, unswaddling it. It glowed in her hand, green and cool. She saw the fire flash inside it, then her own face as it was, hardbeaten and forty, like a fieldhand grown old.

Yet in its reflection her hair was still pretty. She had not yet gone to fat. Her chin held the line of a smooth younger face. Maybe Callie looked twenty to him, by the light of her lamp in the barn. Else what did he see in her, why did he come?

She answered before she could ask it: the first child. The pain they shared, old tired shame. That memory scattered her mood. The crystal stared up, without life, so she wrapped it back in its velvet and put it away.

In the kitchen she found two cold wedges of pone. She crumbled them into a tumbler, then poured in thick buttermilk so the cornbread made a foam, and sweet pills of yellow bobbed up to the top. She ate with a long slender spoon, watching the andirons' trembling shadows, like a pair of large dogs. At that instant she heard the glass quiver, the tapping.

She hushed him through the tiny window, closed the hall door, took up her faded shawl, and went out.

Wind blistered in, as cold as blue light. Leaves shattered rattling over the yard. He stood in the glow of her lamp, unspeaking, his eyes concealed by his gray hat's moon brim. 'You'll turn to ice,' he said, making a cloud.

'Shh,' Callie said, 'just hold me, just please.'

His touch was the end of her waiting, a melting of pain, of the seven long days since the last touch. She marveled at how bodies match. They stood that way, breathing.

'Can't we go in and just talk?' he said.

'Hush.' She pulled from him. 'Let's go to the barn.'

'Just one time,' he said, 'I would love to just sit in your house, drink a cup of your tea, and look in on our babies.' He coughed.

'But they might wake up,' she said. 'You ought not wish for things that can't be.'

He detected her tone. 'Let's go to the barn,' he agreed. 'They all asleep?'

'Sweet angels,' she said, 'but I can't stay long. They're up and down all night.'

They balanced together across the cold grass, under great swaying branches, like town lovers out for a walk with the moon. The barn door gave in with a groan. Three curious cows turned their heads.

Callie hung the lamp on a nail and went to him. His fingertips caused her to shudder. 'I miss you so bad, through the week,' she said, moving away, seeking strength for her news. She opened her mouth but no more words came out.

He watched her there, struggling, said, 'I miss you too.'

She shook her head, hushed him again. She could not look into his face. She reached down in her pocket and felt it, all wadded, a paper the color of lemons. He took it, unfolded it, smoothed out its wrinkles. She held up the lamp. The words made him wince.

DEAR WIFE PREACHER BATES

GREATLY SADDENED STRANGER INFORMS TRAGIC HEART DEATH PREACHER JOSEPH A BATES DURING FINE SERMON BELZONI MISS STOP BURIED NEARBY ELM STOP EFFECTS TO COME

REGRETFUL SERVANT
W A VOSS

He moistened his crackly lips. 'Poor man.'

She took the wire from him, jealously. 'Oh he aint poor,' she said. 'He's got some kind of a heaven at last.'

Callie had not seen the Preacher since July the summer

before, when he rode in with money and stayed for a week. He always sat muttering in this dark barn, fixing harnesses.

Once she tried asking him how he had been. He started in on his one sermon, against a wild hateful God casting out demons, against all the bad souls befouling this earth. He prayed for salvation for both of them. After that, she let him be.

He was a Bates just like Callie, from the opposite end of the same proud old family, gone down to dust. A great-aunt assembled their marriage; Joseph was fifty, alone, and Callie had her own young shame to put right. No one but Callie noticed that Joseph was eaten alive with his God, like a mange. She knew it, and knew it would spread to her if she let it, but she had no escape. After the wedding, she realized Joseph was terrified of her, as well. They spent not a night in the same bed. He left on his buggy, and came back in summer, and left again. Callie's children were Bateses, legitimate Bates, yet he never asked her who the father might be.

'Fell dead in his *sermon*,' came words in the barn.

Her eyes found him. 'You talk like you already heard.'

'I knew it would happen one day; so did you. You had to know. He was pure crazy! Craziest man in all south Alabama. You can't boil the way he did, all your life, and not end up boiled over, someday . . .'

'I had a dream I remember last night,' Callie said, 'but it was of you. Not of him. I dreamt you come in to where I was asleep. You didn't say boo, didn't touch me not once, but you stayed. You stood with me. You sat in a chair by the fire, and just waited.' She brought up a hand to her eyes.

His face found a smile. 'Well, I have done that, hadn't I, sweetie . . . six times. Six sweet angels.'

'Seven,' she said, 'with the first.'

'Seven.'

Her voice held a chill. 'I aint forgot the first one,' she said.

'Now just wait –'

'. . . and here anytime it could come to be eight. I'm feelin all poorly, and wrong.' Her eyes went away.

That news struck him hard, she could see. 'Oh,' he said. His hands sought pockets. 'When?'

'I don't know yet, but I will soon. Now won't that just be a sight, me a widow, and swoll up with child.' She folded her arms. 'I give our last dime to the boy brung the wire.'

'I'll give you money.'

'Oh no,' she said. 'I won't start that.'

'But, sweetie. There's no room left for you to be proud.'

'Oh yes sir, there is,' Callie said, her voice rising, 'when only thing I got that's left me is pride.' The cows turned to listen.

She prevented his embrace. He buttoned his coat, went to the door, then he turned and came back, took her up.

The kiss confounded her. It felt like farewell. 'I got to go get him, the Preacher,' she said. 'Bring him back here, to his home.'

'Let him rest,' the man said. 'At least now you know where he is.'

His words struck like a slap. 'You get out of here.'

'Well it's true,' he said softly. 'He never deserved you.'

'And I reckon you do . . .' She tasted a fear then – that he might heed her words and leave, and never come back. 'All these years,' she said, 'all of these Sundays. And whatever for?'

He looked up. 'For you,' he said. 'Oh, and for me. And for them. Our babies. And for the first one.'

She reached for his arm. 'You reckon it all could be punishment, all these bad years? For that? I wonder –'

'Callie. There's no such thing. There can't be. Not for a thing that was right.'

'Oh no, it was wrong –'

'It was *not*.' His eyes leapt up in flames. 'It was all we could do.'

'You can't still come here,' she said, 'not when this child . . . There's no Preacher now, to keep folks from talkin.'

'Hell with folks. Talk is just talk. I'll come,' he said. 'When have I not?'

'But not if – another child . . .'

He nudged the door. 'I'll come.' He could have reached in for another swift kiss, but his eyes showed a change. Just that fast she felt him leaving, and gone, and coming back never.

The wind killed her lamp. They hurried back over the yard. 'Wait,' she whispered, and went into the house. She found the green crystal and took it back out to him. 'Here,' she said, shivering, 'you take this thing, and you keep it. It's my prizest thing. You hold it, and think about me.'

He slipped it into his coat without looking. 'I'll get you something,' he said, swinging up to his saddle. She felt a vast distance interrupt the air between them. One snap of his reins took him off.

Callie's shoulders sank, and her eyes. She stood in the cold until the sound of him faded away.

The house was warm as morning dreams. She smelled him still, tasted his taste on her tongue. She felt his firm press in the flesh of her arms. With a calm that fell over her then like a quilt, she settled by the dying fire, to search it, to seek in its colors the face of the first child, to watch for the face of a child on its way.

1910

TWO

He did not tap at the window again. Once or twice in the daytime he stopped by, pretending an errand. He stayed in the yard, staring down as if his whispered apologies and excuses were written in sand.

Sunday became just a night of the week.

Callie waited through the long months, and the swelling. By August, she felt all trembly and flushed, so she knew the new child was near. Near her center, she felt its impatient tumbling. She stonily prayed for that first twist of gut – last labor, last child, the last pain. Bring it on. And the last of all waiting, she swore. She kept up her chores and invented new ones, to smooth out her nerves. She chased off Brown Mary, the promise of help. She scolded so much that the children hid from her.

An aching dry sun blasted down from the sky. It was too hot to think or to smell, or go in, or do anything but raise the hoe, and bring it back down. She was all by herself in a patch out to the east of the house, working a long row of peas.

Her heart missed a beat and she knew. She felt just a twinge, a descent, like a flood. She left her hoe chinked in the stiff red clay, and fled through the blackberries, up the long hill. Thorns scratched her legs as she ran, but she felt no real pain. Pitching forward, the bulk of her baby so thrusting, so *down*, she collapsed by the great pecan tree in the side yard.

In the barn, Stella saw. She flung the milk pail away, and ran for the tree.

The horrified children came out from their hiding and closed in a circle. Stella knelt, took up a palmful of sand, raised one fainted wrist and scrubbed at it, scrubbing and crying out 'Mama,' and 'Mama,' and 'Mama' again.

The others stared, then took up the word in a soft little chant.

They all copied Stella – even William, who was a year older, and a boy. The twins stood back with mouths open. 'Brother,' said Stella, 'go run fetch the wagon.'

William unfroze, and ran off.

Suddenly Callie fluttered awake, fumbling in her skirts. Her face was bleached of its color. 'You go – oh, my great God . . .' She swooned off again.

Stella let the wrist drop in the sand. The awestruck children mumbled closer. As if it was something they had rehearsed, they made a sling with their arms, to lift Callie up to the bed of the flat-wagon. Stella climbed to the seat beside William. 'Yall go in the house now and – *listen to me* – go back in. Charlie Boot, you're in charge. Don't you set one foot out, none of you.'

'But I'm as old as he is,' came the whine from Foster, then Charlie Boot said no he wasn't. They started up. Stella said they were both boss, and to get in the house like she said.

William raised a cane pole, brought it down. After that, Stella heard only the steady slow plod of the mare, which ignored all their begging and kept to its laggardly pace. William flailed out, jumped down, and yanked at the traces and cursed. The mare turned to regard him. He climbed up again. They lumbered away.

They bounded through ruts and old ditches, and splashed through the creek at the foot of their hill. The chill calls of bluejays fell down from the trees. Their tiny road joined with a wider one, which led to the hardtop pike into Camellia. For all their long miles in the hot open air, they never saw one other soul.

Then they were there.

The doctor came ambling down from his porch, mopping his face with a rag, beginning a greeting. When he saw Callie, he stopped where he was. He took just a heartbeat to gather himself, climbed up to the wagon, and lifted her skirts. His silver-rim spectacles fell from his nose. 'Everne!' he cried. 'Come get these children!'

His wife came running, and dragging at Stella, and pleading with William, and got them inside.

The child appeared to be dead. It was the soft gray color of

a quail. The doctor sliced the cord, and placed it off to one side.
He fished from his bag a blue capsule, snapped it under Callie's
nose.

Her limpid eyes swam open. The recognition grew, then the
knowledge, and fear. A lone pearl of sweat went down her
cheek. 'Oh bless me,' she said, 'and another one yet. Did it
live?'

Doctor Dannelly did not answer.

The infant made a squeak. It was wriggling. Deep blue. The
doctor took it up in his hands and ran for the door, for his wife.
'Take him,' he said, and went back to the yard.

Everne wrapped the child in her apron, concealing it from
Stella and her brother standing in the hall. She disappeared down
the hall to the doctor's study, shut the door, laid the thing on a
white-lacquered table. She searched for some kind of swaddling.

Everne knew of Callie, the last of the Bateses. A long string
of infants had sapped her of nurturing juices a new baby needs.
Poor thing. And a boy. He was doomed.

She glanced through the window to see her husband at the
wagon, speaking in one of his lecturing poses. The rag was now
wrapped on one finger, polishing in his ear. The girl and her
brother had escaped the house and stood with grave faces,
listening.

A sharp hiccup below sent a thrill through Everne. The child
shone hot and purple on the table. It waved its small arms, and
fought for a breath. Its face was a tiny weird mask of frustration.

She had to hold back a scream. Be a nurse, she told herself,
now, your duty is thinking at bad times like this. Your heart
must be still. She twisted her fingers, drumming home the
lesson, watching the child in its struggle. It seemed to be
winning. She'd never have thought it could live.

The doctor's boots thundered down the hollow hall. Everne
put the child in his cupped hands. 'Look, he's alive!' she breathed.
'You take him.'

She wandered back to the window, absently wiping her fingers
on her skirt. Through the hot wavery sunlight, she watched as
the painfully thin boy got back up on the wagon. His sister
climbed into the bed, with their mother. Everne realized what

they meant to do. 'Oh Bester, good Lord, look, they're going
to leave!' She started to run out, to stop them, but his eyes
stopped her.

'Let them go,' he said, in a strange cold voice she did not
know.

'But, Bester –'

'Everne, calm down. Run back and bring me a cup of strong
tea.' His hands hovered over the child, but he chose not to
touch.

'She shouldn't ride off in a wagon,' his wife said, 'not just
delivered – this child –'

'Missus Dannelly.' He brought his hands up, took off his
spectacles, folded them, tucked them away. 'I told them to take
her home,' he said. 'There's no place here. She delivered fine.
I told that girl of hers what to do. She's done it – what is it, five
or six times. I've done all I can.'

'But *him* . . .'

'Everne. I told them he's stillborn.'

She dropped her eyes. The infant's shade of blue had lessened;
its breathing was quick, fluttery, but stronger now. 'But he's
not,' she said. 'Look. Look how alive he is.'

'Well, he may live to a hundred. May die by nightfall,' said
the doctor. 'I'll do what I can. He won't make it. Too little. She
barely can feed all she has. She's widowed. And poor. Don't you
see? If this child's meant to live, then he will. If not, then not.
Now you bring me my tea.'

THREE

The wagon jounced under the fingers of trees, a forest of green hands above, shielding the road from the fast-failing sun. The stillness gave way to the creak of the wheels and the mare's easy rhythm. Stella cushioned her mother's head in her lap, hearing his words again, like a song in her head: Go home now, go home, just drive gentle and slow, just take care that you drive just as slow as you can, and be sweet when she wakes, use these pills for the pain, now that poor child is gone and it's nobody's fault. I'll be out . . .

They passed through a region of gray stunted trees, with tops broken off by some old vicious wind. They rounded the bend by the Gibsons' small house, starting up the slow red rise to their own. As the wheels dunked in the creek, Callie awoke with a soft startled cry. Stella nestled her close, her thighs numb with the weight, and bent low to speak. 'It's all right, Mama, we near home now.' She leaned back. 'William! Slow up. She's awake.'

A little sound came then from Callie, a sad note like music. It hung in the air. 'Tell me,' she said, 'tell me what it was. Boy or a girl.'

Stella stroked her mother's hair. 'He said a boy.'

Callie sighed, breathing out sorrow. 'I had his name all picked out,' she said. 'He would of been Jack Otis.'

FOUR

Thirty miles north, the great planters once ruled the broad plains spread with silt and great wealth by the muddy river named Alabama. Two days' ride south, foreigners fished in the swamps of the coast. Between these waters, the land was vast and so well forgotten that one road took travelers through.

The trees were too many for axes to matter. Twenty counties, and twenty small towns, occasional fields scratched open for cotton, some churches, some houses, some farms and some dogs – the rest given over to Negroes and squirrels, and bony cows nudging in scarlet ravines.

No one fought for this place. The War stumbled in once or twice, by mistake, leaving only a sprinkling of young amputees. The woods stayed the same and the lives of the people who lived at its edges. What money there was had been brought from the east and was steadily melting, like ice. White people and Negroes all worshipped a God who was sung to in hymns they made up as they went.

Yet good things abounded. Rich dirt made for gardens that yielded the spreads of noon: crowder peas, fat tomatoes, the okra of slaves, snap beans and pole beans and beans without names, boiling greens, potatoes that grew sweetly amber below. Wild deer and birds did not shy from the hunters. Spring-fed streams brought white lilies in springtime and catfish the whole year around.

The summer sun was a legend. It rose early and stayed up too long, and the only escape was the woods – rampant green, cool as a crawl space, gone foggy with gnats and blueflies. The sun sent down columns of light, as solid as tree trunks. Seven-year locusts set time with their throbbing for the noises of secretive beasts.

Into this place, three days after the child came, Stella led the children out of the dazzling heat. In the woods she had only to keep one eye turned to the little ones tottering, stumbling on roots.

William had stayed behind, to sit with Mama, who slept and woke up, and cried out in her sleep. No one dared mention the one that had died.

The twins, boys of eight, ran off to all sides in search of crawling things they could torment.

'Snake! Snake! Run get him!' sang out Charlie Boot, and Stella saw Foster follow him off the path into the weeds.

'Yall gone get bit,' she called, but they were happy, so she let them run. They were smart enough not to touch bad snakes. She drifted ahead, feeling rich and alive, scolding the girls the way they enjoyed. 'Irene, come on, honey,' she said to the smallest one. 'Get your fingers from out that hole. You don't know what might be down there.'

Irene, who was smudgy, and three, pulled her hand back.

Imogene, the proud little queen at five, let go her big sister's hand and went after the toddler. 'You don't know what's down there, silly,' she said, jerking Irene by the hand. 'Now you come on and mind.'

The children could wander like this just as long as they all looked out after the rest. Stella was happy, after the bad days, to be poking along, not chopping weeds, and not watching the pain in her mother's face. The storm of yesterday scalded away when it fell, but it greened all the leaves and made the air feel thick.

Imogene gripped the child's arm too tight. Irene began whining, so Stella slung her up onto her hip, and found her a pine needle to play with. Stella was so used to babies; for most of her thirteen years, one had been at her hip always, or brushing the backs of her knees. She could no more lose patience with their slaps and catcalls than with the gnats that lit in her ears. She knew where babies came from, how they got here, but the part before that between the man and woman seemed useless and vague, and a chore.

Stella was not pretty, but she had never seen anyone pretty.

She was fair, with smooth pale skin, and good bones from all the milk when she and William were the only children. Callie's cool eyes, blue as an April clear day, were handed down to Stella to see things without blinking. Her shoulders were broad, from the seasons of the stubborn mare, when she took turns with William at dragging the plow. She had strong arms, slender hands, a body that felt nice to stretch. She was older than her age. Her pride was her hair. It went way down her back, and swung gold on days after baths.

'Stop it, baby, now stop,' she said, prying Irene's tiny fingers. 'Don't pull on my hair now, be sweet. Imogene, let go my hand. There's a whole big woods for you to play in.'

Imogene obeyed, but stayed just behind.

'Snake snake snake!' came the scream of the twins.

Charlie Boot leapt out, brandishing a small green wiggler, Foster behind him, one clutched in his fist. They danced circles around, waving their creatures, screeching and sticking out tongues. With squeals that stirred the birds from the trees, the girls scattered.

The twins guffawed. Foster spit, as he was learning to do. 'Let's gooooo!' cheered his brother. They stormed off ahead.

'Come on, girls, now hush now, Irene.' Stella knelt down. 'They aint nothin but play snakes, now you aint ascared. Come on.' She got them all started again. By the time they broke out of the tangly weeds, the boys were stripped naked and shoving each other around in the frigid clear spring.

Stella sank to a soft mossy spot with Irene. They could see the glassy pool and each grain of sand on the bottom, the twins daring each other to greater leaps from the rope, Imogene engrossed in a dance of dragonflies at the mouth of the earth where the water came out. What a lovely thing, simply to let them play on.

'Come on, you sissy,' sang Charlie Boot, 'you're just a chicken, chicken! I did a bellyflop and I'm just twenty minutes oldern you.'

'It'll hurt,' Foster said, clinging to the rope.

'Hurt! Aw, you aint nothin cept an old sissy!'

Foster warmed to the insult. He took in a deep breath and

swung way way out, out over the water. At the highest point he let go, entered feet first, and came up all sputtering. 'So there!' he cried.

Imogene squealed her congratulations.

Charlie Boot waded out to the rope, his twig-skinny arms held up in the warm air. 'That wadn't no bellyflop,' he sulked.

Stella leaned against a tree, stroking the baby's bright curls. If she closed her eyes and let their chatter blend together, she could pick out the distant ky-ree! of a bird, and the tweedling insects, commotion above where two squirrels were tussling.

And then behind her, William.

She whirled to him, dropped Irene on the moss, and came to her feet at the awful wild look in his eyes. 'Sister,' he tried, then ran out of air, and fell to his knees.

'It's Mama,' she said.

He could not bring a word out. He knelt there, coughing and struggling for air. Irene sent up a wail. The boys splashed and hooted, oblivious. Imogene watched from the bank with a thumb in her mouth.

'Bring em all quick as you catch your breath,' Stella said, and she was gone, running hard through the trees. Damn damn, screamed a voice as she ran. Damn! Why hadn't she stayed home instead of just playing? Damn *damn*, gone to play in the woods while her own Mama breathed her last breath . . .

She broke free of the woods and stopped, blinded by the sudden brilliance of afternoon. Above the last field, the air trembled and blurred to the orchard, one corner of their roof shining through the upper branches of pecans. Stella tripped, rose again, scrambled through briars, across the ruined old field, and the fence. A buggy stood by the largest pecan tree. She dashed across sand and went into the house.

After the brightness, she saw just the dark. 'Mama!' Her word echoed. Up at the end of the hall, the door swung shut as if some higher power had pushed it. Someone was there. Through her breathing, she could hear him just standing.

'Which one are you?' he said.

'Stella.'

'Ahh yes, I remember. You brought her to me.'

'Yessir.' Somehow, her hands found her face. She forced herself forward.

'You're the feisty one.'

Stella said nothing.

'Where are all the others?'

The doctor. If she could just see him, she would fly up the hall and attack him with fists until he went away and took his dread news with him. 'Where's Mama?'

'Let's let her be.'

Those words struck like bullets. They made the worst nightmare come true. The darkness dissolved into nothing. She lunged up the hall, crying, 'I want my *Mama*!'

His hands stopped her, held her, too gently. She smelled him there, his doctor smell, like the fumes from her legs when Callie rubbed the bug bites away.

'You can see her,' he said, pressing her face to his chest.

Stella felt herself weeping. 'I didn't mean it,' she blurted. 'I didn't. I did the best I could. We whipped the old horse the best we could.'

'I know you did, girl, now quiet down . . .'

'. . . it was just me and William, we just did the first thing we thought of to do. Oh Mama, oh no . . .'

'Now just hush now.' He turned her, his hands on her shoulders, and guided her forward. He opened a door. Light came flooding.

Stella closed her eyes. She willed them to open and closed them again. She saw the cracked bowl and pitcher, the washstand, the faded old edge of the quilt on the bed. And her mother, lying on her side, her face to the wall. One shoulder poked out of the quilt.

'Mama.'

Callie rolled over. The quilt fell away. Her swollen breasts quivered with milk. At one brown nipple, a red ugly infant sucked.

'Stella,' breathed her mother. 'Look here. He's come back. Our baby did live after all. Here. You take him.' She grasped the child by his ribs, detaching him, offering him to Stella like a gift.

Stella shrank back, but then took him. His small life felt hot in her hands. 'Oh Mama, it's true,' she said.

'The sweet doctor brought him back to us –' Then Callie's eyes went past Stella, who turned. The doctor was gone.

FIVE

A December wind sent its sound through the house, a howling like dogs. It trembled the windows and made the roof shiver. On black winter nights, if the last lamp went out, the dining room took on its own special chill.

Down on her knees in the dark, Stella gave up her search. The crystal was gone. She had explored the whole drawer, and it was somehow not there. Three years had passed since Stella touched it last, since she last heard its weird whistling deep in her dreams. If Mama had found out Stella knew where it was, she might have changed where she hid it. A dangerous thing, she said. Thing not for children. Stella got to her feet, and groped into the hall.

The house was divided in two equal halves, with rooms on both sides, a frail porch on the front, the kitchen at back, and the long hall in common. All doors were shut to the cold. Light showed under one – Mama's, and Stella's, and Jack Otis' too. She would look in on the others, then run for the warm.

In the first room, the fire was out. The twins had battled their covers away, and lay with their bony white arms and legs tangled. Stella eased the quilts back over them in a settling cloud. They did not wake up.

Next, the room of the littler girls, who were smarter and warmer, invisible lumps. Stella patted, to know they were there. William's room belonged to William, and she let him be.

The parlor was darker than anywhere else. She dashed down the hall to the last door, and slipped quick inside. A fine fire blazed up. Propped on a pillow, her squirrel-fur cap on her head, Callie stitched buttons on the fly of Charlie Boot's pants. 'You'll freeze your heinie, child,' she said, turning down covers. 'Come in.'

'I was back in the kitchen, tryin to read. The durn lamp went out,' Stella said, snuggling in. Bedfeathers prickled her nose. This seemed the softest place possible except the inside of a cloud.

'Rurn your eyes that way, readin at night.' Callie attacked cloth with needle like the dirt with the hoe. Her fingers were ringed with old calluses. Even in her heavy nightdress, she shivered. She gave up the mending, and plunged the needle in the mattress. 'Bless his heart,' she whispered, rising and going to the pine crib by the fireplace. 'I believe this is the coldest night he's been alive.' Raising the bundle of blankets and Jacko, she came back to bed.

He was growing up fast. At one year four months, he could totter on his feet; running was anytime now. He said 'ma' and 'milk' and 'no,' and something that sounded like 'mother' but wasn't quite yet. His head was still bald and too big for the rest of him, round as a dinner plate. What's in there, Stella wondered sometimes, waiting to get out? He seemed so aware. His nose was flat, as if he had been in a fight. Callie had not tried weaning him yet, since he had a scream and a will to be heard. He wound up now for one of those.

Callie slipped her shoulder bare and leaned back on the pillow. Jacko's mouth went to work.

A grin cracked his mother's face, sly and sidelong. She started to sing. 'Mama's little titty gets colder, colder, Mama's little titty gets cold in bed.'

Stella broke out in giggles. 'Mama!' she scolded. 'That's nasty!'

'It aint.' Callie covered her bosom, and Jacko. 'It's true.' She laughed, a dry sound. 'You hear that up there, dear Lord? Old Callie's raised up a girl with a proper nature.'

Stella lay on her side. 'I aint proper.'

'You are,' Callie teased. 'Nobody'd thought a girl of old Callie's could be so high and mighty.'

'I'm no more proper than you.'

'And that's sayin enough,' Callie said. 'I guess you right. I'm bout as proper as a flower on a good hat.' She closed her eyes, let the pain cross her face. Since Jacko was born she had lived in this bed, summoning that achy look all the time. She kept telling Stella that soon she'd be well – when spring came, when the summer passed, when the new bottle of Black Draught arrived in the mail. When spring came again.

Stella waited on her, accepting the chores without saying a word, quietly proud that she ran the whole house. William stayed angry and out in the woods, doing whatever boys do. Once he snapped at their mother that she could get up, if she tried – but most of the time he did what Stella said, and most of the time she said hush.

'So proper . . . I ever tell you bout the dress my daddy bought me, when I got married? He ordered after it, all the way up to New York. That one dress cost seventy dollars.' Her eyes hazed. 'Prettiest thing . . . made a sound when you walked. Lace all the way to the elbows. I wish I had that dress.' She had sold it last winter, in town, and brought back with her cornmeal enough for the year.

'Mama,' said Stella, holding her breath, 'tell me the story bout Daddy again.' The outlines were so familiar. A strange comfort to Stella, to know he had been.

'None left to tell, sugar. Told it a thousand times over.'

'Just once more, oh please . . . Just I like to hear it.'

'What can I tell that you aint heard before? That he was a fine Christian man, and a Bates just like me? With a red head of hair, and oh he could preach . . .' Jacko grunted. Callie adjusted his angle. 'Like takin the top off a barrel of snakes, once you got him started. He could preach out a sermon like nobody else. He loved God as much as anybody, almost much as he loved you and me. Sometimes more.'

'Howcome he didn't stay with us?' Stella knew the answer. It just felt good to hear it.

'Aw sweetie, I've told you this all. Some folks are meant to stay home, and be just like everbody else. And some like your daddy, they got a purpose. Bigger than any one of us. If we was selfish and kept him for us, think of all the souls that wouldn't got saved.' She wrestled a little with Jacko, who gurgled for the last milk. 'Come away now, that's all.' She pulled him loose. 'I wish there was more. This is some kind of winter. So cold . . .'

She sat him up on her lap and diddled his toes. He burped. 'No, honey, he lived and he died. In Missippi. We were lucky to have him when we did.'

Stella felt the question nag, way in the back, but she knew to proceed gingerly. When the talk wandered backwards, Callie could get touchy as a new blister.

'Mama,' she said, 'how long does it take you to have a baby?'

'Listen at that. Worry me to death with your questions. You seen it happen. With Jacko, it happened real quick. Just like that.'

'No, I mean . . . you know, the whole thing. From the time . . . you know. From when you get it all started.'

Callie smiled. 'So proper,' she said. 'Nine months. Thereabouts.'

Stella sat up and hugged her own knees. 'Well then tell me one more thing,' she said, sensing this might be the time. 'Now if Jacko was born first of August, and if you count back, let's see . . .' Her eyes drifted up to the ceiling; she counted back through the months. 'And if our daddy came the summer before, well then . . .'

Jacko rolled off his mother's belly, thumped his fist on the needle's blunt end, and let out a shriek that brought heat to the room. Callie rose from the bed, snatched him up, muffled him in her shoulder. 'Now look what you done,' she snapped, sticking a finger in his mouth. He clamped down hard with his two tiny teeth. Callie turned a full circle. 'Gol durn . . .'

Stella buried her head. It was just a bitty scratch. She peeped out.

Her mother absently touched the little point of blood, then put the finger to her tongue. She put Jacko back in his crib and leaned over to tuck him, to still his legs with the blankets. 'Gone sleep right here in his own bed, yes, hush up now, hush up . . . getting too big for his crib.' She turned back to Stella. 'Poor baby,' she said, and blew out the lamp. When she settled in bed, a cold space of air separated them.

'Mama,' Stella said in the dark, 'if your daddy had money, howcome we got none.'

Callie turned over. Their faces were inches apart. 'Are you

hungry?' she said. 'You had a big dinner. Go back in the kitchen and get you some more.'

'Mama, I was just wonderin . . .'

'Wonderin why? Howcome? What is your trouble tonight? You're antsier than the baby.' She sighed, and Stella knew the painful look was crossing her face like a curtain. 'Oh me, bless your heart. You want some new shoes. I reckon that's it. Well the springtime is comin, child; maybe then.'

'I hate shoes,' Stella said. 'I just like to hear you tell how all it was.'

'What's gone is gone,' said her mother. 'Don't help to remember. Rememberin only reminds you, that's all. Old times were sweet, honey, but they're all gone. Fine things, it's better you never had em. That way you don't miss em, like I do.' Her warm arms came out; she pulled Stella in close. 'I just want you to remember one thing, and that's all. I got you, growin up just as strong as could be . . . and all of us here, and not one of us hungry. All the money can't buy that for you. One day you'll have some of your own, then you'll know what I mean. Now roll on over and don't hog the cover. Sleep tight.'

Stella felt peaceful. She tunneled in deeper, finding the cool with her feet, drawing them back to the warm. The wind's chorus raised up a song so high and unsettling that Stella imagined the house blowing off its stone pilings. But here it was safe. She was not afraid. She felt the kind of awe she felt out on the porch in summer, when thunderclouds fought in the sky.

Her mind raced away with the wind. The howls rose and moaned, and the hounds became real. They joined in a pack and ran into her dreams, thin red dogs with narrow skulls, chasing each other and each other's tails, in circles, swooping and blending with air.

When a sound cracked the night into morning, Stella found she was wedged way down at the foot, deep in the heat she had made. She slid her hand around. Mama was up.

Then the crack of a gun, a real gun: the sound that had broken her dream. Frantic dog yelps meant hunters were near, maybe out in the orchard surrounding the house.

Imogene yanked at the big toe protruding. 'Stell-a,' she crooned, 'Stellll-a.'

Stella played possum.

The little girl poked her hand in, found Stella's nose, and tickled it. She slid one eyelid up with her finger. Stella blinked. 'What is it, honey,' she yawned, lifting Imogene up into bed.

'Cold, cold!' Imogene thrashed and rejoiced.

'Hoo! Stop that! Go on. Your feet are like ice.' Stella pinched her until she quit wiggling. 'Lie still or I'll put you out.'

'Mama's up,' Imogene said. 'She's already yellin.'

'At who? The cows aint up yet.'

'I dunno.' They lay still a moment, then Stella heard her mother's cry through the window, the voice she used to call pigs. 'I'd just as soon you just took it and went,' she yelled. 'I said we'd get one ourselves when the time comes to have it!'

'But this is the day,' Gibson said. 'I was only just tryin to be like a neighbor. I'd never come up, if it's left up to me. The missus thought you might want it.'

'You tell her thanks all the same, but we can take care of our own selves,' shot back Callie.

Stella nudged the little girl to be quiet, and crept from the bed to the window.

She knew his growl: John Frank Gibson, from the closest house, at the foot of the hill where the road bent toward town. 'I don't care what you do with it,' he said. 'I done shot it and so there it is. Some folks can't take nothin the way it's give.'

On the sand between them, in a scruffy heap, a large dead bird. Gibson slung his gun back to his shoulder, and whistled for his dogs.

Callie snatched up the bird by its neck, shook it twice. 'I reckon I ought to be thankin you now, but I won't,' she said. 'You keep your pity. I don't believe me or none of mine have ever had a hungry minute, and if we do we won't ask none from you.'

A shower of feathers fell from the inert bird.

Stella's breath spread a fog on the glass. She watched the sphere of the largest pecan tree erupt in a rush of brown sparrows. They left all at once. By instinct they closed in a shimmering cloud and flew off to the south.

She eased up the window so she could hear better. Her mother held the bird by its neck, using two fingers. Gibson tucked a smile behind his beard. 'It aint ever day you find two fine fat toms, lookin to get theirselves shot,' he said. 'It bein Christmas, and you with nobody to shoot one for you . . .'

'I got William, when Christmas comes,' Callie said.

He raised his palms, beseeching. 'But that's what I'm tryin to say. This is it. It's today. This is Christmas.'

She dropped the bird, put a hand to her cheek. 'Christmas?' she said in a thin little voice. 'Today can't be Christmas. That's sometime later.'

Then the horror swept her, everything still to do – oranges unbought and the tree yet to cut, the special warm flannel for new shirts unordered. In that instant Stella knew for the first time that Christmas was truly all her mother's doing, in other, better times. After the months in the bed, consumed by the weight of her pain, Callie had simply forgotten. No one had been to the house, not a soul, since Jacko arrived.

They all knew it suddenly – Callie, and Gibson, the girls at the window.

Imogene yanked at Stella's nightshirt with both hands. 'Christmas!' she cried. 'Oh Stella, it's Christmas!'

Stella could not yet believe that Christmas was only a day on the calendar, back at the back of the third kitchen drawer, and no one had looked to see when. 'Not yet, baby,' she said, guiding Imogene away from the window. 'Christmas this year is a special surprise. Now you got to promise me. Promise.' She leaned down to Imogene's large solemn eyes. 'Come on now, and promise me you won't tell. We gone be busy all day, gettin set. If you tell, Santa Claus might forget you. You promise?'

Imogene nodded, enthralled at the secret. She hugged Stella so hard her knees nearly gave.

'Run put on your britches, and that blue shirt. Run on. I'll figure out your special job.'

Imogene hurried away. From the crib came a stir. Jack Otis

had heard all the talk. He put out a fist; clutching the air, sensing its chill. He made his peculiar grunt, kicking at the covers. Stella took him up, murmuring, soothing him down. He searched her shoulder with his tiny hot tongue. He seemed almost feverish warm with the leftover heat of the covers.

She carried him to the back porch. The air held a freezing surprise when she opened the door. 'Mama!' she called, gulping in. 'Jacko wants breakfast!'

John Frank Gibson strode off with his dogs at his heel. Callie stared after him, one hand still clutching the bird.

She turned and came back to the porch, trading the dead turkey for Jacko. 'We gone be havin this bird for our dinner,' she said. 'I would be so proud if you'd just go out and pluck him for me.' Her face gave nothing away. She shrugged Jacko up on her shoulder and went in.

Stella hid the bird behind the steps, rubbing a hand on her thigh as if to rub away the warmth of it. She would wait until it cooled for the plucking. Inside, she sneaked all the way up the hall to William's room, and rattled the frame of his thin iron bed. 'Burnin daylight!' she announced. 'Get up.'

His eyes struggled open. 'Huh, what you say?'

'Burnin daylight.' She jerked the covers away with delicious cruelty.

William's chest broke out in goosebumps. 'Sun aint up yet,' he moaned. 'Leave me alone.'

Stella's voice darkened. 'Brother, now listen. I need you today. A whole lot's been happenin while you was lyin here, sawin your logs.'

William woke up and covered his boniness with a blanket. 'What's the matter?'

She told it all, Gibson's gift and his news, the sound of Mama's anger as she drove him off. When she said Christmas, William sat up. 'You don't mean she just forgot it?'

'That's just what I mean,' Stella said. 'Now Imogene knows, and you know, and me, but we can keep it our secret. It'll be the worst Christmas, unless we do.'

He was out of bed, pulling on pants.

'I'll run chase after Mister Gibson,' she said. 'He was all mad when he left. I'll run thank him. You get up the others and start figurin somethin.'

'I aint gone do it,' he said in a rush. 'I'm through bein mama and daddy in one. She lain in the bed this whole time, while we worked . . .'

'You hush and do like I say.'

'You don't know it all,' he exploded, 'you don't know anything.'

'What do you know, Mister Big Skinny Britches? Daddy and mama, that's funny – I'm pullin the plow half the time, just like you. More than half. And we got Ben –'

'Lazy nigger.'

'We got Ben,' Stella said. 'Now you put on some clothes and you do like I say.' She saw steam swelling inside him. His face was like hers, except that his cheekbones poked through. He was skinnier than any living human ought to be.

She'd pushed him too hard. 'I don't mean to be bossy,' she said, 'but come on, please, brother. Pitch in, this once. For the babies, or Mama. For me. You don't want to spoil Christmas.'

'I aint the one spoilin it,' he sputtered.

Stella left the room before he could think of more to say. As she laced her shoes, Imogene appeared, wearing her good wool dress backwards. 'I'm ready,' she said. 'What's my secret job?'

'Go back and put on somethin you can't mess up,' Stella said. 'Go put on your pants. Ask William. He'll find you a job.' She flashed past the little girl, fast up the hall through the front door, so she would miss Callie. She hadn't decided yet what she would say.

She went down the front steps in twos, across the brittle grass starting to thaw where the sun touched it. She knew a spot where the barbed wire was down, and hopped it.

If there were no woods, Gibson on his porch would have looked up the hill and admired the Bates place. Half a mile's tangle and pasture divided the houses. Stella suspected that even though his house was newer, and lately whitewashed, Gibson might envy their hill. No matter how their place ran down or grew up, it had a kind of loftiness up on its rise. And she knew the first Bates to come here had owned all the land, every deer, creek, and pine tree for miles. Callie didn't care for neighbors: she said they were nosy. The children knew better than to wander down there. Still, she also taught manners, and a gift deserves thanks. When she cooled off, she would be proud of Stella.

Gibson's hounds bayed ahead, wanting breakfast. She caught up with him beside the cold running creek, where he stood detaching brambles from his legs with the gunstock.

'I thought all you chillun was still in the bed,' he boomed.

'They all are but me,' Stella said. She batted a dog's nose away from her legs.

'Bayard,' Gibson thundered. The dog slunk off.

'Cold mornin,' said Stella. 'I was watchin from the window, from Mama's room. I might shouldn't have, but I was. I think it was real sweet of you to . . .' She paused to catch breath. 'I thought I ought to run after you. Tell you how sweet it was . . .'

She saw the twist of a withheld grin in his face. 'Your shoes,' he said, 'would you look? Must of grabbed your brother's in your hurry.'

Stella's ears burned. She looked down. The brogans were large, brown, and crusty with mud. 'They used to be William's, but I got em now. Charlie Boot needs mine now it's cold.'

His smile died away. She could see him thinking: Not even good daylight yet and already I've embarrassed two Bateses. 'Those your shoes?'

'Well yessir,' she said. 'They're a mile too big, but Mama says the hard toe keeps the hoe off my feet.' She had seen him from a distance, but now it struck Stella how big Gibson was. He towered above her, three heads taller, at least. His thick tangled beard hid the line of his mouth, with threads of metal frosting it. His nose sprouted hairs. In his eyes she saw tiny gold flecks, old hurt. The sympathy in them was new, she could tell.

'You ought to have a lady's shoes,' Gibson said, shaking his head. 'If you lived in my house I'd see you had you a decent pair.'

'They're all right for shoes,' she said. 'I hate shoes.'

She knew that no swinging-rope hung from the tree in the Gibsons' yard. They had no children. His wife wore a pinched look, and screamed at the chickens. She chased the children away from their watermelons every summer, waving a stick. 'Is it really true Christmas, Mister Gibson?'

'It is,' he said, 'else why would I be out on such a cold day? Shot two in a row, just that quick.' He let fly a cough, then sucked the spit back through his teeth. 'Big old tom come struttin out of the trees. Last strut for him. Got him dressed and cookin, right now.' He stuck a thumb over his shoulder.

'Well ours is just fine. I got to go pluck him,' she said. 'We're mighty grateful, just never mind what Mama said. She gets riled up if she gets caught with somebody else knowin somethin.'

Gibson said, 'She must got more worries than I even thought.'

'She's been poorly, you know, our last baby and all.'

'I member. I heard. But still – ah well, hell. I never heard of nobody just up and forget Christmas. All you chillun to surprise.'

'We'll have us one anyway, thanks to you.'

'Some folks just ought not have chillun,' he said, 'that would let Christmas slide by without even a bird.'

'We always have ham,' Stella said.

Gibson took her by both shoulders. She felt the heat in his hands. 'We'll have us a Christmas, down at our house, girl,' he said. 'You remember that. Yall could all stop down tonight, if you want.'

Stella felt a rush of blood, shuddered, pulled back. 'Rabbit ran over my grave,' she said.

His smile returned. His breath put a shine in his beard. 'Let me get you somethin to remember by,' he said, jacking up his shotgun, aiming for the sky.

Stella dropped to her knees. The gun exploded. She smelled its hot smoke. It shook the whole world, then died off in the trees.

Through the roar she heard Gibson's deep growl: 'Take this back up there. Tell em you pulled it yourself.' He scuffed through the leaves to the edge of the creek, and fetched back a spindly branch. White waxy berries were bunched at one end. 'It's mistletoe,' he said.

'William calls em squirrel berries.' Stella's ears sang.

'It's mistletoe,' Gibson said. 'It grows up there all year long, but only time it's any use is today. You tie it up on a string in the door. Anytime somebody comes to stand underneath, you go up to em and lay on the biggest, most Christmas kiss you know how. It's the rules.'

Stella smiled. 'I heard about that.'

'I'd stop by, to collect on mine,' he said, 'but maybe I better not. Yall come down, your mama too, if she wants. I shot us down some, but it aint much use, just me and the missus . . .'

'I hope we'll be able, Mister Gibson,' Stella said, looking beyond him. 'But I think you'll be out in the woods all day, chasin them dogs of yours.'

He turned. His hounds danced away in opposing directions, barking and waving their tails.

Stella took off running, back up the hill, and felt him still standing, just watching her run. He paid no mind to his dogs. Poor man, she thought – two dogs for children. Oh, Mama was right about that.

The flush of full morning hung over the yard: smoke from the chimneys, William grim in the chickenyard, scattering seed, the embrace of hot biscuit when she pushed in through the back door.

'Bring a stick with you,' Callie warned.

Stella retreated to fetch an armload. 'I'm comin through,' she called, bracing the door with her knee. Charlie Boot met her and took half the logs.

'Where you been at, Stella?' Imogene shrieked.

'Yeah, where you been at?' said Irene.

The twins pounded fists on the table. Stella made a face. 'Get on with you, Foster. I seen you and Charlie Boot nekkid as jaybirds last night. Lyin from out of the covers, just shakin. And ever quilt down at the foot. Irene, wipe your nose . . .' She made sure to leave none of them out of her teasing.

At the stove, consumed by spattering grease, Callie managed three skillets. She wore a clean apron. It was the first meal she'd cooked since the day Jacko came. 'While you been out gallyvantin,' she fussed, 'your brother's been doin what all needed done.'

Stella knew then that her mother was well. She heard the silent plea – please keep our secret, I'm back at the stove now, please please don't tell. 'You need to get to the churn first thing. Charlie Boot, finish your eggs or get down. I don't want to watch you make up a mess. Imogene, wipe that child's nose.' Callie spooned eggs onto plates, snatched biscuits barehanded out of the oven, and poured strong coffee in a pair of blue mugs. 'No butter for biscuit,' she said as she sat.

'I like mine plain,' Stella said.

She spent the day prodding the children through a long string of chores, some real and some invented as distractions, and stealing away for whispers with Callie and the anxious Imogene. She talked sweetly to William all day. He was quiet, and drawn up; she could tell he was thinking and keeping his thoughts to himself – just as well. She finally coaxed him to ride the miles in to Kline's store, to fetch oranges, and whatever looked like presents.

Jacko's whining made music, hour after hour, like a mosquito in a night room, refusing to light. They all took turns hushing him. He tumbled out of his crib to the floor, in his rage. Stella found him there, crying to hear himself cry. 'Poor baby, be good now,' she said, putting him back. 'This is Jesus's birthday, now hush.' She passed Callie at the door. 'He's gone drive me crazy,' she said.

'Guess he knows somethin is up,' Callie said. Her voice dropped: 'You send William off?'

Stella nodded. 'I made him a list. I hope Mister Kline will be open.'

'Don't worry,' said Callie, 'he'll open, all right. That man would put down his fork, slide his chair back, and skip a good pie just to make him a dime.' She picked up the high-whining baby. 'Jacko, you just aint much help today, do you know that?'

At last the sun sank, as if it had tired of trying to warm the air. The children bounded in from the pasture, crowding the kitchen, cheering the moist golden bird on its plate.

'Mama, where's William, how come we got turkey?' said Foster, tugging her apron.

Callie shooed him, sprinkled flour in the skillet, whisked the rich grease into bubbling gravy. At last all the pans, plates, and bowls were filled up. 'Come on now,' she hollered, 'it's ready for eatin. I'm not gone to wait. Wipe off your hands fore you come.'

The thunder of feet brought a boisterous wail from her room.

'Yall go on and sit,' Stella said. 'I'll run see about him.'

Jacko pitched his fit on a raggedy blanket, the only one he hadn't kicked to the floor. His face was scarlet from the long hours howling. She took him up, kissed him, and walked him around, crooning the saddest soft tunes in his ear. As soon as she hushed, he would whimper again. She brought a lamp to his crib.

The light startled him. His eyes clamped shut. Stella stood the lamp on the mantel, moved the crib an inch closer to the low-burning fire, then gave in to the musical lure of chatter, the pinging of forks against plates down the hall. She started the cradle with her hand. 'Sweet dreams.'

Callie's face had lost its wrinkles in the light from candles. She was not used to smiling, so she didn't smile, but her eyes danced and lit her face. Surrounded by her children, basking in them, she seemed for an instant a child herself. 'Come sit before it gets cold,' she told Stella. 'Foster, pass your sister the pickles. Now there's a sweet boy.'

Foster melted into his plate with the praise.

'Everbody is on their best behavior, Imogene; stop eatin your peas with a spoon. A spoon is for soup. You need more dressin?'

'Yes ma'am.' She held out her plate.

Stella saw that Imogene's secret had not long to live. Her face was tight, as if she'd had to pee for a week. She glanced from her mother to Stella and back again, dying to tell.

Stella tried a distraction: 'Imogene, pass me that bread. I hear it callin at me now, you hear it? It's sayin, "Get Imogene to pass you some of me. I'm just the best bread . . ."' The little girl giggled. They talked about all they were eating, and went back for thirds. Their bellies were glad, and their eyes glimmered bright as the candles.

'Imogene,' Callie said finally, 'I see you got you a secret to tell.' The children quieted. 'I see that ol secret wormin on out of you, and I reckon you would die before you told it.'

'Yeah, Imogene,' Stella said. 'You look like you swallowed a hen.'

The little girl swelled up and begged, 'Can I tell?'

'Pass the biscuit,' said Foster.

'Pass the biscuit what,' said Stella or her mother.

'*Please.*' Foster rolled his eyes and peered down on Imogene. 'What's the big secret, dumbhead.'

'I aint no dumbhead. I know somethin *secret*. You tell him, Stella, tell him I known it all day.'

'She's right, Foster.'

With exquisite hesitation, Imogene raised her fork, a string bean impaled on each tine. 'Welllll,' she said, 'like I said, I got a secret. And nobody knows it but William and Stella. And Mama, cause she known it first.'

'What the duke are you talkin about.'

'Charlie Boot!' Callie swatted at him with her napkin. 'Swear at this table!'

'Well she's just settin there so high and mighty –'

'If you just shut up, I'll tell you,' said the little girl. "What it is . . . is . . .' She made sure they all were listening. 'It's *Christmas*!' Her hands flew up.

'What you mean, Christmas,' said Charlie Boot.

'It aint done it,' Foster said, his eyes widening.

Only Irene, mushing hands in her rice, seemed not to have felt the shudder of the word.

'Imogene, you a lie; it aint Christmas. We din get no presents.'

William spoke up from the head of the table. 'We got presents comin,' he said.

Foster shoved back his chair. 'Mama,' he wailed. 'It aint fair! Howcome she known and we didden.'

'Shut up, Foster,' William said.

'I won't. I won't. What you mean, Christmas. They wasn't no present, they wasn't no oranges, and Christmas don't happen without you get oranges.'

'We got oranges comin,' said William.

'Well I don't *want* no Christmas then.' The volume of Foster's anger made everyone take in a breath. 'Christmas comes in the mornin, and you can just *have* it!' He flung down his napkin and fled the room.

The wonderful food was forgotten.

'Yeah, howcome you told Imogene,' Charlie said, 'and you didn't tell us?'

'It was a special surprise,' said his mother.

Imogene turned on him then, with sweet vengeance. 'Well, I'll tell you why, you old dumbhead. Cause Mama *forgot*. Me and Stella found out. And William found out later on. So there.'

'Forgot?' The word hung before Charlie Boot like some weird shiny thing. Christmas was not something to forget or remember. Christmas happens when it does. He jumped from his chair, and followed his twin from the room.

The fire in the hearth burst just then in a shower of sparks. William hopped up to stomp out the rug. Callie watched him, unbreathing, her face growing older, consumed by the pain. It came down all at once.

'Mama,' Irene said, 'peas, peas, peas.'

Stella took the child's hands from her plate. 'You eat what you got, then there's more.' She glanced at her mother – alone now, and old.

'I'm sorry, Mama,' said Imogene, winding her face up to cry.

Stella felt pity for Callie, the children, especially poor Imogene. And for herself – the whole long day wasted, ruined, just that quick. 'Mama,' she said, 'I think the baby has fever.'

Callie put her hand to Irene's forehead. 'I don't feel it,' she said.

'Not her. I mean Jacko. I held him and he felt all hot.'

'I held him all day, and I didn't feel it,' Callie said. 'But he's been fussin too much, now you say it. Maybe you're right. I'll run up and see.'

'Mama,' came a voice at the door. 'Me and Foster, we're hungry.' The pair of small heads appeared around the door, a plea in their faces.

'We're sorry,' Foster said. 'Can we come back?'

'Come on, then,' Callie said. The room brightened. 'Mind what you say with that smart mouth of yours.'

They scooted in, bringing the lighter air with them, and everyone went back to eating again. Soon they were talking, then giggling, and then Callie reached for an empty white bowl. 'I'll get some more peas, and look in on him,' she said, rising.

'We was up there,' said Foster. 'He was asleep.'

Callie's skirt rustled. She passed from the room.

Stella turned to the toddler: 'It's *Christmas*, Irene. You know what that is, don't you? Sure you do. Presents, and oranges, and all this good food. And if we're real good, maybe Santa Claus comes.'

The name made sense to Irene. 'Sanner Claus!'

'Why look here, baby, he's done been and gone.' Stella got up, and went to the sideboard. 'Look here what he left us! No, over here.' She drew out the cluster of berries. 'Now this here is what you call mistletoe, baby. Santa Claus shot it down when he come by today.' She found a nail in the doorframe, and hung up the little bouquet. 'Now anybody walks under here, they get kissed. It's the rules.'

Irene slid from her chair. 'Mister toe!'

The twins hooted into their plates.

'Sanner Claus! Mister toe!'

Charlie Boot snorted. 'Shot it down, huh – I bet, what the duke,' he said. 'That stuff come off of a bird?'

'Now I'm up under mister toe, here you go, darlin. See? Now you give me a kiss.'

Irene flung her arms around Stella's neck. Then the world stopped. A deadly sound came from the front of the house, a sound that could only be Callie.

A scream.

Perhaps it is true that a blue bolt of lightning can fix a face forever in a windowpane. This vision, exploding in fire in the hall, stayed with Stella through all the dark nights of her life.

Her mother emerged from her door, now silent, so slowly, raising her arms and entirely on fire. Her hands were consumed by a bright cloud of burning, an offering, held up in flames. Jacko. Jacko on fire.

Fire licked down her arms. It ate at the dry patterned cotton of her dress. Callie just drifted away up the hall. She did not seem to mind. She was led by her bundle of burning. She halted, then went, then stopped again, as if to consider a change of direction.

Her door poured its fire on the floor of the hall. When it met the pine boards it blew up again. The front door was stuck. Stella heard Callie moan, pound the baby hard into her bosom.

The sound of the fire was all crackle, all spitting and roaring. White smoke came as fast as the flames back to Stella, there still on her knees in the door, with Irene.

The children still babbled behind her.

The door gave way in an instant or a lifetime, and Callie flew off the front porch into night. Stella tried to yell fire. No sound in her throat but a rasp like the rattle of snakes.

She chose without choosing, and felt her legs straighten. She ran up the hall, away from the others, to Callie, to Jacko, so fast through the fire she felt none of its heat. The door did not resist her. The black air outside chilled her hotter than fire.

She saw her mother then, out on the grass in the yard, rolling and rolling and rolling, setting up little fires, wrestling the child as they rolled on the grass.

Stella flew down the steps, seeing nothing but the fires in the grass. The smoke followed her out. There was light in the yard, so she saw them.

Her mother was still. Her fire had gone out. A haze of soft vapors arose.

Stella fell to her knees. Jacko's charred blankets peeled off like cornhusks. The innermost blanket protected him – oh he was there and alive, untouched by the fire, smooth and too warm, like an organ exposed. He lay breathing softly, alive and not crying, a look in his eyes she would never admit – as if he could know it, the fire around him. As if he had waited for fire to come. She felt a vast surge inside when she saw him, but turned away then to her mother, to where vapors rose up and all hope burned away, to where nothing was left but a smell.

Clamor came from the house, a whole world large and dark and far distant away. The high-rising shriek of Irene came cascading out over the yard.

Jacko lay motionless there on the grass. He seemed to be hearing some voice. She gathered his blanket and wrapped him up in it and turned, as a witness, to see.

From the front of the house to the back, all the rooms were alive at their windows with fire: orange, and yellow, with purple

and black. The house was invisible but for its fire. Crosstimbers
framed infernos, stark squares of bright burning. The cloud
rushed from front to back, fast as a cloud that will cover the
moon. Then Stella watched the roof fall in. The house was eager
to burn. Like cards, the walls collapsed.

She took Jacko up to the edge and they stood there just
watching. The settling mound of fire shone in his eyes. It made
fireplace sounds. The shrieking had vanished along with the
walls.

She could witness no more. She felt herself turn. She heard
nothing else. By the barn now, she saw the shape of the wagon,
the shapes of the children, lined up in a row on the bench, not
moving or speaking. Just waiting for her.

She gave them Jacko, then went back to Callie, and dragged
the still form through the sand. The silent children helped her
lift their mother up to the bed of the flat-wagon. She thought
she saw one of the twins dart across to the barn, but she must
have imagined it, since they were all sitting there. She harnessed
the mare and climbed up to the bench. There was room for
them all without crowding, somehow. She wished they would
say something.

The mare knew to move. The wagon pulled forward. They
trundled out past the pecan to the road. Stella looked back to
see the beautiful heap of hot glowing, alive. She watched the
dark orchard shrink down, until it was only a black dome that
capped their round hill. She looked to the sky and saw stars
going out.

Halfway, the wagon wheels dunked in the creek. The splash
sounded out through the cold windless night. The Gibson house
shimmered through trees. Three lights waited in windows.

Gibson called out her name from the porch. He asked her
why she was all alone there, like that. He brought his hand to
the rail of the wagon and looked in the back. She knew from his
face that he saw.

'Where all the chillun?' he whispered.

Stella turned for an answer to William, to someone, but no
one was sitting beside her at all. Jacko lay in his blanket, a smile
on his face, as if he'd just wakened from sweet dreams.

The other children must have got down somewhere along the road, but Stella had not noticed, somehow. She knew she had felt them there, sitting beside her, but how could they leave without saying goodbye?

SIX

He filled his pen with fresh ink. A cold morning light sliced across the blank page, revealing invisible flaws in its surface. He started again.

Here below us Callie Bates, late of this life, who gave her

He set the pen down. Before the ink lost its shine, he snatched up the paper, crumpled it, tossed it into the fire. He watched it blacken and curl, fall apart.

Here beneath us lies Callie Bates, late of this life, born in the year

But he did not know. This page, when he burned it, took an odd spherical shape, a hot orb like a tiny world melting from inside.

To think they might go to their graves without words to tell who they were, how they died. How she seemed to choose death for herself. It was unthinkable.

Here beneath us Callie Bates, late of this life, born in this district shortly past the Great War, died in the Year of Our Lord, 1910 A.D. This Mother of seven gave her life for that of her youngest Child. Seeing flames communicating to the infant, and losing all interest in her own safety with greater regard to that of the Child, she extinguished the flames, and then traveled with her Children to the House of the Lord. With her, in blessed eternity, Charles Booth Bates, Foster Lee Bates, Imogene Ivory Bates, Irene Dolores Bates.

He knew what Dewitt the stonecarver would want to cut the

whole thing, but he knew he would pay it, whatever it was.

At the end, he added 'Rest in Peace.'

He carried it in his vest pocket until nearly dark, when he drove into town. He stopped the buggy in front of Gadney's Hardware, and climbed down. The narrow door off to one side was unlocked. A light showed in the glass of the door at the head of the stairs, so the *Gleam* was still open.

Pal Herlong looked up from his chaos of papers. He smiled when he saw who it was. 'Another poem?'

'Not this time.'

Pal opened the folded white sheet. When he was through reading, he whistled out loud.

'That's mighty good,' he said. 'Makes you wonder.'

'It does.'

'You planning to have the whole thing cut that way, in the stone?' Pal said.

'I am.'

'Well I say, if you'll pay to engrave it in stone, I guess the least I can do is to print it. You want your name on it?'

'No.'

'I would, if I'd written it,' Pal Herlong said. 'Doc, you've done a fine charitable thing, let me say.'

The doctor turned and went back down the stairs.

SEVEN

The world shrank to silence, but Stella's ears sang out an endless high drone. She wondered if soon she would not hear a thing. Birds left their branches without making sound. Their wings took them off, but did not disturb air.

The Gibsons passed by where she sat in their parlor. Their shoes made no noise on the floor.

One morning, she brushed too close to the kitchen table, and watched the slow arc of a glass as it fell. She watched the fragments explode without sound.

Miss Ethel looked up in fright from her darning. She always wore one of two faces: fear or disgust. Her eyebrows were spread out like buzzard wings. Snuff made her eyes glitter. 'Now look,' she said.

Stella stood among the bright glass shards. She barely heard Ethel. 'You reckon I could of hurt my head?'

Ethel stared. 'Hurt it how?'

'I can't hear nothin,' said Stella, poking the sharpest piece with her big toe. 'I didn't hear when it broke.'

'You hearin me now, aint you?'

'Well . . .'

'Well see there.' Ethel reached for her little tin box. 'You can hear good as the next.'

Stella fought the surge in her hands, the desire to strangle. 'No, what I mean,' she said, 'nothin makes noise. I can just barely hear. I might could of hurt my head that night, some-how.'

'That's peculiar.' Ethel slid her lip back, tucked in a dainty green pinch, and took up her husband's dark sock.

'First Jacko won't move, and now I can't hear.'

'It aint the same,' Ethel said. 'You want coffee?'

'You know I don't,' Stella said. 'I don't want a thing in this world from you.'

Miss Ethel screwed up her face, yanked a rag from her pocket, and sneezed. 'John Frank says the folks in Camellia will help. Some are goin in on it together, to buy em a stone.'

'I know what it is,' Stella said. 'I can't hear any babies.'

'He said the word's out,' Ethel said. 'Folks want to do what they can. Said the doctor done wrote to the state.'

'I wish I could just hear some babies.'

'Tomorrow's the new year,' said Ethel. 'Oh me. I reckon I'll boil us some blackeye peas.'

EIGHT

The dress belonged to Ethel. Stella would not wear it. Nothing was wrong with it: to wear it made sense: she would not. Not because of its stiff black wool or its dozen frustrating eyelets up the back – not just because it was Ethel's. Stella had no dress except the one she wore from that night.

Ethel said, 'This is silly,' and 'You aint goin near a churchhouse in that awful burned dress with them poor ugly shoes,' and even *'Take yourself in there and put on that dress.'*

Stella shook her head and barely heard. 'I don't care who looks at me,' she said. 'They can look all they want.'

Ethel said either she wore the dress or she stayed home. Stella said she would stay home. Ethel said no, she would not. Not from this. Stella covered her ears with her hands.

Ethel said well, she would talk to John Frank about this. She grabbed her snuffbox and marched from the kitchen.

Most of the time, she tried hard to seem nice. Stella knew how hard it must be to try, from the fear in her eyes all the time. John Frank Gibson looked secretly glad she and Jacko were there. The niceness was deafening.

Maybe she should give in to it. Maybe just wear it. Maybe they'd leave her alone.

She scuffed down the hall to the little room she shared with Jacko. She pulled off her dress with its perfect round holes from the embers, and tossed it over a chair. She wrestled Miss Ethel's dress over her head, cursing the way it bristled and the blackness, the blackness of it.

Jacko slept. She took him up in her arms and carried him into the kitchen. The Gibsons sat at the table with coffee cups. Their eyes watched her.

'I wore your dress,' Stella said. 'I reckon we'll go ahead on.'

'It aint time,' said Ethel, her eyes triumphant. 'Whyn't we leave him here. He's asleep.'

'We can walk,' Stella said. 'It aint far.'

'Well if you will just wait –'

'Let her do like she says.' John Frank cut her off. His eyes lifted. 'We'll meet you up there.'

Stella drifted out past them, and into the yard, where the grass shone like stiff frozen hair. The mud of the road was stone hard. She turned east. As she walked, she slackened her jaw, then popped it, trying to clear out her ears. Once, she caught herself looking behind, for the children.

She came to a place where the line of gray trees broke for a skinny dirt road, leading shot-straight to the face of the Antioch Church. Plain as a drawing in pencil, the church faced the road whitely, precisely, as if the nudge of a breeze might send it toppling back.

To one side, a black iron fence ringed the graveyard, beneath the nude limbs of an old huge oak. Just beyond, creosote posts were overnetted with chicken wire, on which church ladies in summer spread tablecloths and set out food. A chilly wind sang in the wire. Stella walked down the long hall of trees.

Past the clutter of old stones and newer markers made of Birmingham iron, she saw the chests, arms, and heads of two Negro men. They seemed to be digging a hole. Even in the cold, their arms glistened with sweat. Their shovels made solid connections in dirt. They made some noise between them that might have been laughter, or singing, but Stella could not tell which.

She opened the gate, picked her way through Mullinses, Collinses, all the Fails in their neat plot with its white edging of bricks. She stopped to inspect the rusty iron kettle containing Mullie Z. Jernigan Waites. Stella supposed she could lift up the lid by its handle and peer in on Mullie's white bones.

The Negroes propped elbows on their spade handles and watched her come.

She saw there were five holes in all – four small ones, and one that was larger, each attended by a mound of red sandy dirt. 'What kind of noise are yall makin?' she said. 'You gone wake up my baby.'

'Might sorry, missy,' said the bigger Negro. Even knee-deep in his hole, he was nearly as tall as Stella. His skin was rich sweaty brown, except for a scar that traced down one arm from his neck, like a crooked pink worm.

'Yall been hard at it,' she told him. 'That looks like some diggin.'

'Yassum,' was all he could think of to say.

'I didn't mean to stop you.'

A grin eased its way onto his face. 'We be might glad all the stoppin we get.'

'Yall was singin,' she said.

'Make the time roll on by.'

'Well go on,' Stella said. 'Just please sing out so I can hear you.'

The men traded glances. The smaller Negro was the color of coffee with one spoon of milk. 'Hain proper to sang in a grave-yard,' he said.

'You aint gone bother nobody,' she said, shifting Jacko, who still had not stirred. 'Yall dig for a livin?'

The larger man took up his spade. 'Nome,' he said. 'Mostly we cuts cotton for Muster Arant. Sometime we come to dig pits.'

The other man muttered at that.

'Shoot yeah, I rackon,' the larger one said. 'We built a house or two, now and again. Bet this hole last heap longer.'

'Yall know Ben?' Stella said.

'Nome,' said the big man.

'I thought you might know him. He works for my mama.'

His shovel forced down into dirt, and scraped against some-thing. He worked around it.

'Yall ever find any bones in them holes?'

'Nome,' he said, 'nare a one.'

'Iffen we do,' said the smaller man, 'we put it back.'

'Don't let me stop you singin,' she said. 'We'll wait over there.' She wandered with Jacko back under the oak tree and sat, going deaf again, smelling the cold.

Soon a wagon arrived, with the boxes.

1911

NINE

Ethel stood flexing her hands. 'He rode out this far, now, you come on and talk.'

'She'll talk, give her time,' said the doctor. He squeezed Jacko's tiny bare leg. 'I know how she feels.'

Gibson towered above like a tree. 'She's got where she'll talk some, but it comes and goes,' he said.

'You don't know the way I feel,' Stella said. 'Nobody knows.'

Ethel recoiled. 'Don't you talk smart to me, Miss Priss. I'll take you out back –'

'Shut your mouth, Ethel, you make it worse.' Gibson bent down, but Stella turned away. 'Come on now, girl, talk to him. He come to help.'

The parlor was small, and now it seemed to shrink. Miss Ethel had got out her best chenille cloth for the table where Jacko lay, motionless. He had not moved since that night, except for the blink of his eyes.

'Well shoot, I'll tell you if she aint,' said Gibson. 'They thought he took with a fever that day. She aint sure. Said he felt hot. Kep on squallin. Said he kicked all of his covers from out of his bed.'

'A fever,' said Dannelly.

'I aint seen nothin like it.' Gibson backed away from Stella. 'Course we got none of our own, but I always had heard that babies was hard to keep still. Not this one. He aint moved a muscle, or let out a peep. It's spooky, I tell you. Some way.'

The doctor brought up his wrinkled brown bag, made of leather rubbed raw at its edges. He opened it, took out a white napkin, and spread it beside Jacko.

Ethel spoke from her corner in a tight voice: 'I washed the tablecloth, special.'

'Yes ma'am, I see it's clean. But this one's sterile.' The doctor reached deep in the bag, and removed an assortment of shiny tools – tiny probes, tiny needles, clamps with fish-teeth, pinchers, wicked devices with points. He arranged them by size on the napkin, then turned back to Jacko.

That brought Stella to her feet. 'Don't you hurt him,' she flared. 'I'll talk, I promise. He did move. But just a little. I saw it.'

'When?'

'Last night.'

'I told you she'd start,' Gibson said, turning. 'Howcome you didn't tell me?'

The doctor's hand poised in midair. 'Mister Gibson, you've been a big help,' he said. 'Maybe just Stella and I need to talk for a while.'

'Whatever you say. You're the doctor.'

'Come on, John Frank,' Ethel said. 'I'll make up some coffee.'

'Some tea would be nice,' said the doctor.

'Aint got no tea.' Ethel retrieved her tin box, and stalked out of the room. John Frank followed.

The doctor's pale eyes went up to the ceiling, then he closed the left one down in a wink. 'That is one strong-minded lady,' he said with a smile. 'No wonder you don't want to talk.'

Stella did not answer.

The doctor returned his spectacles to his nose. He took up one of the smaller pinchers, and he talked as he worked. 'This won't hurt him now, I promise. He won't feel a thing. With children his age, it's all right. They feel it the same as we do, but they can forget.' Gently, he closed the jaws of the instrument on the flesh of Jacko's thigh. Jacko blinked.

'Hmmm.' The doctor shook his head. His hand moved down the chubby pink leg. He pinched again. Jacko did not stir. 'I'll bet it wasn't his legs that he moved, am I right?'

'His arm,' she whispered.

Dannelly dropped the clamp back in the bag, took another, and closed it on one small fat arm. Jacko's eyes loomed. His mouth opened. His scream made the window glass tremble.

'Stop it! You hurt him!' Stella lunged for the table to stop him, but the doctor had already removed the clamp. After another good lungful of air, Jacko grew quiet.

'Now see there!' the doctor said. 'You see his arm move, the rest of him not? That's good news now, I believe it. He's not all paralyzed. Only his legs don't feel. Something is wrong, that's for sure. Don't know what . . . but this narrows it down just a bit.' He pried Stella's fingers away from his wrist.

He did not miss an inch in his inspection. He talked to himself, and did not seem to mind Stella's silence. At last he reached for his bag. 'That's all. Take him back to his bed. That's plenty for now.'

Without speaking, Stella gathered the little limp boy in her arms. She stood, watching Dannelly retrieve his tools.

'Oh yes,' he said, looking down, 'one other thing. I want you to know . . . just how sorry I am. No, that's not the right word. Just how badly I feel for you. Don't you be worrying about him now, he'll turn out. We'll figure it out before long. But the other . . . you know. Well I can't find my words. Bad time. I know that. I see you there burning, inside . . .'

He stopped to wipe his forehead. 'What I said. I say it all wrong. What I'm trying for, dear, and so badly, is you ought to know that you don't grieve alone. Just you know that. Remember. The good Lord, he works out his mysteries. When you feel ready – you'll know when it is – I'll be right there to hear anything you want to say to me. Just come by. You know the way. And I'll come back to check on your boy. I'll come Sunday. Maybe we'll have us a talk.'

He snapped the bag.

'I'd best go to speak to the Gibsons,' he said. 'You ought to be patient with them. And I know – they're like strangers, like all of us must seem to you. But they're being good as they can, I can tell. Take care. I'll be back out.'

Stella shifted Jacko to her hip. 'I sure thank you,' she said, but her throat did not work. She wanted to go to him, hug him, but she was afraid to touch anyone for fear they would not be there.

TEN

Stella was lost in a glimmerless fog. She came to feel glad when the sun went down, glad for the end to an unending day. At times she could remember everything, down to the smell of an egg that she burned on the stove, the day she turned five years old.

Other times, she could not think how to breathe.

Her nose was always bleeding – from all the weeping, she guessed. She let it bleed. She soaked rags with the blood, then tucked them away with the few things she saved from that night.

One morning, Stella discovered black spackles of blood on her cot and nightshirt and the floor. Different blood.

She was dying. She prayed that Jacko would die with her, so they could all be together again.

Then she discovered the source of the blood, and remembered Callie's whisper: *It's a curse* . . . Stella had always hoped she might be spared. Somehow, it did not seem right. Blood is meant to stay in.

She scrubbed hard at her nightshirt, and wept.

On a calendar in the kitchen was a colored picture of some big kind of statue, a lady in robes, with a torch in one uplifted hand.

One night the lady came into a dream. The torch looked like Jacko on fire.

Stella woke, crept into the kitchen, ripped down the calendar, and burned it in the stove.

She figured ways to keep her mind empty. She counted the things in the Gibsons' parlor: the long paisley sofa, a ladderback chair, the marble-top table, the lamp, a dull rug, a striking-clock just like her mother's – but louder, percussive. A spittoon, with spit. An umbrella holder, with a black umbrella. She lost count and started all over again.

This time she counted the clock shelf as one, and the Bible supporting the lamp. She counted herself as a thing, and that made fourteen things. Her age, come July, her next birthday.

If she counted the doorknobs, the windowshades, all the gray rabbits of dust that lived under the chairs, maybe she could figure out how old she would be. If she counted the stars on the wallpaper, maybe she'd live to be that many years.

As noises returned, she counted them too. She sat very still in the mornings, not breathing, while Ethel and John Frank were out in the yard. She counted twenty sounds, blending together: Ethel's shrill voice, Gibson's rumble, the chickens, the pigs, and the clock, and the clock . . .

After weeks of this mist, when she thought she had forgotten how feelings feel, she detected the slice of something inside, new and sharp as a razor – sharper than sorrow or anger or loneliness. It felt like hate. Stella hated them all – Mama for dying without words, William for burning and leaving no trace, the others for seeming so real on the wagon bench, and then disappearing.

She would whirl to the sound of their teasing, or Charlie Boot's abandoned laughter, but she never turned in time to see their faces.

The months passed, soothing, blunting the edge of her fury, until it lay sullenly curled in the place where her heart used to be.

Moonlight rippled the ceiling of the little room off the hall. From the rocking chair, Stella listened to the faint rise and fall of Jacko's breathing.

Jacko.

The only one left.

What if he . . . if something happened to him . . .

She had lived fourteen years in a high dreamy cloud, a soft place where people you love do not die. Then the whole cloud burned away in a night.

A fist pounded hard on a door. Stella slipped up the hall to the parlor, blue dark. A wet nose snuffled along the threshold.

The door burst with the force of John Frank Gibson staggering in, roaring and waving his arms. His words made no sense. His dogs nipped his elbows. His wild eyes searched the room, but the dark was enough to hide Stella.

He lumbered past, muttering. When she heard his bedsprings cry out, she dragged the hounds by their tails, shut the door, and went to her room.

She sat rocking, holding Jacko's foot in her hand. It must be a strong madness to seize John Frank Gibson, to consume the man who once shot mistletoe from a tree, as a gift.

Stella's eyes followed the wavery patch of moonlight across the ceiling, until it touched the far wall. She thought of the girl who ran home with the branch of white berries. That girl was gone too, as far as the kind giant man with the gun.

Stella's fingertips grazed the skin of her throat, then moved down, trembling, discovering places so soft that the slightest touch started a terrible shiver. She was not the girl her hands remembered – more tender in places, more round. Soft, like a woman, but harder inside.

ELEVEN

The day held a promise of spring: a sky of thin haze, a lightness of air. Stella sat by the window, praying for sun. With each week that passed, she had felt the melting of silence – her ears slowly clearing, the rage fading. Her plan gave her comfort, and so did Jacko.

The rest of him moved now, but his legs did not. A few words came back to him; he learned 'dog' and how to wave with his hand. Except for the legs, he was fine.

Stella took care of him, which was all right by Miss Ethel, who seemed to grow more out of sorts every day. And John Frank's face changed, along with the weather. His beard had more silver. His eyes narrowed down. He stopped trying to talk to Stella, even when she began answering. He came in at night, ate his supper alone, then went straight to his bed without saying good night. In the mornings, he left before Stella awoke. He spent his days out in the woods with his dogs.

She felt like an open sore, painful to see.

A cloud moved. The air beyond the window began to brighten. A moment of sun passed across the new grass.

Stella turned with a smile to the crib where Jacko lay snoozing, so quiet and sweet. Gibson had brought the crib in from his barn. He explained that he'd kept it for company. It was hand carved from golden pecan, sanded and gleamy with wax.

Jacko's eyes opened, and then his mouth, in an O. He yawned with a pleasure that made Stella yawn. 'Mornin, boy,' she said, 'are you wet?' She felt, and he was.

He liked to be changed. As she worked, Stella tried to not bother his legs. The rest of him had outgrown them. His knees were white knobs, locked against bending; the white little toes had just started to curl. If she touched the legs, Jacko shivered inside.

She powdered him well, and he sneezed. 'The sun's out, boy, can you feel it? It's so warm. Let's us go out for a ramble, what say? Maybe that's all our poor bones need, is sunshine.' He burbled and cooed as she fastened his eyelets.

In the way back of a drawer she found the wool bundle, the blackened remains of the blanket that saved him. It held her few things – a tortoiseshell hairbrush with a few strands of Callie's own hair still webbed in its bristles; a smoke-stained white napkin; three tiny white berries . . . and now the sling harness she'd fashioned for Jacko, made of two belts she found in a shed. She placed Jacko in it and buckled him on. 'Hold on now, get ready,' she said. 'Fixin to go.'

She heard Miss Ethel outside with the hens. 'You hear that?' she said. 'Jacko, listen at that. She's been out amongst them chickens so long, she's startin to talk like them.' She stole from the front door, and escaped across the road. Ethel did not see them go.

Stella slid down the muddy small slope to the path. 'You never been up this trail, have you, boy? There's not but one thing to look out for. Snakes. Charlie – Charlie Boot used to say girls was ascared of snakes, cause we look just like them . . .'

Jacko, slung up between her shoulder blades, saw it all in with wide eyes. She took her time up the long gentle hill, across the chattering creek. She smelled rotting bark and the sting of pine needles, a trace of far woodsmoke, her talcum-sweet boy. To the left, an old furrow led off to the spring, but the fork to the right beckoned home. Though she'd pictured it a hundred nights with the house burned away, Stella had not returned. But today, with her mood lightening, and the air, she felt ready.

She told Jacko of the day at the spring, when her fear for their mother had brought her fleeing this way. She told him of kites, how they soar from your hand, rising with every breath, high and higher, until you get tired and set the string free. She stopped to point out a forsythia blooming too early, the yellow of lemons. 'I guess any day now you'll start in to talkin,' she said. 'And, boy, I wonder what all things you could tell.'

The last rise, and home. For the first time since that night, she saw the big old pecan trees marching fifty deep, uninterrupted except by the barn. Where the house ought to be, just a sullen rectangle of mounded ashes, blackened boards angling up, and three lonesome chimneys.

Stella pushed herself on, dragging her feet through weeds. She did not want to go closer, but now she knew she had come this far and would not turn back. One day, she would have to see, and this felt like the day.

As she drew near, she saw that the mound of rubble was several mounds, with paths scraped clean where the hallways had been.

From behind a smooth hill of ash, John Frank Gibson rose up to full height. His expression sounded out like thunder – a wild angry look, tightened eyes. In one hand he held a shovel. 'What in the holy hell you doin here?' he demanded.

'Well I'm sorry –'

He cut her off. 'Somebody send you out lookin for me?'

'Why no sir –'

'Well then, what the hell!' He waded toward her on one of his paths, bearing the spade like a weapon. 'You know that child aint well, slingin him up thataway, what's the matter with you? You go on back to the house!'

His dogs bounded in. Jacko waved one fat hand. Stella backed away, groping for some explanation. 'The doctor – he said it's all right if we did,' she invented. 'He said Jacko needed some air for his legs.'

'Not in my hearin, he didn't.'

'He said it to me.' She felt for the buckles, unfastened them, took off her coat and spread it on the ground. She wanted to find out what she had discovered. 'I'll only just stay just a minute,' she said. 'This thing, it rubs on my shoulders.' When she placed Jacko on her coat, he waved. 'What are you lookin for, please, Mister Gibson?'

With the spade, he looked like a farmer of ashes. His face was a solid dark wall, staring down.

'You lookin for William?' said Stella. 'Cause he aint up here. He's gone, along with the rest.'

'Hell no he aint,' John Frank thundered, 'or else we'd of found least some part of him, least one damn bone of him.'

'Don't,' Stella said.

'He run off.' Gibson jammed his spade into the mound. 'He took scared and run off and just left em all burnin –'

'You hush!' she flared. 'You don't know! Nobody knows! And it's nobody's business but mine!'

'It aint him,' John Frank shouted, marching his path to the back of the patch. 'It don't matter bout him. He's the simple one.' Gibson stalked up his path, wheeled, and went back. 'Here.' He took two steps to the side and held out his trembling hands. 'Here's the table. The girls on this side, and them twins over there like you said. You tell me if I get it wrong. And your mama gets up, and goes into the kitchen, and walks right up here, up the hall' – he stopped, swinging right – 'to her room. No sooner gets through the door than she's out in the hall and on fire, and with *him* . . .'

His blazing eyes fell to Jacko. 'It's him,' he said, in a painful cracked voice. 'It's him that don't figure. It's him she was comin to get. It started in the room where he was. And he's the one come through it without not one single scratch, not a burn on his hide. It's him that don't move his legs, when it's done.'

'I did,' said Stella. 'I come through it too.'

'But it's *him*.' Gibson stepped from the ruin toward her. Stella knelt, lifting Jacko. Gibson was out of his head. Pure plain crazy. She'd discovered him sweating, wild, as if he were a murderer tearing with fingers at the dirt where his victim lay. 'Stop where you are,' she hissed. 'You just stop.'

He obeyed. His hands disappeared in his pockets. For a moment, he seemed to recover himself, then he shuddered and whistled out high, for his dogs.

A gust of yelping blew in from the south. Bayard and Big Help came bounding, wagging, yapping, their homely hides eaten by mange. Big Help's whole head was bald pink. They circled and barked, seeming glad they were ugly.

'Daw,' Jacko crowed, in a clear little voice. He waved. 'Daw!'

'That's right, dog,' Stella said. 'See the dog?' She watched Gibson's face take a turn, an odd bend. The dogs waggled up, leaped for the hand he extended.

'Go on,' he muttered. The dogs skittered off and came back, barking and jumping.

Gibson hollered hush but they kept up their frantic yelping, as if they smelled blood on his hands.

Then a sound came, a choking, *ark! arrrrghl!* With a murderous snarl, and a vicious shine in his good eye, Bayard lit out after Big Help.

'Mon now,' called Gibson, 'come back! Hyuh! Giddown!' He started after them, ambling, running, then chasing their tangle of snarls in its wide circle, back toward Stella. She froze, her back to the tree. Jacko dangled from one arm.

'Daw!' he said.

Stella heard teeth ripping hide. The wild swirling funnel swept past, Gibson shouting behind.

'Giddown!' He snatched a limb from the ground and laid it down hard on the maddened dog's spine, but Bayard ignored him and went for the throat. Big Help fled shrieking.

Thwack! the limb struck, and tha-*whack!* again harder, hard enough surely to split Bayard's spine, but the dog got away and went straight for the fence where his prey struggled, snagged on a barb in the wire.

Gibson scrambled after, screaming, flailing with his stick, but Bayard set jaws into meat and tore his companion free of the fence. John Frank tried to climb it, but caught his own leg in the wire and fell, pulling a fencepost down with him.

Big Help's piteous howl drowned in gurgling as his throat was opened. Bayard snatched him up, shook him to know he was dead, then stood wagging his tail, and panting.

Another howl rose in the orchard. 'Now look what you done!' Gibson cried to the sky. He untangled himself from the fence. The dog did not run from him. Gibson's left hand clamped his neck and lifted; the body of Big Help came up in the right. He stepped across the fallen fence, holding the live and the dead one before him. He walked an unvarying line to the garden of ashes. With infinite care, he lowered the body of Big Help to

sand, took up the shovel. His other hand pinned Bayard's neck.
The dog did not resist.

Thud. Stella turned her eyes away. *Thud*. She cringed, and
waited, but two was enough. She made herself see. John Frank
left Bayard there, skull hidden under the shovel blade, and came
toward Stella with Big Help's body. She knew she should run.

'You wait there.' Not loud, but cold as white ice. Black blood
oozed down his wrist. His eyes shone, hard and dark. Stella
could not break away from their grip.

'Good Lord,' she said. He came near. 'Please. Oh please
don't. Please, oh, take it away.'

He held it close to her face. Blood dripped on the sand. 'That
was my dog,' he whispered.

'Oh I know,' she said. Run, run away – but he held her still
with his stare.

He knelt before her. 'My dog,' he said. 'That was my *dog*.'

'Oh I know. I never seen a dog do that way . . .'

His eyes came up again, melting. She watched a tear tracing
down to his beard. He was not looking at her. He was not even
trying. The twist of his mouth made him look almost as if he
was smiling. He saw only Jacko.

Stella whirled, took off running, and faster, so fast that the
barbs in the fence missed her feet stumbling through. She
hugged Jacko. He began whimpering. 'Hush,' she said, turning.

John Frank still knelt in the sand by the largest pecan, stroking
the ears of his dog.

TWELVE

Stella ran down through bushes trembling with buds, past a forsythia blooming too soon. She ran to the fork in the path without stopping. She could not go back to Gibson's house, not till nightfall, at least. Give him time to get down there, give Ethel time to see how bad he's gone in his head. Surely she'll see, and talk sense into him. She's peculiar enough, on her own, but surely . . .

The right fork. The spring, for a while, just to think, and to let Jacko sleep in the air. She fastened him into his harness. He let out a sigh that seemed gray as the gathering clouds. Wind from the west brought a message of rain. She hurried her steps, and soon reached the mossy lip of earth above the spring.

It was not like she remembered – a mirror as flat as those dead metal eyes. She tried to recover the mood of those fine distant days when she brought all the children to swim here, but John Frank kept crowding it out.

Digging in ashes for some kind of clue, but to what? What was he hoping to find? Why did it matter to him, how they died? He could dig down to China, or hell for that matter, but all the dead would stay dead.

Stella shuddered. The blame for his dogs, in that last awful stare. He put no blame on the killer. He blamed the most helpless creature of all. Jacko. A baby. Her boy. Her sweet only boy. Maybe some sickness had seized Gibson that night, like the one that came to Jacko's legs, only it touched Gibson somewhere way deep, and it took time to show.

A single huge droplet shattered the glass. Perfect rings floated out. Another drop bounced and fell in, and another. The rain made a spatting on leaves, and then suddenly the whole sky was full of its falling. It grew to a roar, blurred to sheets driving sideways, made new little rivers that ran for the spring.

Stella searched in her mind for a roof, any roof. She tried to be Jacko's umbrella, hugging him close, taking off the way she came. Her foot struck a slimy place. They went sprawling. Jacko spilled out of her grasp and fell hard, but he laughed, and Stella laughed too.

Her barn! It was there, and much closer than Gibson's. They could wait through the storm and dry out. She gathered Jacko, so wet that the rain did not matter at all. Still, Stella ran all the way home.

Gibson was gone. His paths were melting, the ashes diluting into a gray milk.

The roof of the barn poured a line of small waterfalls on the sand. The door gave and swung in to darkness and old hay, the smell of cows not long gone. Stella sank to her knees with Jacko. 'Both drenched to the bone,' she told him, but he did not mind.

His clothes came off quick as cornshucks, and then her own, which she spread on a bale of sweet hay. She took her boy into the curve of her body, curling around him, warming them both. Rain drummed above on the tin, and occasional thunder set the roof to buzzing.

They breathed together. She sang him some nonsense until he quit shivering. Naked, they'd never be warm. A horse blanket, maybe, somewhere in the barn. She crept to a corner, found a musty wool heap with her hands. The instant she pulled off one blanket, Stella shrieked and jumped back. Her hands flew to cover her.

Floating there above the mound was a pair of old eyes, yellow and crusted, and sly like a cat's. They blinked coolly.

In her panic, Stella nearly stepped on Jacko.

'Hold on, nekkid white gal! Got nothin to fear!' said a gleeful dark voice, past strange.

'Who are you? What you doin in here?'

'Hooo, the same thang as you, ceptin I got some shirt on my back,' it said. 'Wrop up yo hide in this here, swee petunia, and po little crupple boy, wrop him up too.'

Stella was glad for the blanket, but returned the stare with

suspicion. A tiny and ancient and possibly Negro old woman
stood up then, her hands on her hips. Her face was the cracked
brown of yard eggs, but wrinkled and scaly, more like the skin
of a snake – a face that seemed as friendly as it was ugly.

She pulled back her chin, outlining four chins, grinning wide
pink, with one tooth. 'I come from outen the rain, child, the
same as you. White or some else, hit don't differ. All wet when
it rain. Be a wonder if po crupple boy don't take down with some
chill.'

'Why you call him that?' Stella said. 'How do you know?'

'Hooo, gal, you tell you a lot, just by lookin. By lookin, I say
he be – oh, he ain two year, the most. Took down with fever,
back long about Chrustmastime. Had him a high boy ol fever, I
say right? And set to his wailin and thrashin like ol Mistah Devil
come set up a camp in his belly. I speak it right? And then,
hooo! He don't move. Don't nare wiggle. Don't nothin at all
ceptin lay in the bed. Now tell me, child, tell me – do I speak a
lie?'

Stella clutched Jacko. 'How you know all that?'

'When some babe done touch by the fire, swee pea, Mary
make it her business to know,' said the woman. 'He done been
hit, done be touch by the flame. A heap of old cheeruns I brung
to this world, but hain seen too many get touch thataway.'

'What you mean?' Stella inspected this creature who dressed
like a boy: overalls held together by a dozen patches, a bright
crimson shirt, brogan shoes, and a flat knitted cap. Like an
ornery prideful smart wrinkled brown boy, with old eyes that
smiled.

'Powerful lot,' she was saying, 'got troubles. Yo boy there,
he troubly, but he be all right. Hain gone know what it was to
just get up and walk. So it hain gone to matter the day when he
don't.'

'You crazy, old woman,' said Stella. 'His legs are sick, but
they won't be for long. The doctor says they'll get better and
he'll learn to walk.'

'Once some thangs die, they be dead,' said the woman. She
stuck out her hand like a prize worth accepting. 'You call me
Little Brown Mary. That's what all my cheeruns call me. Yo

Mistah Doctah Man there, he be rile should I come in his house. He be jump in the air, say, "Here, devil, get gone!"' Her eyes narrowed down, then she reached out to Jacko.

Stella pulled away.

'Now looky, see how his legs? Once they do thataway, bendin, well that's when you know. That's when the life juice done gone, hain comin back.'

'You don't know better than the doctor,' Stella said.

'Hoo-hooo, petunia, I known me some *thangs*!' Mary cackled. She hooked her thumbs through her overall straps. 'When you get old like I do, you come to know a whole heap. Heap of thangs comin yo way all the time, comin *at* you. To where if you don't know em, it's yo own fault.'

Stella sat down on a bale. 'You seem awful much at home here,' she said, 'for an old Negro woman in a white folks' barn.'

'Hooo!' Mary's whistle was clear as a train in the night. She rolled her eyes. 'Lissen at big talk. Just lissen at her.'

Jacko squirmed against Stella's bosom. She slid her thumb into his mouth.

'And he won't quit till he's had him some eat. You can't blame some baby his age, want his dinner.'

'I give him breakfast already,' said Stella.

'Hoo, girl, don't say it! Now you speak a lie! You ain got the titty yet, given no milk.' She laughed so hard all her wrinkles shook.

A blush crawled over Stella. 'I give it from our neighbor's cow.'

Mary settled a claw on Stella's bare shoulder, squeezing and cackling still. 'Din mean to say you was shy on yo titty, gal. Comin along. You be makin the white boys to smile.'

Stella brushed the hand off. Callie once teased her the same easy way . . .

'Now don't get like that. Why you'd thank I said bad. Look at you, sissy old thang with yo babe, and ol lip done poke out like a baby yoself. Come on, sweet tunia, give on with yo smile.'

'You give on,' Stella said. 'You stop makin fun. You the meanest old thing that I ever have seen.'

'Now, gal, I ain done it,' Mary wheedled, crouching. 'What I say wrong? Just tell it back to me.'

'You sayin Jacko's a cripple, and all. Like you known us before. Like he won't never walk.' That was a thought that she constantly hid from her mind. 'You said it almost like it was somebody's fault.'

'I hain say fault now, cause hain no fault, ceptin ol Mistah Devil. He come up to breathe of some air and done touch on yo boy, that was all. Leastway, he gone. He done gone off of here.'

'Who . . .'

'Tell me his name, cause I caint. That white skinny boy, you know him. That boy. Yo brother. Din they find ever last bone ceptin a one from that boy?'

'William,' Stella whispered. 'You don't know a thing. He burned along with . . .' She stopped, cleared her throat, and went on. 'The fire was too awful hot. That's howcome they didn't find him. That's all.'

'I be beggin yo pardons, done talkin too much,' Mary said. When she stood, all her joints cracked. 'Don't mean to talk bout yo kinfolk like he was the devil. You right, some fire just too hot for bones. And Law, ain we all of us dance with the devil a time or two, sometimes, one time in our life.'

Stella felt tears in her eyes, wanting out. She squeezed them in, holding Jacko still closer. 'Aint you got no place to live but in here?'

'Live where I breathe,' Mary said. 'Late times, though, well I tell it, they been bad. Been havin myself what some folk calls a *difficult*. Folks all be holdin they babes for the springtime, nare too much business for me. Had me a regular place I could lay down my head, but done got run off. Old black preachah done run me. Say he was the man who done own where I stay. Like any man, white or a colored, don't matter, could own him a piece of this earth for hisself.' She cackled at the idea.

'But Law, din ol Mary put word on him, though. He come with his talk – say, "Come on now, Suster, you pay me some rent, or I thow you right off." Back and a forth, you know, him talkin God. So I says I aint fear no God that *he* know. But he kep on, come on bout getting to heaven, say, "Pay me some

rent or I send you to hell." This what I told him, now lissen:
"Mistah Black Preachah," I say, "then go on and send. If hell
got no rent, I the first on the train!"' She folded over, clapping
her knees, making the funny high whistle. Her glee shamed a
grin out of Stella.

Mary tottered to her feet again, displaying her yellow palms.
'So then's when I come to stood here in yo barn. I could see
you was got not too much use for it, since you done down to
that house with yo babe.' From her bulging bib pocket she drew
a soiled leather pouch and a whittled cob pipe. The stem was
brownish and greasy, chewed down to a nub, the bowl charred
down to a fragile thin rim. 'Yes ma'am, be one fine old
barn. Gettin right crowded, though, longer I stay. Twix that
old white falla diggin, be lookin for gold or some worse I cain
guess, and that big color man come to tend for yo cow . . . and
here come you outen the rain with yo babe.' She shook her
head, as if fate were a hairnet, then dug the pipe down in the
pouch.

It came up stuffed with a moldy gray weed, wicked tobacco
with a strange sweet smell. Stella had seen men smoke pipes
before. She held it as an instance of grown-up foolishness, like
drinking whiskey, which smelled like something to burn and left
Negroes upended, giggling in roadbeds, like june bugs flipped
onto their backs.

Little Brown Mary snapped her fingers. A magical blue flame
sprang out, touched the pipe. Harsh smoke erupted. Stella
coughed. 'That stuff smells nasty.'

'Brang yo sweet boy and come seddown with me.' Mary
offered a grin and the bowl, leaking smoke. 'Come on and have
you a smoke with Brown Mary. I never did mean to bring sorrow
to you.'

Stella wrinkled her nose, shook her head. 'I don't know how
you stand it,' she said. 'Yack.'

'Hooo, child, I tell you, it help when you po.'

'Smells like it would choke a dog, to me.'

'Hit do, now you say it,' Mary sputtered.

Her high cackle faded, and changed to a sigh. She was tiny
and feisty, and acting so funny that Stella could not help but like

her, right off. 'I reckon you stay here as long as you want,' she said.

Mary looked up. 'Well now bless you, petunia, I plain be beholded. This be yo whole barn to give?'

'Yes ma'am, it is,' Stella mimicked. Jacko snored.

'Gal got her a barn, well that's some mo than most. I thankin you kindly, but I be all right. I got mo cheeruns, spread out in these wood. Got two boys up North there, just fine boys, real big. And three fine gals, purty, in Montgomery City. Ain really my cheeruns, no, mine done and gone. Dead and buried, like yourn. But I brung some down.'

They sat for a long moment, tasting the gloom. 'What you do, swee petunia, if you ain got no babes – oh you will, sho you will. But if you just don't, just make sho you brang down a whole heap of cheeruns. That way you always got someplace to go.'

'Yes ma'am, I won't,' Stella said.

'Hooo, gal, now lissen,' said Mary, inhaling. 'I think you and me here, the pair of us both' – her fingers danced as if she were leading a tune – 'we make up a fine pair of niggers, just fine.'

'Who you mean?' said Stella. 'I aint a nigger.'

'Why you and me, gal, and that sweet crupple boy! The niggerest folks to set foot on this earth.'

'But I aint a nigger. I'm a Bates. And a Bates is some things, but not niggers.'

'Hooo, now you talkin, but liss what I say! A nigger is any old body that ever done seen the upside down side of a white man shoe. And that is us, gal, just as sho as can be.'

'Well I aint,' Stella insisted.

Mary took a long draw. Smoke oozed from her nose. Her lone tooth slid out. 'All right, then,' she said, reaching out for Jacko. 'Me and this boy, we be niggers our own selfs.'

Stella let her take him, though no one had held him but her, since that night. His legs dangled naked and ugly, so limp. His bare bottom sagged, wrinkled and loose as Mary's old face. He did not mind awakening in her hands. She bounced him; his eyes jiggled dizzily.

'A fine little nigger,' said Mary, 'sho fine. And life of me, I cain see nare one burn spot on him.'

Stella leaned back in the hay. 'He didn't get burned.'

'Touch by the fire, and free from the burnin.' Mary grabbed Jacko's foot. 'Now see there, I tellin? Just look here. The life juice done gone, and it ain comin back.'

Stella bristled. 'He'll walk, you wait,' she said. 'He'll walk right up to you one day, you'll see.' She liked the sound of it, hoped it was true. She reached out for Jacko, took him in, gently nuzzled his head, catching wisps of his silvery hair in her teeth.

'Rain quit,' said Mary. 'Look see.'

Stella rose, collecting blanket and Jacko. She nudged the door open. A sprinkling of drops still fell from the eaves, but the sun was out, shining the grass. 'That sure was fierce, to pass by so quick,' she said. 'Reckon if our clothes are dry.' She turned. The barn was empty.

Jacko said, 'Wuh wuh wuh wuh.' Stella set him down, went to the pile of old blankets – nothing but blankets now. She climbed the rickety ladder to the hayloft – hay, but no Mary. Gone, just as quick as she came. 'Well if you're still here,' Stella said, 'I wish you'd come by and see us sometime.' She climbed down. 'Boy, we best get on back. They're liable to be out lookin for us.' Her clothes were clammy, but she put them on. What a funny old woman! Something familiar: the smell? A whistle like that you could never forget. Just when what looks like a friend comes along, she ups and disappears.

Stella sang songs to Jacko all the way back down the hill. She stopped when she glimpsed the white house through the trees. Something was wrong. Bad bad wrong.

Miss Ethel was proud of her yard, but now the green of its grass was laced with muddy ruts. Wagon tracks. It looked as if a herd of drivers had raced through the yard, and half had got stuck, and the rest pulled them out.

And a silence, too loud – not the kind in her head. Not even the faraway chonk of a cowbell to break the hard quiet that covered the place. No dogs. No Miss Ethel, clucking. No John Frank there, muttering low to himself.

The wagons were gone, the town and the field one both. The pair of rockers was gone from the porch. Gone, gone, all gone but the house. A wind might have sucked the house clean. She stepped up on the porch. Her footsteps made loud hollow sounds. The door squealed. A square paper stared up at her from the parlor floor. The rooms had been emptied of everything else. She picked up the note.

Stella.

The bugs is eaten John Franks crop. He says they are hear to stay now for good.
He has better place in Clarke Co.
Good bye.
He says we have got to go where no bugs. The Dr look after you and baby. I left yr things back in the kitchen. Go look. Come see us some times. God will forgive.

E. Gibson

PS *We are not afraid. We catch it all sides. John Frank sed he cleared the place where yr house. Maybe you build you one there. God bye.*

Ethel had scratched out the last words and spelled them again, but Stella kept reading them the way they were first. God bye. Oh God help me. God come and take me away. God bye. Gone, and as quick as if they'd never been! How could they gather all the things and leave in the time it took the storm to pass?

Unharnessing Jacko, she sank to the floor. She cried awhile, soft as music, without tears, because it seemed the right thing to do. God bye.

She wished she was back somewhere, back in the past – not to the time before that night, not then, but back to the time when they all were new dead, and lived on just as real, in her mind. When her life seemed a dream of the dead. If she could dream her own family now, they would never be able to leave.

She heard someone coming, and stood. Through the screen she saw Ben! Their own Negro, who helped with the plow. The last soul alive on the earth. He dragged up slowly to Gibson's front porch, as if every scuff of his feet was a job. He glanced around, expecting a ghost. He filled up the door. His head was so tall that Stella could not see it. His corded neck muscles wound into his shoulders like roots. He put a hand on the knob.

'Ben? That you?'

He did not jump back. Ben never moved fast. Every blink of his eyes was the product of a deliberate thought. She remembered the field, the children all pestering, buzzing around him like gnats. The beat of his powerful hoe never changed.

She spoke through the screen. 'I got caught in the rain,' she said. 'I thought of your house first, but I couldn't remember where it was.'

'Be where it is,' Ben said, bending to peer in.

'I guess I've never been there.'

Ben did not answer. His hands hung helpless beside him, unoccupied without a hoe or something to hold. He folded them over his broad chest.

Stella nudged the door. He took a step back. 'Well go on, then,' she challenged, stepping out after him. He retreated down the steps. 'You act like you afraid of me.'

'Where Muster Gibson.'

'He's gone,' Stella said.

'But where to?'

'I don't know. Just gone. I thought you might could tell me. Sometime since this mornin, they picked up and went.'

Ben's solid face told her nothing. He blinked. 'Muster Gibson, I talk to him day befo last. He owe me a dollar for milkin them cows.'

'How much?'

'A dollar,' he said. 'It's a dollar a month.'

'Well you welcome to come in and look,' Stella said, 'but I don't believe he left you no dollar.'

'Nome.' Ben's eyes looked past her, taking in all the emptiness. 'But it look like he'd say where he gone.'

Stella turned from the door. 'I got to go get my boy,' she said. 'I'll be back out.'

She did not notice how Ben's nostrils widened at that. Jacko greeted her with a sharp burp. She gathered him up and went out. 'Look like they took it all but him and me.'

'Look like it,' Ben said, his eyes to the ground.

'Those cows are mine and not his,' she said. 'Now listen. You keep em for me till I get a place. I'm gone build me one up there, as soon as I can. I'll pay you your dollar just soon as I can.'

Ben stayed quiet.

'I might come get us some milk, time to time.'

He nodded.

'I reckon we'll walk into town, to the doctor's. You know where he lives, don't you, Ben?'

He said nothing.

'I bet he'll let us stay there for a while. Till I can get me some money somehow. Soon as I do, you can come work for me, like you did for Mama. I'll pay you.'

Ben examined the tracks in the grass, shaking his head.

'Why not, Ben? You like me all right, don't you?'

'Some thangs change,' Ben said.

'Aw Ben, come on. You afraid of a ghost?'

'Aint talkin no ghost.' His eyes lifted. He stared with passion, the same kind of passion as Gibson, at the boy she held in her arms. As if he were seeing some great fearful storm. 'He really do live and breathe, like they say.' He turned. 'I gots to be gettin along.'

'Don't go, Ben,' Stella said. 'Just please stay for a while.'

But he was moving away, to the road. Ben never ran, but he trotted off now and he never looked back to see Stella, who watched.

THIRTEEN

Hooo, such a sight for some po eyes to see. White folks done roasted alive, such a sight. Nare such like that since a way long time back, since the niggers was all runnin scared from the white. Then it was all the thing you ever saw, folks totin torches and white womens screamin, all kind of shootin and hangin and such.

Least way back then you could make you a band. Cause niggers, they runnin so scared they would listen, and sign down they X's, and meet you at night. Then come the fightin, and all them such stop. Niggers set free. Or else thought they was, hooo! Like some lanky old white man could sign down his X, and free would fall down out the sky, like some rain.

White folks and niggers all got to be po, spendin day in the wood, shootin squirrel. Just tryin to get from today to next week.

Burnin and shootin and such settle back. Place got too quiet, it all stood the same. You can't make up a band out of folks that aint scared. Gone join nothin, nare such, ain no way. Hungry and scared – them some two different things. Hungry folks don't want no trouble. Just eat. If shootin and hangin gone start up again, why some niggers get riled. Then maybe join up a band. White folks burnt up, why it could be a sign. Could be some things would get troubly again.

Old joints done froze up. Been settin too still like. All crack. Gettin old. Hooo! Colder than most nights, some colder than most.

House done burnt up, but they barn be all right. White gal done give us the sayso to stay.

Member her mama, a right sweet white gal. Plenty of babies, bring down all the time. Till that one old hot night. Got run off.

Don't need no white mama runnin me off. Plenty of cheeruns spread out through some wood.

Ain come around, ain no way. Till tonight.

One time, done give that white mama some prize. Best kind of witchy ball, best kind. Do burn just to member. Then she done run this gal off. Wonder them witchy ball burnt in them fire.

Gone stay in that barn. White mama, she owe it. She dead but still owe her Hoomama. She say get gone, you done known too much, Hoomama. I tell you, child, ain nothin so bad what I saw. Ain a thing to worry yo lifetimes about. Just a thing you might do, was you stuck in a bad kind of place.

And she was. And done gone up in smoke. Left us some warm kind of barn, cow to lay down here with. Fin to sleep up next to em. Sho be glad of some warm.

This place done touch by the fire. By some bad kind of warm. Like a sign, or some such.

FOURTEEN

Everne emerged from a tunnel of scuppernong vines in the yard to one side of her house. She crookedly carried a woven straw basket, spilling a trail of green fruit. A smile slipped onto her face. 'Now look who's come callin,' she sang, 'and me in the yard with no shoes!'

Stella glanced down at Everne's chubby feet, crisscrossed with tiny blue lines like a map. 'I'd sure love to be barefooted myself, Miz Dannelly,' she said, 'but we've come a ways –'

'Why just looky at him!' burst out Everne. 'And how you got him slung! Isn't that a notion! He's got so big I just can't help but wonder. And looking so good I barely recognized him.'

Stella reached into her pocket, and offered Miss Ethel's last message. Everne squinted down. Her smile died. 'Well me, that's odd, isn't it,' she said, 'just up and leaving, that way. Bugs in his cotton . . . Well come on in the house, child.' She set up a chatter that led to the porch. 'Now sit yourself down – Aurelia, I need you. We'll sit in the swing till the doctor comes home . . .'

She talked without stopping until the tree shadows stretched out and the nightbirds were starting to sing. 'He'll be back soon,' she promised. 'He'll know just what to do, wait and see. Why don't we put the child down on the loveseat inside.'

The doctor stayed gone until well after dinner. He showed no surprise at his guests. 'I knew that man Gibson was funny somehow,' he said, then, 'Well you know you're both welcome here, long as you like. Bless your hearts.'

The next day at breakfast, Everne announced that she was glad, after lo all these years, to have someone more lively than the help around while the doctor was off on his calls.

The doctor fashioned a crib for Jacko from heart pine; the Gibsons had taken theirs with them. He sanded and sanded, buffed the wood until it shone like sateen. Stella and Jacko were installed, with this fine construction, in a small room by the kitchen. She gladly adopted it, hiding her things in a place where the molding misjoined with the wall.

She ate from the generous stove of Aurelia, a woman the color of bourbon who wore red bandannas and doted on Jacko. Stella's hair lost its harsh cast and grew soft again, golden, with a feel like combed cotton. The flesh came back onto her bones.

For the first time in Stella's memory, no one expected an ounce of real work. She felt like a queen in a book. Aurelia cooked; her man Cleo did everything else. Stella had hot tea whenever she wanted, like that, simply by asking. The table was spread with a cloth and bright silver. The yard was swept every morning by Cleo, who took away leaves that had fallen at night.

Everne took Stella into Camellia, to Front Street, for an afternoon at the Planter's Mercantile. While Stella chose among millions of dresses, Everne told her ways people act while in town.

Then it was summer, a swim every day in a creek that ran cold, half a mile from the Dannellys' house. She took Jacko, who loved to splash and scream.

Then it was autumn. The trees grew new colors. The Gibsons' hard faces were fading away, so Stella quit trying to conjure them. No message came, from Clarke or any other county.

The rush of new things brought a healing – the hot baths, the teacakes at four, the prospect of school.

Mama never believed in school, when there was work to be done at the house, and besides, town was a seven-mile walk each way. And anyway, she already could read every word in the Bible, said Callie, and that was enough. But Stella had always wondered what it would be like to sit still all day while somebody talked to you.

Now she found out. It was terrifying. She stood up in front of those eyes, wiggled toes in her rigid new shoes while Miss Maysie Broyles introduced her. She blushed at the sound of her name. She was taller than Miss Maysie, taller than anyone except one lanky boy in the last row. She tried folding her legs under the little desk, but they would not fit. She heard snickering.

Miss Maysie wasted no time to begin. 'Seven times nine,' she called, 'seven times nine.'

A drippy-nosed girl in front thrust her hand high in the air. 'Sixty-three,' she cried.

'Thank you, Nadine,' said the teacher. 'Who's next? Class? Four times nine! Luther Herlong? Sit up straight, sir, and tell me what four is, times nine.'

Nadine jabbed with her hand. 'I know it, I know –'

'Four times nine, sir, or have you gone deaf?' Miss Maysie clapped her hands: crack!

The lanky boy blinked. 'Ma'am?' he said.

'Four times nine!'

'I . . . I don't know. Fifty-five. I don't know. Fifty-two . . .'

'I know, I know!' cried Nadine.

'How about our new pupil? Does she know?' Miss Maysie pointed to Stella.

Stella suddenly realized it was just four nines put together, but just as she started to answer, Nadine yelled, 'Thirty-six!'

'Thirty-six,' Stella whispered.

'Nadine, we must give other pupils a chance,' said Miss Maysie.

Stella saw the lanky boy pretending his face was not red. Their eyes met. They both looked away. She was glad someone else here was too tall and did not know answers.

After the first day, she wondered if she would survive this room and its stale odor of milk every day until spring. But then she started to read. She raced through Miss Maysie's bookshelves, past the slender big-lettered books, straight on to the fat books, which mostly were stories of young girls named Eloise or Marguerite who got mixed up in some kind of trouble, but always got out just in time.

There were three fat blue books on the shelf yet to read, when spring came out of nowhere, and school was over.

Spring brought in bugs, a voracious new breed, to chew into green cottonfields all around. They hatched inside the white bolls, ignoring the green leaves and stalks for the precious white fiber.

These tiny gray dragons held farmers' red necks in their vigorous minuscule jaws. They ate the only rich thing in the land as if they had been built by a god for the task. Farmers went to their fields every morning, hoping for nothing but one more night's growth, but the first pass of mules down their rows made them stop. They would snatch off a boll, peel its husk, and find inside a white useless sponge. They hurled bolls and curses to the earth. None of them ever had seen an invasion.

When cotton failed, they looked around them for something to sell and regarded the woods with new eyes. Trees were the stuff of this land, so they cut them – trees with more shades of green than had names. The lumber brought money, but took away something. The trees blunted wind, softened the blow of rain. When trees fell, a destruction began. The farmers who always had beaten back woods soon discovered that they missed the cool of its shelter. Ravines opened up. Shacks stood poking from newly cleared woods like bad teeth.

Beneath its cover, the earth here was red – bright crimson when turned, then it rusted – all but one swath, a freakish black band, rich as the soil to the north along the planters' river, cutting from west to east like a buried black snake. Yields from the crops on this stripe were far better. The cotton grew stronger, the bolls more resistant. A farmer might puff up in pride at his skill when a good crop came in, then look over his fence to his despondent neighbor, who damned the cotton and dirt and himself.

Among this blend of good soil and hard clay, there grew creatures so small that no human eye saw them. In sunken wet places, they found their best homes. Their numbers divided, divided again, then flew off in the bellies of bugs that consumed them.

So many things lived their lives out in eyeblinks; the ones that were felt by the people were few. Yet these specklets governed like tyrants. Their touch could bring death.

Every summer, mosquitoes attacked, bringing malaria with them. It weakened the people and turned their attention away

from one or two children who grew still, and died. Other plagues
came, with unspellable names.

Now their power throbbed. They seemed to lurk on every
chance breeze, on the rims of all cups, on the lips of all those
who might say howdy do. A man would give his wife ten children,
in hopes that three might survive all the summers.

Without announcement, a new plague had arrived.

It had touched Jacko first, then curled up into night on a wisp
of white smoke. It descended again in a year, but found nothing
so frail as to tempt its discreet appetite. It withdrew – feeding,
dividing through seasons, breathing the air as a fire breathes a
draft, until it had numberless numbers.

A swift march of years, the world growing older. The untried
malignance grew strong. In steaming July, in Camellia's Negro
quarter, a small mulatto boy felt its touch. His fever gave him
six nights screaming. His hollering woke up white people on
Front Street, four city blocks from the house where he died.

His brother soon sickened, and lit half the windows in town
with his cries. A third child was stricken – a small pretty girl
with skin like old chocolate, known in the town for her sassy
young mouth and pink dress.

The people of Front Street heard mutterings among their
servants and met with the doctor. He went to the house and
was puzzled, gave shots for the pain, then carried the violent
creature away when he left.

It raced through the town like a wind.

In three weeks, the doctor turned old. His silver-blond hair
bleached to white, all at once. He found that his spectacles would
not decipher the parts of the *Gleam* that were set in small type.
His ears caught just those things he chose to hear. His sweat
tasted saltier. He slept fitfully, some nights not at all. If he fell
to dreaming, the faces of sick children woke him. He preferred
not to sleep, to drive sickbed to sickbed, noticing nothing he
saw in between. The children, the children . . . an endless
parade of dim unknowing faces, upturned to the cool of his
hand.

Jacko became just a child among many.

Some citizens packed up their households and left, then some more. They cluttered the road with their wagons, their drivers happy to believe they'd left all the troubles behind.

While most counties fell to the jaws of the dragon, no other was stricken by two plagues at once. In many minds, both the contagions were one. Whatever fell, cotton or children, it all was the same – all ruined, all blight. New farms were waiting, and even new children. The old land held only a curse. Those who remained watched each other with hot anxious eyes. Some muttered to others, dark talking.

1917

FIFTEEN

A hot night. The burden of August hung down. The doctor strode into the hall from the kitchen. He stumbled on something, peered down: a leg white as milk. Jacko: the round pinkish face with a brat's bold expression, the tangle of frothy gold curls, a pair of ears jutting like cup handles, eager blue eyes that seemed black when they flashed. Half strength. His shoulders were strong, and his arms, from pushing, but as if a line had been drawn at his waist, everything below was shrunken up, drawn.

The big foot had come down with full weight on his calf. Yet the boy stared up with a painless undisturbed look. 'Where's Munner?'

'The kitchen, the last time I saw her. I didn't mean to step on you, boy. What were you doing in my study?'

Jacko's eyes blazed like the sky before stars. 'Just lookin,' he said.

Despite the dozens of stricken legs the doctor touched and massaged every day, he stared down with something near to revulsion. They looked like normal legs, but they were too small by half, splayed out on the floor, the toes clenched into a fist. Before he learned he knew nothing of this affliction, the doctor had thought they would heal. He thought fresh air might interrupt their bending, so Jacko wore blue denim dresses Aurelia made for him. The hems reached to the knobs of his knees.

'You'd best go back, get your supper,' said the doctor. 'And you stay out of my study. That's no place for you.'

'What's that green thing?' Jacko said.

'What green thing?'

'In yonder, in the pitcher.'

'I don't know which of the pictures you mean, boy. Go on

back, now, and get you some supper.' The doctor stepped over the legs. 'You want a lift?'

'I can go.' Jacko planted fists on the floor.

'Careful where you put yourself, Jack. You like to got run over.' The doctor stepped into his study, eased the door shut, sat, and shook out the *Gleam*. Then he heard a sound come in from the hall – the thump of fists on the floorboards, the legs dragging after: thump-shhh, thump-shhh . . .

Jacko pulled toward the beckoning clatter of pans from the kitchen. 'Munner?'

Stella turned, her hands consumed by soap bubbles. 'What you want, boy?'

'Just a cool drink of water.'

'I give you one, not ten minutes ago,' she said. 'You are more trouble tonight.' But before she was through saying it, she moved for the galvanized tub by the door. She brought the dipper too full. 'Careful,' she said, bending. 'I swear, you'll wet the bed.'

'No I won't,' Jacko said, starting a pout.

'You wet it three times last week. One time you wet so much it woke me up.'

'I din meeeean to,' he said, winding up for a wail.

'Shh – be quiet. Miz Dannelly's got her sick headache, and Aurelia's sick for real, and doctor's got three calls tonight.' Stella touched her brow, frosting it with soapsuds. Troubles passed by every day on the road and lately they seemed to be stopping at night.

'But I din mean to wet –'

'I know you didn't. But you just can't have thirteen drinks of water before your bedtime.'

'I want a peach, Munner. Peel me a peach.'

'Peel me a peach what,' said Stella.

'*Please.*' Jacko rolled his eyes.

'There aint no more peaches.'

'Howcome?'

'Because. There just aint.' She turned to the dishpan.

'Munner. The doctor. He stepped on me, Munner.'

'Well he didn't mean to,' she said. 'I told you, he's got more troubles than you. You ought to stay out of his way.'

'But, Munner, it *hurt.*'

Stella dropped a saucer. 'It *what*?' she said to her face in the window.

'It hurt. He stepped on my leg and it hurt.'

'Are you sure now, boy – you mean – did it really –' She turned away from the window. From the sly look in his eyes, she knew he was telling a lie. 'Oh me, don't tease tonight, Jacko, now please.'

'It *did*,' he insisted. 'It hurt.'

'You a lie.'

'No I aint.'

'Yes you are.'

'No I *aint.*'

'Jacko, hush. I swear it, I'll put you to bed.'

'But –'

'Just hush up a minute, you hear? If you hush your mouth, I'll tell you a story for boys who tell lies.'

Jacko loved stories. 'I'll hush,' he said, dragging nearer to her feet.

'All right.' Stella put her hands back into the basin. 'Mama used to tell us this story when we would lie. And she said it was true. Don't know where it happened, don't matter. It did. There was this little old boy, bout your size, and this whole town full of folks that was scared of the dark. So scared that they all of em took turns at night, watchin out. One night it was this little boy's turn, so they set him out there all by his lonesome on a stump.'

'What was his name?' Jacko said.

'Don't matter. This was before they had names. But anyhow, this boy was sneaky. And wantin some fun. It wasn't much fun just to sit in the dark there, and watch. And before long he thunk up a joke he could play. Just to get him a laugh.'

'He run into town, quick as lightnin, and yellin out, "Woof! woof! woof!" loud as he could, like a woof was about to eat him.'

'What kind of woof?' said Jacko, in his trance.

'Well now, he didn't tell em what kind, he just yelled, and the folks come a runnin, bringin their guns, and lookin out sharp for the woof. They met him out there, but wasn't no woof – just that old boy, and him just a laughin. Slappin his knee, Lord, and havin some fun. That made them mad. His mama, she whooped him, but folks in the town, they decided they'd give him another chance watchin. Him bein so little and all. So they put him out there the next night. Along about midnight, he commence to yellin it, "Woof! woof!" again. And it brung em all runnin.'

Jacko's eyes sparkled as he pictured villagers rushing with pitchforks and guns.

'Well what do you know? There he was, just a laughin again. And no more woof than a man in the moon.

'Now some of em said, "Take that boy out and drownd him, or least whoop him good for his lies," but some other said, "Aw now, he aint no more than a baby, let's give him just one more last chance." Don't ask me why. I reckon they was short on guards. But they put him out again, warned him real good, told him this was the last time for him.

'He hadn't even got settled down good on his stump, when what should come runnin from out of the woods with his teeth out, and all kind of slobber and all, but a big old, nasty old, real-life old woof. Fixin to eat him some *boy*.'

'What kind?' Jacko said.

'Any kind. It didn't matter to him. Hush till I'm done. Well that boy, he set in to runnin and yellin for all he could do – "Woof! woof!" Hollered till his voice give out. And what do you think? Them folks in the town was just settin at home, listenin at that boy a yellin, and tellin each other: "Hear him? Playin the fool, that's three nights in a row. Let him play."' Stella placed hands, soap and all, on her hips. 'So you see?'

'See what? Did he get a whoopin?'

'Well no, boy, cause he was eat up.'

'Well who eat him?' said Jacko.

'The woof did, you dummy,' Stella said.

'What kind of a woof?'

She groaned. 'It don't matter what *kind*.'

'I just wondered,' he said.

'I'm gone quit tellin stories. You aint got nothin but questions.'

'Stella? Where are you?' A high, bothered voice. Jacko pulled out of the doorway just as Everne came through, breathless and moving too fast for her size. 'There you are! Did you take Aurelia her dinner?'

'Yes ma'am.'

'Well was she any better?'

'None,' Stella said, reaching for the dishcloth. 'She said she was sick as three dogs.'

'Oh my stars,' Everne said. 'Just when I need her the most. Did you take the doctor his tea?'

'It aint done yet.'

'Isn't done. It *isn't* done.'

'Nome.'

Everne fluttered up to the stove. 'Well, honey, you don't just boil it with the tea just floating – oh, bless my sweet loving stars.' She snatched the boiler and crossed to the door, dumping the liquid outside.

'The tea ball come open, I guess,' Stella said.

'You're sposed to watch out for things like that. He'll be back from the Gossages' any minute.'

Stella put her palms together. 'I didn't know he was gone,' she said. 'When did he go?'

'The tea was for when he got back from the Gossages'.'

'Jacko saw him just a minute ago, in his room,' Stella said. 'Didn't you, boy?'

'He stepped on me and it hurt,' Jacko said.

Everne regarded them both like a pair of curtains she no longer wanted. She stalked across to the hall. 'Bester, you there?' she called.

The doctor answered, but no one could hear.

'Well bless me,' his wife said, 'I told Fred Gossage you'd be there by time they got done with their dinner. They're needin you, darling. Their little girl just took down with it today.'

'I'm coming.' The doctor's voice preceded him through the door. 'Now just calm down. Who is it I am supposed to go see, and what time was I supposed to go?'

'The Gossages.' Everne stepped across Jacko. 'It's their Louanne, their youngest. Darling, she's their pride and joy.'

'Every last one of them is somebody's pride and joy,' said the doctor.

'I know . . .'

'Every one.'

'I'm sorry, Bester, I know. But it's Fred –'

'I've been thinking,' the doctor said, folding his arms, peering down at Jacko through his glasses. 'There has to be a way for this boy to get about, better than just on the floor.' He knelt beside Jacko's legs. 'I think all you need is some wheels, Master Jack,' he announced, as if he had just reached his life's best decision. 'A wheelchair won't do. You'd just get sores. No, what you need is some kind of platform with wheels, down low, down close to the ground. That way your arms could keep on getting stronger, but you could stretch your legs out while you rolled.'

Everne cleared her throat. 'Don't you think it's time to go? Fred and Elvera are sitting there waiting.'

'They'll wait.'

'But, sweetheart . . .'

The doctor stood. 'Missus Dannelly, please,' he said. 'I'll go in just a moment. Fred's child is here on my mind all the time. I just picked this minute to think about something else.'

Everne set her jaw. 'Of course, dear,' she said. 'You know best.'

'Matter of fact, I was wondering whether Fred might have a pair of old roller skates he won't be needing –'

'Why, Bester!' Everne's hand flew to her mouth. She was stricken.

'Well they've got so damn many children,' he said. 'I thought surely . . . I mean, I only was –'

'Lord God! My stars! What a *terrible* thing to say! Sick as she is!' Everne snatched the apron from Stella, and tried to make the ends meet at her own back. She failed, and flung it away. 'Child's near to dyin, and all you can talk about is some old skates!'

'I meant for the wheels,' came his befuddled answer. 'Maybe a pair they'd outgrown. I didn't mean –'

'You all go up in the parlor, and read from the Bible.' She pointed the way.

'I done heard it,' Jacko said.

'Not the whole thing,' said Stella. 'Hush your mouth.' She

retrieved the apron, draped it over a chairback, then stooped down to lift Jacko.

The doctor waved her away. 'There's no need to go,' he said, watching his wife. 'You won't hear anything you haven't heard.'

'We'll go.' She lifted Jacko.

'I wanna watch em. They're fightin.'

'Hush, boy!'

The doctor sank to the chair. The apron slid to the floor. 'I swear, I've done about all of my fighting for now,' he said.

'Oh dear.' Everne went to his chair, placed her hands on his face, and buried it in her bosom.

Jacko squirmed to the floor. 'You mind me,' said Stella.

'I wanna watch em. They're kissin now.'

'Young man.' The doctor sat up. 'The parlor is up at the end of the hall, and the Bible's the word of the Lord. You go on.'

Stella took Jacko up, hurried him out. 'Your smart mouth is liable to get us both killed or else thrown out in the road,' she said, swatting him with her free hand. She gripped so hard that he could not hit back. 'Who you think you are, sassin that way? If Mama was here, she would tear up your hide.'

'Well she aint,' Jacko offered.

'Well no sir, she aint, and you better be glad of it too.' She pushed the screen open with him, set him down on the porch. 'I swear, you act so bad, Mama would whoop you from time you got up till you went off to bed.'

Jacko inched away from her reach. 'Did she ever whup you?'

'Not me, but I never talked back like you do.'

'She ever whup William, or Charlie Boone?'

'Sometimes she'd whoop Charlie *Boot*,' Stella said, pronouncing it. 'He used to put snakes and such in her bed. But she didn't get holt of him much. He was quick.'

'I bet I'm quicker than him,' said Jacko.

Stella eased down with her back to the wall and put her feet out. They sat in the dark and listened to thunder a long way off in the black night. The side of the sky flashed with heat lightning, yellow as fireflies. 'Lord, though,' she said in a while, 'she'd always catch up to him, one way or the other. She used to give him a knife from the kitchen. She'd make him go cut his own switch from the yard.'

'Howcome?'

'So id hurt more, I reckon. One time, he brung back this libitty switch, no more than a twig. Said it was the one he wanted. Mama helt that thing out to him, just raised up, and told him if he didn't go out and bring back a real one, she'd find one herself. Lord, it scared him so bad. By the time she finally hit him, I think he was glad.'

Jacko broke out in a laugh, but then he saw the moony look in her eyes and fell quiet.

'She always said, "Spare the rod, and you spoil em," and I know what she meant by that. She meant it for bad boys like you.'

'But I din do nothin.' Jacko attempted a pout.

'Not since we seddown,' she said. 'How long's that been now? A minute.'

From the yard, a noise – a wagon rounding the curve in the road by the sycamore, toward the house. Stella could not see into the deep black. A voice called the horse to a halt. 'I'll get a light,' Stella said. 'I'm sorry it's dark.'

'I can see,' the man's voice said. 'Who is that?'

'Stella,' she said. 'Stella Bates. Who are you?' She could not see past the steps.

'Joe Espy. Hold on, and I'll tie up.'

Stella moved to the door. 'I'm gone run get the doctor.'

Jacko could see, but he could not be seen. He stretched out on his side so he could see past the uglyberry bush to the big horse showing its white teeth and prancing, as if it smelled something. A man came around with the rein.

Jacko stared at the animal, which showed the white part of its eye and backed off, into its traces, away from its master. 'Hey there, you horse,' Jacko murmured.

All at once, it reared on its hind legs, pedaling air, slamming down, coming up again, screaming the scream of a horse.

'Ho down, down there,' the man shouted. 'Goddamn!'

Jacko's eyes dropped. He heard the horse settling down.

The doctor pushed through the door. 'Hey, Joe, wait there, I'll come give you a hand,' he called. Stella came after.

In a tight angry voice, the sheriff threw curses at the twitching beast. 'Goddamn,' he said, 'goddamn horse. Think I's a snake, way you act.'

Stella lifted the lamp so its feeble light spread on the yard. She leaned down to whisper to Jacko: 'You do somethin to his horse?'

'Uh-uh.'

'You tell me the truth.'

'I am.' He folded arms, and stuck out his jaw. 'I din do nothin.'

'You wantin a whoopin?'

'No!'

'Cause I believe you bout ready for one.'

'You won't hit me,' he said.

Stella crouched. The lamplight made him cringe. 'I might,' she threatened. His hand protected his eyes.

'Spose it's this damn muggy weather has got him so antsy,' the doctor said. He led the man to the porch.

'Nosir,' said Stella, 'he's only actin the fool.'

'Not him. I meant the sheriff's horse, there.'

'Who yall talkin about?' said Joe Espy, squinting up. He was tall, thin as a plank, and he carried his hands in his pockets like guns. Stella knew him. He and the doctor were friends, of a kind. He cursed all the time, as if those were the best words he knew.

'This here's my brother,' she said.

'Hm. Seem like I remember bout him.' Joe Espy scraped one long foot on the heel of the other, solving an itch. 'How you comin along?'

'Just fine –'

Jacko broke in from his place down below. 'Where your guns?'

Joe Espy squatted on the topmost step. 'In the mail,' he said. 'I had to mail em away to the Riley Gun Company, all the way up in Chicargo, Illinois. Hammers need filin.'

'Howcome you din keep one to shoot people with?'

'Boy, you hush!' Stella popped him a good one.

'Well he can't be sheriff if he aint got guns!'

A clicking throat sound, a dry nervous laugh from Joe Espy. He looked beyond Stella. 'Who's talkin up there?' he said. 'That him? Goddamn! Boy makes some sense, don't he now! Boy, rest your mind. I got plenty of guns at my house.' He chuckled.

'It's a good thing he don't wear britches,' Stella said, 'else he'd be too big for em.'

The doctor broke up the chat. 'Sit down, Joe, let's talk.'

'Here, with these chillun about?'

'Well, it's the middle the night, my wife is near fit to be tied, and we got us a cook playin sick in the back. I suppose there's no better place they could go.'

'We aint listnin,' said Jacko.

'Whatever you say, doc.' Joe Espy spat, and hung his hat on his thin knee. 'You think there's call to do what you said?'

Stella retreated to the wall beside Jacko, studying the sheriff's shiny head.

The doctor sank into a rocker. 'Joe, you know me. I wouldn't have asked you to come, not at night, if I wasn't sure it's the only solution.'

'Just can't see where it makes that much difference, this point.'

'Well neither did I, till today,' said the doctor, removing his glasses to polish them. 'I swear. I don't know. Every fever I've heard of but this one, it was enough just to keep the live cases apart. And that's what I've done for three weeks now.' He coughed. 'Today I stopped over to Fred's place. His youngest girl took down this morning. We went over every single human being she's seen, or talked to, or been near in a month. And not a live case among em. That can't mean but one thing.'

The sheriff untied a small leather bag, and wedged a wad of tobacco up into his cheek.

'Means it's everywhere,' Dannelly said. 'Not like malaisma, carrying from one person to the other, or yellow fever, or diphtheria. Or anything else I can think. I have been reading till my eyes are shot. They're doing work down in Panama, blaming malaisma on mosquitoes. Maybe that's it.'

'Doc, I don't see where a skeeter would have room to carry much else but his biter,' said Espy. He laughed.

The doctor went on without even a smile. 'That's got nothing to do with this,' he said. 'We had new cases at Christmas this year. You find a mosquito at Christmas, I'll give you a prize. Hell, even Jack back there. Same thing. His fever hit him at Christmas.'

Joe Espy sneezed. 'I aint follerin you.'

'All I'm saying is I don't know anything, really. Nothing for sure. Who does? It could be you're carrying it. Or else me. I've thought it. Who else has been to see every last one of these children? Makes sense.'

Joe spat a clean arc. 'Aw shit, that can't be. There's niggers took down. Took down first. You aint seen the niggers.'

'Oh yes I have. Every one.'

'Well *I* aint,' the sheriff said.

'But that's beside the point. Anybody could be carrying it. Or it could be something we don't even consider. The milk. The water they're drinking. But I don't think so. I think we may all be the carriers. We'll see. If everyone stays away from everyone else, it will stop spreading. Have to.'

Joe Espy eased up to rock on his heels. 'It aint gone be easy to tell healthy folks that they got to stay inside all day. Can't go to town, can't go visit, can't nothin. We'll shut down every store on Front Street if we do.'

'Don't be silly,' said the doctor. 'There's not a business left open on Front Street to shut. Haven't you noticed, Joe? Everyone's leaving. Face it. If this thing keeps up, I won't have a patient left. There won't be a soul for you to arrest. Except for the children. You seen the children, Joe?' He stood. Sweat ran past his eye. 'Everyone's leaving this madness as quick as they can put a horse at the front of a wagon. Somebody has to do something. I asked if you'd help.'

'Yessir.' Joe Espy spoke with an edge. 'And that's the reason I'm here.'

'Well then, let's talk about how we can do it, instead of the why.'

'Hell, there's no need to get your hair up.'

The doctor exhaled. 'Oh, you're right. I'm sorry. I apologize. I'm just so tired. Like one big raw nerve. Guess I'm too old.'

The sheriff stood, smiling. 'Young as you feel.'

The doctor brushed at his hair. 'Wait'll you have to tell old Missus Frick that she has to keep her busy nose to herself.'

'Well if I got to tell her' – Espy laughed – 'then you got Miz Hartselle. Sweeter than pie sometimes, but she can be mean as shit if you cross her. And talks . . .' His hands went back in his pockets. 'I tell you, doc, it's gettin where I don't know whether to talk to folks any, or not. Nobody's mindin a soul but theirselves, I was thinkin. That boy just might speak the truth. I might ought have my good guns.'

'You can't shoot a fever,' the doctor said. 'I got Pal Herlong to print up some signs. When I said what they should say, he looked like he'd seen a ghost. Like I'd gone out of my mind. Said, "Jesus Christ, doc, you might just as well tell the sun to stay down as to tell folks to stay home." God, I hope he was wrong, for all of our sakes.'

'He's been hearin the talk, then,' said Espy. 'You hear what they sayin? It aint me I'm worried about. Hell, it's you. Folks talkin. They talk, when they want. And you the one brings bad news. Got the first fever right livin here with you. Hell, even Fred. He says –'

'I don't care what he says, or anyone else.' The doctor released a long painful cough. 'I don't want to hear talk, not tonight.'

'Nothin else counts, not round here.' Joe Espy let fly with a proud curve of juice. 'Wellsir, I got me some miles to get covered tomorrow. You leavin the county to me, I'll have to start early. Reckon I ought to just make some good time and just unhitch the wagon, but I don't know but what that damn animal might not throw me, actin so fidgety.'

'You ought not talk ugly to him like you do,' said Jacko from his place.

The doctor stared down, amazed.

The sheriff tried to choose something to say, and at last he said, 'I don't talk ugly to him.'

'Yes you do. I heard you,' Jacko said. 'And you beat on him sometimes.'

Stella spoke. 'Boy, you hush.'

'A right sassy boy there, for not much to look at,' said Espy. 'Somebody ought to show him how to act.' His glance found the doctor. 'Says too much what all he thinks.'

'I swear,' said the doctor, 'sometimes I don't think he says the half of it.' Everyone stared down at Jacko. At last, the doctor: 'Boy, go on in. Stella, take him. Then bring me my bag.'

Joe Espy went down the steps, and turned. 'Don't worry bout other folks' horses,' he said.

Everne appeared at the screen door. 'Evening, Joe. Care for some dinner?'

'Nome, thank you, good evenin, Miz Dannelly.' He swept his hat to his chest.

'What is it, Bester, what's wrong?' she said.

'Nothing that's new,' said the doctor. 'I'm gone. Joe and I have some news to spread in the morning.'

'What news?'

'Sweetheart, we have us a quarantine.'

Everne took hold of her fingers and whispered the word.

'Now listen to me,' he said. 'Pal Herlong will bring by some signs that he's making for me. Should be anytime. You pay his bill, but check the signs first to make sure he spelt it right.'

Everne said she would look it up. The doctor took his bag from Stella. 'I'll ride with Joe,' he said. 'I'll be back. I don't know when.'

'If anybody comes,' said Everne, 'what should I say?'

'Say to wait.' The doctor mounted the mare gingerly, like an old fieldhand climbing a fence. The sheriff's horse cantered off with a fast frisky step.

'What's a quartine?' said Jacko.

Everne turned. 'Hush.' The door cried. Her steps clicked away.

They listened to silence. The air in the yard was so still, unmoved by the breeze that churned at the branches above. 'Munner, what's a quartine?' said Jacko.

'I aint sure exactly, but I think it's bad.' She fingered her lip.

'Is it like lightnin?'

'No, boy.'

'Is it bad as a whoopin?'

'Don't talk no more.'

'We didn't do nothin wrong, Munner.'

'Oh Jacko, we didn't mean to,' said Stella, 'but I got this feelin we did.' She wrapped his neck in the crook of her arm, and felt the dark wind washing down, full of heat.

SIXTEEN

Pal Herlong sent his boy out with the signs. Luther rode the long mile from Camellia four times in the dark, two boxes each trip. The whole county knew Luther. He brought the *Gleam* every week, wires from the depot, and prescriptions to the infirm. The rasp of his bicycle bell meant news – good, bad, or old; folks came to their porches as soon as they heard it, to find out which kind.

Stella knew him from the glances they'd shared in school. While she'd grown bolder, Luther stayed six feet and three inches shy, scratching his head when Miss Maysie called on him, slouching in his desk.

The first three times he came, Stella accepted his boxes in silence. His fourth trip took longer, so deep in the night. He tottered in, empty of breath, past the sycamore, balancing the load on his handlebars, then he struck a mild rut and collapsed. The boxes fell one way, the bicycle went the other, and Luther sprawled flat in the grass.

Stella ran to him. 'You ought to have come in a wagon, dumb boy,' she said, kneeling. 'Four trips. That's silly.'

Luther croaked for a drink of cool water. She fetched it. He gulped, spilling half of it down his shirtfront, then propped himself up on his elbows. His eyes watched the dipper. 'Thanks,' he gasped.

'It's free,' Stella said. 'All you want. You're brave to make all of those trips by yourself in the dark.'

His breathing eased some. He stood, collecting the boxes, avoiding her eyes, as if the word 'thanks' had drained him.

She raised his bicycle, leaned it against the porch steps, and put her thumb to the bell – zing! 'Come set a minute and catch your breath before you go,' she offered. He nodded. They went to the swing. Luther perched in a corner.

'You want more water?'

He nodded. This time he drank without spilling, and smiled.

'Luther, I'm only one up,' she said. 'Miz Dannelly's down with her headache, and the doctor's gone on a call. I hadn't got money to pay you.'

'Don't matter,' he said.

'The doctor said check the way yall spelled it,' she said, grasping a flap of the nearest brown carton. It was glued too well. 'I'll run fetch a knife.' She tiptoed back to the kitchen. Jacko's faint sleeping sigh made her feel safe.

The knife made quick work of the box. She slid one sign out, and dropped it as if it were hot.

QUARENTINE.

bellowed letters as big as her hand, solid black in a field of bright yellow. And a smaller line:

KEEP OUT OF THIS HOUSE.
BY ORDER OF BOARD OF HEALTH.

Then an impossible scrawl, the doctor's, nudged by a caption:

County Health Officer.

'Oh me,' said Stella, 'that's fearsome.'

'It is,' he agreed. 'It gave me the willies to print it.'

So he did have a voice! Stella smiled. There was life in those eyes, or in what she could see of them behind his spill of brown hair. A gentleness in them made her want to shiver. His front teeth were split by a space, and a promising mustache made fuzz of his lip. 'It looks like it's spelled right to me,' she said. 'I wish Miss Maysie was here. She could tell.'

Luther just grinned, with his space.

'It was scary the way Miz Dannelly looked when the doctor said "quarantine,"' Stella went on. 'Troubles and more top of those. You write the newspaper, don't you – you reckon howcome?'

Luther just shrugged, all lank and soft eyes.

'When you write on a newspaper, you must find out lots of things,' Stella said, easing down to the swing by him. He inched away to his corner. 'Reckon why all of it happens to us?'

'Don't know,' said Luther. 'But I know one thing. There's troubles all over the place.'

She started them rocking with her toe. 'Well tell me.'

'Well there's a war on, for one,' he said. His voice was light as smoke.

'I heard there was. Doctor said it was real bad.'

'Daggum right,' Luther said. 'It's awful. I get the dispatches off of the train.'

'Well long as they aint fightin here, it's all right, I reckon. But it must be bad, anyway, the way he talks.'

'Daggum right,' Luther said. 'You know they're makin a law up right now, up in Washton, DC, and it says that the Army can up and tell any man he's got to leave home and go join up with em, go fight in the war? It's the truth. No matter what he wants to do. And if he don't, well then, they chuck him in jail.'

Stella snorted. 'That's silly. Silliest thing I ever heard. They can't just make you go, if you don't want.' She'd never heard a whole sentence from him; maybe he wasn't as shy as he thought.

'That's what it says in the dispatches.'

'Well now, you know you don't want to go fight folks you don't even know,' Stella said. 'They'll get somebody else. You just ought not to do it.'

'And get thrown in jail?'

'Joe Espy was out here tonight,' Stella said. 'He sent his guns off. He can't make you go.'

'It aint just Joe Espy,' he said. 'It's bigger than him. It's the United States of America Army.'

Stella sat back. 'Shoot I aint believin it,' she said. It sounded like kidnapping! No wonder they wanted the men, she considered; men were the only ones stupid enough to go.

'Well that's what I heard, anyway.' He stood up. 'I preciate the drink. I got to get back.'

'It sure was nice talkin,' said Stella. 'You know a heap more than folks said you do. You come back out sometime and we'll set here and just talk.'

Luther nodded. He seemed to have said enough to last a year.

'When the doctor gets back, I'll tell him it was you that come,' she said. 'I bet he'll bring you a dollar tomorrow.'

Luther ran down the steps, climbed up on his bicycle, prodded a ring from the bell, and rode off.

Stella reclined in the swing, holding her feet in her hands. The whole house was sleeping, but she was so wide awake that she felt she might never sleep again. QUARENTINE screamed up. She slid the sign back in its box.

She knew what the word meant, from summers, from signs that said YELLOW FEVER or DIPHTHERIA. She knew every house would be branded and marked, each one an island of sickness. She tried to imagine the large trouble coming. The sheriff was right, with or without his guns: folks don't like staying home if they have to.

Edging the boxes back next to the house, so the rain she smelled coming would not reach the signs, she crept down the hall to the doctor's dark study and went to the white hulking cabinet. It was unlocked. She considered awhile, then brought out the small sparkling glass and the bottle of the doctor's best bourbon whiskey. He used it as medicine, and sometimes treated himself. After flirting with Luther that way, Stella felt grown up, and ready to try the things grown-up folks try. Maybe the yawning would start.

It reeked like a fuel. She swallowed it all in one gulp in the dark, and sweet Lord Almighty it burned: an explosion of warmth in her throat, then a burst through her chest, then a last golden salvo, way deep. Her head swam a bit, then she grinned, full of sin, happy to have shattered several mirrors at once. In the final glow that extended to her elbows, she knew why so many grown people drank whiskey. If you needed killing, it would be the way. She made a vow to stay away from it. It made her feel too sweet, like a coconut cake, and anything that sweet was bound to rot you, inside out.

When the heat faded, Stella gave in to a memory, from when she and William were the only children. She acted like him.

Mama would dress them, fussing with their buttons, shooing them out to the yard, where they tussled and fought. When they tired of that they would torment some chickens, or look for someplace to jump off.

William was bravest at that. He taught her what a dare was and made it sacred. He got a mail order umbrella for Christmas that year. It bloomed in his hand like a black shiny flower, and he held it up to slow his descent from first the porch, then the ladder, higher and higher each time. Stella followed his leaps from each perch, imitating his joyous look at the landing. Each time, her heart seemed to crash through her ribs, but William had dared her, and she trusted him.

At last there was no higher place than the roof. William shinnied up the gutter pipe. He looked so small, way up there, scrabbling slick shoes on the ripply tin. She tossed his umbrella to him.

He crouched for a while, taking time, mulling the jump to be made. Even back then he was skinny, just bones. He squatted, considered.

Callie heard some voice just then and stepped out. She looked to the roof and saw William there. 'William,' she called, 'what have you got in your head?'

'I'm own jump off a here.'

Stella watched, praying.

'Now, William, you don't want to do that,' said their mother, just as calm. 'You'll bust your neck.'

'I got my umbreller.' He held it up. A light breeze tugged it.

'Now that won't stop you from bustin your neck,' Callie said.

William inspected the distance down, looked at his mother, and made a decision. The umbrella wilted. He tossed it and swung down from the gutter.

Now, in the dark and the whiskey, Stella remembered how ready she was to climb up the pipe after him and make the jump. He caved in so fast! It was awful. She wandered on around the house by herself, and flung her arms out, and started to spin. She spun very fast and then faster, until the world spun and she pitched to the ground. She pressed a cheek to the sand, to keep from throwing up.

The world went past in bright loops of wild color. She loved it, this feeling, this absence of right side up. It touched a hard place, a wildness inside her. Down on her belly, she felt she had reached the true place she belonged, while the earth did its spin and held everything to it by spinning. How hard it is to feel that pull, and still stand on your feet! To look at the sky, and then lower your eyes and pretend it is only a roof overhead, it does not go on forever. You can forget it, and walk underneath. She had no caution or fear, and would spin herself sick just to feel the fast rush of the things she could never decide.

SEVENTEEN

The night passed over to morning. An insect slept between two blades of grass arching up so their tops touched. Then the light bleeding blue across the yard began to strengthen and warm. The sun cast a beam, announcing the shimmery carpet of dew.

Raising its head, the insect cocked its hind legs, and sent the first meager cheep of its day. An insect nearby, at an oak tree, returned the tentative greeting. A third sent its song from the region of the well, and a fourth, and a fifth, until all the insects in the doctor's yard were sending forth harmonies in collision.

The chorus raced past the sycamore, along the red road, across the creek, spreading in wide pools to other yards further, to woods and then woods beyond those, until at last all insects in yards everywhere sang a song to the sun.

A bluejay fell screeching to swallow the insect that started it all.

It might have been this noise that woke Stella from the violent dreams of her long restless night. For an instant, she saw all her dreams before her, stitched by their convergences into a brilliant quilt, but at once the details of the stitching went blurry. The picture faded. She lay very still with her eyes closed, as if by will she could glide into darkness and bring all the dreams back together. Moments that shone bright a moment before were now delicate husks of moments: some feeling of falling, the very last dream – a loud noise, like a gun going off, but more subtle, alarming. An animal sound?

She slid down again to the comfortable web, and slept for a time without dreams.

When she returned to the world again, she felt just tatters of dreams, as if she had heard a long, intricate story but could not remember a word.

Her face felt distinctly cool, too cool for August. She woke
with a jolt. It was not air, but the bed that was cool. Cool, she
discovered, and wet.

She propelled herself up in disgust, and settled back onto her
heels. Jacko's sweet upturned face gave no clue; he lay in a
circle of dampness, unconscious. 'I *told* you,' she scolded, but
he did not stir.

The ugliness faded as fast as the dreams. To wake him now
would be cruel. His face was twitching with dreams of his own.
She contented herself with a yawn of distaste, rose and went to
the washstand, splashing and dousing until she felt clean. The
sheet? Let it be. There are other, more dangerous things yet
to do.

She dressed in the pinafore sewn by Aurelia, covered with
bright crimson flowers of three petals each on a pure field of
coolish white cotton. She was up first. The kitchen was empty,
the stove cold. On the back porch, the air moved with its first
breeze. The yard was littered with sparkling jewels. Her toes
turned to numb little knobs as she picked her way up the path
to the small whitewashed hutch. Inside, she heard her far trickle
of water, then a pock-pock from outside – Cleo, chopping stove
wood.

But when she emerged, she saw him down at the garden's
far end, with the mule. Someone else, then, in the woodshed.

She went to the side with no wall, and found the doctor there,
down on his knees. Bent over a square of good lumber, he was
working and did not see Stella come up. Four tacks lined his lips
like gold teeth. In one hand he wielded a ball-peen hammer; in
the other, a spotted calfhide.

'Mornin,' she whispered, too softly to startle him. His exhaus-
ted eyes came up. From their red, she saw he had not slept.
He worked up a faint smile of greeting. 'What you makin?' she
said.

'It's a surprise,' he said blearily, 'for your boy Jack. I've
figured it out at last.'

Stella knelt by him in the sawdust. 'What is it?'

He turned the board over. Silvery swiveling wheels were
nailed on at each corner. He spun one with his thumb. 'You see,

I was right,' he said. 'Fred did have a pair of skates that all his children had outgrown. See there, how fine? Now all I need do is to put on this batting, stretch the hide over, and tack it around. Your Jack'll be able to get around as well as anybody.' His exhaustion was gone. 'You watch. He'll be to scooting before we know it.'

Stella grinned. 'That's the sweetest thing,' she said. 'You stayin up workin on that, and him the thorn in your side.'

'I must admit, it's a clever design,' said the doctor, replacing the tacks in his teeth. 'These could be useful for all kinds of crippled people.'

She winced at the word. 'Well you are sure enough sweet,' she said.

'I'll be needing you today, Stella.' Creasing the hide, he nailed the batting with short precise strokes. 'You heard what we said last night. The signs are spelled wrong, but you know what they mean.'

'I knew I ought to have looked it up,' Stella said.

'No matter. They speak loud and clear.' His eyes never swerved from his project. 'Most times I'd go do my duty alone, but I've got some ground to get covered today. Have to tell everyone in Camellia. You're going with me. Missus Dannelly'll look after the boy.'

'He's gone be hell to pay, soon as you give him that toy.'

His eyebrows rose. He studied her. 'Where did you learn to say that?'

'What, hell to pay?' she said. 'I guess from Mama.'

He smiled. 'I bet she had a right righteous look when she said it.' He made swift work of the last three tacks.

'I'll be proud to ride with you,' Stella said, 'but I aint sure what help I can be.'

'You'll drive the buggy for me. I need to move quick, so everyone finds out about the same time and no one gets their feelings hurt. And so those who – who decide to leave, so they'll have a day's notice. It starts tomorrow at sundown.' He slapped the dust from his hands, and rolled the platform a little to show that it worked. 'Now look, how fine.'

Stella nodded. 'It is.'

'While I'm up telling the people, you'll take this hammer' – she took it – 'and nail up the quarantine signs. One for the front door and one for in back. Just nail them on up there, don't mind what they say. A quarantine isn't legal unless the Health Officer fixes the notices. That's me. And you'll be my agent.'

'I've never been nothin before,' Stella said. The idea thrilled her. 'I aint sure I can.'

He coughed and stood, brushing his knees. 'Oh, I am,' he said. 'Let's go in, get us some cornflakes.'

'I'll run wake up Jacko, tell him I'm gone.'

'Everne will tell him when they get up.'

'But he gives her fits.'

'She'll survive.'

'Well I ought to at least comb my hair.'

'Do that,' said the doctor, 'and get your shoes. I'll be right in.'

Stella dashed for the house, buoyed up and bound on a mission. At last she could do something besides watch wagons pass, help with the dishes, and keep Jacko quiet.

He lay with his mouth open, leaking a snore. He smacked his lips and rolled over. She pulled on her flat brown school shoes, then kissed him and whispered, 'Be sweet, boy. Back soon.'

The doctor sat crunching a spoonful of dry flakes. 'Fetch us a sack with some apples,' he said, 'and see were there biscuit left over last night.'

'Shouldn't I ought to wear britches, if I'm gone be gettin up and down off your buggy all day?'

'Shoot no,' he said. 'You're a pretty girl, Stella. Nearly a grown-up woman. Folks need to see what one looks like.'

She blushed as she gathered things in a small burlap bag. He was so sweet, and never a thought to himself. She went to the yard, where she found Cleo cleaning his stuff-loader gun. He was old and bent, with eyes that bulged from his face. 'Run fetch the buggy,' she told him, 'and hitch up Annette.' She followed his slow amble. 'How is Aurelia this mornin?'

'Slep good,' Cleo said.

'Is she well?'

'Been worse and been better.'

'You reckon she'll get to the kitchen today?'

'She might, less she don't.' Cleo fastened the traces with old swollen hands.

'I wish you'd look in on my boy today,' Stella said. 'I got to go with the doctor.'

'That boy fine by his lonesome.' He cinched the bridle.

The doctor came out, and told Stella to take the driver's seat. She clambered up. Annette was her friend, of a sort, the mostly ungrateful recipient of apple peels and one-sided discussions. The mare lumbered off with no spring to her step, but on this warming morning, on a mission, Annette was a steed, prancing and prissy, pulling a fine golden ambulance wagon, and Stella became a brave noble girl driving. 'I can't wait,' she burst out.

The doctor regarded her sideways. 'This will hurt,' he said. Stella drove on.

EIGHTEEN

The Hobarts all lived in a shack by a tree. Stella counted eleven children, all sizes, in colors from pink to bad sunburn. They had gotten up early, it seemed, just to come out and lie down awhile. Near the chimney, which let out a pencil of smoke, three or four of them pulled each other's hair. The rest were drowsily draped on the porch.

The doctor selected a fat red-haired boy who was picking fleas off a small dog. 'Where's your mama?'

'Inside,' the boy said.

'Your daddy aint home?'

Stella marveled at how the doctor's voice had changed; aint was not one of his words.

'Nawsir, don't never come in till round noon.'

'You run tell your mama the doctor is here.'

The boy took his time getting all the way up, but once he got started, he moved. The doctor told Stella to bring on the signs.

She froze, dropped the hammer, grabbed for two signs, and a yellow fan spilled from the buggy. '*Now* look,' she swore at herself, starting over.

Picking a path across the yard, Stella saw a stick-thin woman peering out through the screen door.

The doctor lifted his hat. 'Mornin, Miz Hobart,' he said. 'I won't take more than a minute.'

'We got no sick.' Mrs Hobart kept her bony hand up at her throat.

'I know you don't, ma'am; that's lucky,' he said. 'Stella, hand me that sign.' He held it up. 'Now it says "quarantine," see what it says? You know what a quarantine is.'

'But we got no sick.'

'I know you don't, Miz Hobart, but I'm here cause this fever.

You're just the first to get notice. The onliest way we can beat this thing back is to quarantine all of Camellia. The whole county too.'

Her voice trembled: 'Howcome we first?'

'Cause yall live the closest to me, is all.' Goggle-eyed children packed murmuring up to his knees. 'My girl Stella here will put her sign up, and yall will have to stay home till we come take it down. Unless in case of emergency.'

'Hobart aint home yet.' She slapped at a child.

'I know, but when he comes in, you tell him I said he's to stay put right here. And what else . . . Tomorrow at sundown, then's when it starts. Yall get what you need from the store before then.'

'You mean he can't go out,' said Mrs Hobart, 'not even at night? He aint gone to like it.'

'None of us like it, Miz Hobart. You tell him the doctor said stay put, or Sheriff Joe Espy will lock him in jail. If he's got anything to say, he can tell it to Joe.'

'But how bout his cards?'

The doctor began backing away. 'Just – please ma'am – tell him the way I told you.'

Stella flathanded the poster against the skinned log that supported the Hobarts' porch roof. 'Mama, the sign, what's the sign say?' screamed children.

'Run round back and we'll be gone,' the doctor said, trailing three noisy attendants. In back, the fat boy asked Stella if she needed any kittens. She said no. As she went back around, she heard Mrs Hobart hollering, 'Get yall ass back in the house.' None of them minded her.

Stella climbed up to the buggy and let out a breath: one house marked. 'You did that just fine,' said the doctor, echoing her little pride. 'That no good Hobart hasn't been home longer than it takes him to sleep it off. Not in five years. Don't know if we did that poor woman a favor or not.'

Stella laughed.

'There's a whole mess of Martins up here on your right,' he said. 'Remember that boy that cuts firewood for me? Stop her in here.'

The Martin clan lived in three neat square white houses, set back from the road on a big clean-swept yard. The doctor explained at the door of the first, then both other doors opened. Martins filed out. As if places were marked on the ground for each one, they lined up to watch the departure.

Stella spoke when they were well out of eyeshot: 'I swear, it's likely to take us a week.'

'Just wait till we get into town,' he said. 'The word will get there before us, you'll see. Can't keep a secret for long around here.'

They stopped at all houses, Negro and white, whitewashed and gray. Each had a dog waggling greeting out front. Each owner looked different when he heard the news.

At the top of a long hill, the Gossages' place spread out, finest in all of Camellia. The main house seemed fine as a castle to Stella, its enormous white columns marching across the broad porch, and surrounded by green close-cropped grass. Besides serving as mayor, Fred Gossage owned two sawmills, Planter's Mercantile Store, five buildings on Front Street, and who knew what else. He came out sweating and stripped to the waist, a mist of sawdust in the hairs of his chest. 'Seem like you left here not more than an hour ago,' he called. 'Scuse my appearance. I been to the mill twice this mornin already. Some niggers won't work until you show em how.'

'It's been more than an hour,' said Dannelly, slipping back into his own voice. 'How is she this morning?'

'The same.' A tight smile showed his pain. 'I'm sure glad you're back. This fever is somethin.'

'Fred, I can't stay. We came with the notices. I've got to cover the whole town today.'

'That's fine, doc,' said Gossage, 'no really, it is. There's more than us that have sickness.' He looked past the doctor, surveying the town as if rust on the roofs was a mark of the fever. 'You do what you got to,' he said through his teeth. 'I see you brung the young lady.'

'Howdy, Mister Gossage,' said Stella, but he just looked out at the view.

'Yessir, she keeps me cheered up,' said the doctor. 'I made her my agent and my chief driver.'

'The doctor said you give us those roller skates,' she said, counting out tacks in her lap. 'My brother will thank you when he gets a –' She saw the doctor's eyes: *Hush*.

'What you mean?' Fred said.

'She means nothing.'

'Now you just wait, just a minute . . .' Something in Gossage's eyes leaped out, streaking for Stella – a dark chilly stare. 'Doc, what say you and me step round back for a minute, please sir.'

'Why, Fred –'

'Just a minute, please sir. If you can spare it.'

They walked away, Gossage leaning in urgently. With every stride their discussion grew fiercer, and softer, from down in their throats. They talked all the way to the back of the house.

Stella stared up at the columns, and wondered how fine it must be to have a house that big, and with stairs – downstairs or up, when you pleased! Like two houses stacked, one on top of the other. The windows were all draped in black, admitting no daylight. At one, the curtain parted and a small face appeared, then it vanished so quickly she might have imagined it. She shivered, hearing the argument swelling out back.

The doctor came storming around, turned for one final word, threw his hands up, and stalked to the buggy. 'Get her up and let's go,' he said, swinging up trembling mad, landing hard beside her.

'But the signs –'

'We'll bring em later.' He snatched the reins and yelled, 'Get up! Go on!'

'Don't yell at her, doctor. It makes her more antsy.'

'Damn it, I know my own horse!'

Annette heard the sound of his anger and heeded it, clanking off down the long gravelly drive.

Stella folded her hands, and did not breathe out until they seemed to pass some kind of boundary and she felt the heat in the doctor subsiding. He inhaled, looked around him, settled sad eyes on her. 'Oh me, I'm sorry,' he said. 'Damn Fred, got my hair up.'

'What was the matter?'

'Oh nothing,' he said. He shook his head. Stella felt a fine spray of his sweat. 'Just talk. Silly talk. Like a woman. I couldn't take the time to come sit with his Louanne, was all, and a whole town full of children every bit as sick. Sicker. I don't know. I swear. A man gets some money, and soon gets to thinking the world owes him more.'

'Oh.' Stella didn't believe him. She'd seen the change in Fred's face.

The doctor read her mind. 'I guess I shouldn't have bothered the man for a pair of old skates,' he said. 'He yelled at me because he's upset about his girl, and I turned around and yelled at you.'

'Howcome you didn't tell him why you wanted the skates?'

'Just keep on like you are, being a help. Don't mind what I say, don't mind anyone else. An agent and driver has got to be tough.' He handed the reins back to her, then smacked a fist into his palm.

'Yessir,' she said softly. He had been right: this was no fun. 'Why'd he look at me that way?'

'You look fine, Stella, now just drive on.' He stared straight ahead. She'd seen him angry enough times to know just to leave him alone until his mood dissolved.

They reached Grant Small's house, the last before town. He would be nice, anyway. But when they drove up, Grant Small sent his wife out to greet them. Folding her arms like a shield, she listened, then answered him, choosing each word like a brooch. 'Hmmmm,' she began, 'Mister Small already mentioned that this was a possibility. As we were speaking about it, he wondered if it were not – how should I say it – unusual – well, kindly strange, if you will. That we'd be included in your edict. Well, frankly, I'll tell you, doctor, we have no living children. We know that you know that. And this disease strikes children, as we have understood, does it not?'

'That's been true up to now,' said the doctor, his patience intact. 'But you must know I know so very little of this fever. It's new to me. I think it's transmitted from one person to the next, just as possibly by grown folks as children. I'm doing what I think is best.'

She smiled. 'Oh, and far be it from us,' she said, 'to question your judgment. We know you must be worn out with the questions themselves. Still we have them.' She smiled harder. 'Please do forgive us.'

'Yes ma'am, I sure will.'

Stella noticed the damp ovals under his arms, and all at once he seemed to want for his coat. 'And I hope you'll forgive me looking this way,' he said, in retreat. 'Please give my best to Grant. Tell him my wife pours his honey on our biscuit every day, same as always.'

'I will.' For the first time she noticed Stella. 'Hello there, honey, how you?' Stella said nothing. She nailed up the sign. 'Isn't she getting to be the young lady.'

'She is,' said the doctor. 'Good day now.'

As they rode down the slope toward the creek, Stella pondered what she might say about Mrs Small. 'I sure do like Mister Small,' she said.

He smiled wanly. 'So do I,' he said.

The day was steaming when they reached the pleasant small stream that bounded the town on the south. It was too shallow for boats, and clotted with persimmon trees overhanging, but perfect for swimming on hot August days.

Stella spotted them first: four or five wiry gangling boys, shouting, showing their white everything, just up from the bridge.

The doctor sat straight. 'Watch the road, now,' he said.

Stella giggled. 'It's nothing I hadn't seen,' she said. Then she saw his eyes grow. 'Back home, I mean, back at the spring. We all used to swim nekkid.' She glanced again. 'Kind of funny lookin, anyway, if you ask me.'

'The human body's a temple,' he said. 'I don't think a temple can be "funny looking."'

'I just meant those particular ones . . .'

'Hah-haaaa . . .'

Stella had not heard him laugh in such a long time that it alarmed her, somehow, when he did. For a moment, his face found its youth, then the look faded like last night's warm glow of whiskey. 'Oh let's see,' he said, 'let's do the worst and be done. Turn in up here, at old Missus Frick's.'

'Even you call her old,' Stella said. 'How long has she been old?'

'Long as I've known her. Some folks are born old.'

She looped Annette's tether on a crepe myrtle. 'You want me to run ahead on with my signs?'

'No, I'll spare you this one. You just stay here. And peel us an apple. I'm just about starving.'

'Lord, so am I.'

He was back in a minute. 'Not home,' he said. 'She must have got wind of us. I bet she's spreading it now. Where's that apple? And fetch me out a biscuit. You bring the honey jar?'

'No sir, but they're real good plain,' Stella said.

The little meal left them still hungry. 'It's a good thing Sara Lizabeth Hartselle is just up the road,' said the doctor. 'That lady can some kind of cook.'

'No wonder you never eat dinner,' said Stella.

'You better not give my secret away.'

'Promise.' The road spread out, paved in gravel and mud. The weathered signboard gave greeting:

THIS IS CAMELLIA. WE ARE PROUD OF OUR CHURCHES, OUR SCHOOL, & OUR HOMES.

The courthouse rose in the square, a high pile of massive gray stones with a clock tower crown, flanked by two small white churches. Past it, on both sides of Front Street, a scattering of large white houses, and then the three blocks of storefronts, and on down to the railroad trestle, and Camellia ended. Except for the Negroes, most people lived just a block or two from Front Street, and Negroes had their own quarter past the depot.

The doctor told Stella to stop first on a side street, at a small cottage set up on thin stilts. 'Now we'll get dessert, I'll bet,' he said. 'This is Miz Hartselle.'

Stella knew Sara Lizabeth was sister to Polly Mae Hartselle, whose talent for gossip was second to one – Mrs Frick. Sara loved to help Polly beat old Mrs Frick to the news. She came to her door with a blessing of teacakes, bright gold and warm on a blue-bordered plate. 'Come get em, they're hot,' she sang.

The doctor corrected his draggly tie. 'Well now, Miss Sara,' he said, 'how'd you know we were coming?'

'A little bird told me,' she said, winking to show them she didn't mean a real bird. 'But he said there'd be just one of you, though. Come right on in!'

'Where is Missus Frick, anyway?' the doctor said non-chalantly. 'We stopped by, but she wasn't at home.' He peered around the tiny parlor. 'She still here?'

'No, and when she left, I don't know . . .' Miss Sara heard herself then, and nearly dropped the teacakes. 'She only said you'd stop by,' she said, reddening.

'That lady's ears would hear grass growing,' said Dannelly, trading a cake for her smile. 'Stella – here, take one. They are magnificent. Thank you, Miss Sara. Did Missus Frick say why we're here?'

'Well not really, no sir. Just said Annie Louise Martin – now listen at me, there I go, telling again. I never was much good at keeping a secret.'

Stella thought: Neither is old Mrs Frick.

'Well what I said to the Martins is true,' said the doctor, declining a chair. 'We have a quarantine.' He made his speech fast by now. He sympathized with her dilemma, the church ice cream social postponed and the dismal decline of the town's social life and the dearth of business in the stores. Stella went out to the porch with her hammer and signs.

'That yellow is kind of pretty,' said Sara Lizabeth. They agreed it was. 'Here, take one more cake . . .'

As Annette came back to life, the doctor let out a chuckle. 'She could hardly wait for us to leave,' he said. 'We set her straight on the details. We gave her the pleasure of beating Miz Frick, and her sister as well. Ah, it's ladies like that who make up for the Fred Gossages of this world.'

Sure enough, Stella looked back to see Miss Sara hastening to her fence.

The ladies of town were mostly friends of Everne. Stella remembered their names from long teas and endless luncheons. On Front Street, three or four big white houses signaled all that remained of Camellia's wealth, perching on undersized lots as if they had not decided whether to stay. Husbands in these homes were not home at this time of day, just past dinner. Black maids came to their doors, and went off to announce callers.

'Do come in, the both of you,' crooned a fat lady with silver hair and a tinkly laugh. Stella knew her, but the woman eyed her strangely.

'Missus Middleton, you know Stella,' said the doctor.

'Yes, oh, of course!' she tinkled. 'Come right on in, darling. It must be just *marvelous*, doctor,' she said, taking him by the elbow, 'to be blessed with servants who help in your work.'

'Oh no, she's not a servant . . .' His eyes begged Stella for patience. 'She's my – well she lives with us . . .'

'Of *course* she does, doctor. And now I really must tell you. These pains. Very bad. The most excruciating ribbons of pain, in my back and, you know, way down low. Entirely new. They just scare me to death. I wonder if you might not . . .'

She chattered on until she needed breath, then the doctor took over and did not relent. '. . . and you stop by the house one day next month,' he finished. 'We'll have a look at those pains.'

When Stella nailed Mrs Middleton's signs, she made sure to knock dents in the plaster columns.

On through town, house after house, working all the side streets, they brought news. They never saw old Mrs Frick, but Stella imagined her scooting one yard ahead of them, making the story better every time. Each lady knew more details than the last. Mrs Castille spoke up even before the doctor, to ask how long the quarantine would last. Mrs McMurphy said she'd heard that only white folks would be quarantined, and wasn't that awfully unfair? The doctor assured her all houses were marked equally. Mrs Faye Dupree, a slender flushed woman with hair like rose petals, offered iced tea and then turned to Stella with a kind smile. 'When you put my sign up,' she said, 'please take care you don't tump over my geraniums.'

Where Beech Street met Elm, a swatch of dead grass wrapped the corner. Matched furniture sat on the grass, arranged like a parlor without a ceiling or walls. A black shawl hung on the door.

'Stay here,' said the doctor.

Stella did not know the house or the woman who answered his knock. The woman bowed. He stepped in, to deep darkness, a room without furniture, lit with dim candles.

After a time, he came out by himself and stood blinking, his hat in his hand. 'No one will come to this house, anyway, for a while.'

'Who are those people?'

'Just people,' he said.

'Did somebody die in there?'

'Yes.'

'From what?'

'I'm not sure.'

'Oh,' she said, 'I didn't know this fever could kill a person.'

'Well it can.' Weariness swept him then, weighing his face so it sagged in its wrinkles. He sat on the buggy seat, too tired to speak, allowing the mare to nibble a mimosa.

Stella covered his hand with her own. 'How you doin?'

'Phew.' He slicked a strand of white hair. 'Hot.' He could not summon more.

'Reckon we ought to go home now, and rest?' She thought of the stores still unmarked – and the newspaper office – but he seemed weary past caring.

'We're nearly done,' he said. 'Just Front Street, and the quarter.'

'There's no use you gettin all worn out yourself,' said Stella. 'They need you. Everybody. You're the only one who aint either stupid or sick, or else both.'

'Now Miz Dupree was nice –'

'Dumb old geraniums.'

'And Miss Sara. And most folks are taking it better than I thought they would.'

She pulled her hand away. 'Reckon it's old Miz Frick, givin her warnin,' she said, watching him. 'Only one who seemed surprised was Mister Gossage . . .'

He coughed. 'I guess you're right, Stella. Let's head home. We'll come back later this evenin, to finish. Maybe I'll get me a nap and some dinner.'

'Get up,' she said to the mare. They clopped to Front Street and south, to the square. The streets were deserted, every house marked by its bright yellow sign. She pictured the people behind the veiled windows, packing to flee the town and the new plague. How nice it would be to ride through Camellia with nobody there. You could pick out which house you wanted. But maybe it would be too lonesome, more lonesome than out in the country.

The doctor sagged in his seat, lightly snoring. She drove across the bridge. The boys were gone. The sun shone white and still, nearly hot as noon. They were well clear of town, nearly cool and nearly home, when she rounded a bend and saw Joe Espy attack his horse.

It reared and screamed, but a rope held it to a fencepost. The sheriff used just his fist. He stood in a hard shaft of light in the dirt of the road and assaulted the flank like a man he intended to kill. 'You goddamn horse!' His voice cracked with pure rage. 'You stupid goddamn no good lazy son of a bitch!' The horse lunged. Its tether held it in place.

Annette made a sound in her throat, an odd whimper, and stopped.

Joe Espy's fist thudded on flesh. He paid no attention to the wild flail of hooves. He yelled a plentiful string of profanity, ending with 'heathen goddamn fit for glue!'

On the seat beside Stella, the doctor awoke. His mouth fell open. He moved. She could not. His foot missed the step. He came down on one knee, then up quick as light, moving fast, bellowing as he ran, 'Joe Espy! You fool! You stop that!'

He grabbed the sheriff's arms. Both men shouted as the horse bucked and danced. The doctor bent over, to try for a stronghold, and they both fell off to one side. The horse lunged again, and rose high, and came down, and its hoof struck a skull with a sound like a split-open melon.

They fell tangled, in dust. Stella could not tell which one. The horse stood over them, grinning, terrified, stamping and screaming its chilly horse scream.

Her foot touched ground: she flew effortlessly: the sheriff untangled himself: oh the doctor. Her heart flooded numb. 'Oh sweet holy,' she cried.

'He's all right,' the sheriff shouted, a nauseous quiver disturbing his voice. 'Oh doc, you're all right!' He reached down. His
hand came back red. It jerked at the end of his arm as if scalded.
'Oh shit, oh Jesus, he's all right!' he yelled. 'Goddamn you,
horse!'

Oblivious to Stella kneeling by the doctor, he stood up, intent
on killing something. He reached to his hip for his gun. It was
gone. He looked wildly around for some weapon. His eyes
settled on Stella.

His horse jerked its head. The rope snapped. The animal
bolted away down the road toward the doctor's house.

The head was so large on her knees. Stella made herself look
at the wound. Her heart jumped. A simple smooth crescent the
length of a finger, not nearly as wicked as the splitting sound.
He did not feel dead. Blood seeped into the white of his hair.
His spectacles, shattered to cobwebs. She placed a hand to his
lips, and felt breathing. 'Oh quick,' she cried, 'he's still alive!
Bring the buggy!'

Joe Espy came out of his trance. 'I'll kill it,' he said, 'I will kill
it. I never seen no horse go crazy like that!'

'You beat him!' Stella hissed. 'He should have come down on
you. Oh Lord, come on please now, doctor, wake up –'

'He'll be all right,' said the sheriff, then he leaned over and
threw up his lunch.

'Run get the buggy. I can't pick him up by myself. Oh holy
holy, oh please . . .'

Joe Espy did as she said.

Stella drove.

NINETEEN

Some power done spoke from this broke-down ol fig. Way down in the root. Say here a sweet root, come get him, come on here and dig. Some mo kind of tea come from here! Dirt be all smelly good, smell like some worm. Just look good down at it, watch it to crumble, like fingers was meant to be poke here for root. Ain seen nare like this one, looky here. Drink me some mo kind of tea from this here.

Hooo, come some noise! From the road. Noise ain seen this gal, no, be unvisible, glad of this fig for the hidin. Some white man, skinny, done tie up his beast. Gone to cussin and swingin, and beatin like he be to kill him. Gone wild or else what them hoss done afflic on that man?

Here some buggy. White-hair ol man, sawin log, wake up there – hooo, now he wakin. That gal be – whoa devil, stop it and see! White dress nare red flower ain fool me. Know them gal. Brung her down with these two hands. Right smart gal, member her plum naked, back in them barn. Mama and cheeruns all roasted, left one cripple baby, touch by the fire.

Now here come whitey hair, stop him some beatin. Cain stop no white man who made up he mind!

Hooooooooooooo. Ee. Done rear up, brung down, done hit some white hair.

Gal come a hoppin now, seen so much troublin, ain cry. Seem like ol devil just stay by her side. Gone now, Mister Hoss. Snap some rope clean. Run off like you know where you bounden.

Gal, she be look for that hoss, where he run.

Member that shovel-hold man, by them barn, had some dog, hooo, be memberin all from that day. Done set in to fightin, done tear out some neck. Nare soul but that yonder gal and that man.

And. That shrivel-leg boy.

He talk to them dog? Set em up to a fight? He talk to this hoss here, say kick you some hair?

Cain be. Just some ol boy.

But done touch by the fire.

Come on here, root, we gots travel to do. Could be old root never said nare word. Could be some power done talk in its place.

Ought to kep up with them boy.

TWENTY

The mare made each stride do the duty of three. Stella drove standing, half-balancing, locking her knees against bends in the road.

'Slow down,' said Joe Espy, crouching by the doctor, who lay on the seat, his wound oozing.

'You shut your mouth!' Stella never once feared him – just tasted that cold metal taste, the bright hate. When this was done she would have time to hate him completely, time for the fester and swell.

'Gone tump us out –'

'I said shut up!' The sycamore, one last bounding. 'Miz Danly!' Stella screamed. 'Come out, come quick!'

A horse, Espy's horse, grazed beside the front steps. It turned, showed its white eye, nodded once, then took off, pounding so close past the buggy that Stella smelled it. The sheriff just watched with his jaw hanging. The horse met the road, sprang up, floated over the fence to the pasture, and fled in a pall of fine dust.

Stella ran shouting, 'Come quick!' She flung the door open and sprawled in a heap.

'Munner?'

They lay knotted together. 'Oh God, Jacko, damn it!' she cried, scrambling up. She hopped him, and dashed to the third door, pounding. 'Miz Danly, oh please!'

When she opened the door, Everne's face was compressed by the pillow, her headache, confusion. 'Why, child, what in heaven –'

'Outside. It's the doctor.'

Everne's face went blank. 'Oh bless me,' she whispered.

Jacko had righted himself but they struck him again in their

flight up the hall. He tumbled over, and started to cry. But they
did not hear him. He felt for his legs, pulled them under him,
planted his fists, and dragged to the parlor where he could see
out. They all must be scared, all that yelling. He pulled to the
low window, and set his chin on the sill.

The sheriff rose up and fell out of the doctor's buggy. The
doctor's wife shrieked like a bluejay, climbing up where he
had been, leaning down, taking something between her
hands.

Stella stood off by the mare, looking down at the sheriff, who
hunched on his knees in the grass. He was sick. She said
something. His head came up, then went down.

Jacko heard only Everne, whose wild noises dwindled to
weeping, who held something in her wide lap. A white head.

Who could fix a sick doctor? he wondered. And a sick sheriff,
besides?

The sheriff spit on the ground and strode off the way his horse
went. Poor horse, to get beat on that way and cussed. Maybe
he'd run so far no one would find him. Run on, run quick as you
can.

Munner's meanest voice: 'You wait! You help me!' The sheriff
came back and they climbed up to pull Mrs Dannelly off. The
doctor's rear end hung down as they carried him. Jacko could
not tell if he was dead or just asleep. He would not like being
carried that way.

Cleo came over to take the feet. Munner ran up to the porch.
Jacko pulled toward the hall, to see. He could not pull fast. They
thundered in.

'Watch his head – grab him, no, right back here,' Stella said,
'no, Cleo, watch out! Oh watch out!' The hall floor went kathoom!
when he fell. He would hate being dropped. A wave of shrieking
blew in from the porch.

'Munner!'

'Goddamn it,' Joe Espy said. 'Don't look like he weighs that
much.' Was he crying too? His voice was shaky.

They managed to raise the doctor again, carried him back to
his room. 'Now lay him down easy now,' Stella said. 'Watch it!
Easy!'

Everne came after them, her face changing from scared to all sad, and then back.

The sheriff shrank into the narrowest corner. His face paled. He ran from the room. Cleo went the other way, down the hall. The doctor lay still on the white chenille cover, his mouth slack. A glassy red bubble appeared on his lips.

When Everne leaned in, her cheek popped it. 'Bester,' she moaned, her hands sliding up under him. She kissed his neck, set her knees on the bed.

'I'll run get alcohol,' Stella said. She needed only one moment to breathe, to stop her heart fluttering on her bones. When she opened the door to his study, the corners of desk papers lifted. The sun had collapsed just outside, in the woods; the whiteness of the room was fading.

She found the right stoppered bottle. What else? Bandages. Oh drawers without labels . . . She rummaged for clean white gauze. Hot water? That was for babies. Smelling salts. What else? Everne was the nurse. Maybe if she could find the words.

But she lay on him now, murmuring. Stella's eyes fell. She did not wish to see. Still, he would want her to do something quick. 'Get up, Miz Dannelly,' she said, 'come on. We got to do somethin for him. Come on, now.' She embraced Everne as far as her arms would reach. The three of them huddled there. Stella's mind tumbled. 'Come on, now,' she pleaded.

Everne turned her face. 'Please,' she said, 'leave us be. Please just go on.'

'But no ma'am, he aint dead now, I promise.' Stella pried Everne's fingers away. 'Please, we have got to do somethin. He's breathin. I swear it.'

A dry cough came from his chest, as in answer. His wife sat back, then climbed down from the bed. A light came on deep in her veiled eyes. The folds of her face seemed to gather. The ruined look vanished. 'Oh bless me, you're right,' she said. 'What is that bottle?'

'Alcohol. And here's the gauze.'

'My no,' the doctor said.

His voice froze them in place. 'My no mama,' he said, 'no away.'

'Oh Bester, sweetheart, come on now, don't talk!' cried
Everne.

'Give em best way,' he mumbled. 'And proud.' His voice was
dreamily clear, his eyes closed.

'Now, sweetheart, it hurts you to talk.' Everne dabbed at his
wound with moist gauze. His face did not change.

'We need a doctor,' said Stella.

'Oh sweetheart . . .' Everne sank down beside him on the
white blanket. 'Oh I am sorry, oh talk to me, Bester.'

'There's one in Dead Fall, I bet,' Stella said. 'I'll get Cleo to
go –'

'My, my,' the doctor said, blurring. 'Oh some stay – stay –'

'Sweetheart, what is it?'

He did not answer. Stella saw it fall over his face, smooth
as drapes falling across a window. Everne kept begging him,
pleading, but Stella drew back. He was gone.

TWENTY-ONE

His wife wept, a crooning smooth as a pond, with sobs that broke it like ripples. 'I told you,' she whispered – to whom? To the doctor? To Stella, who stood at the door undecided, who wanted to steal out and never come back?

A fly spiraled down, humming, weaving. It chose to alight on the doctor's forehead. It rubbed its hind legs, then forelegs, balancing unsatisfied on the pair in between. Stella leaned in. Its body was covered with furry gray stripes, its eyeballs two dusky red orbs. It had two wings that seemed spun from glass. She snatched it before it could cock them to fly.

'I'll be on the porch,' she said softly, feeling its prickle against her palm's crease. She would take it out and free it, so one thing from this room would live.

She carried it up the hall, but stopped at the sound of a cool voice just beyond the screen.

'. . . and then, what you think hap?' it said.

The next voice was Jacko's: 'Tell me!'

'Hooo, then come a skinny white boy, come shootin out back with his heinie on fire, come runnin so fast he like probly still runnin tonight!'

'Howcome?'

'Well just put on yo thankin head, honey, and thank. What that boy flyin from?'

'*Tell* me,' begged Jacko. Stella stood, listening.

'I ain fin to do it,' the voice said. 'You gots to thank. Lissen, swee pea, you gots to be thankin. I got a suspicious that you could do more by just settin up thankin than most folks get done if they work up a sweat. But I'll tell it. That boy was chase by a big ol red devil, done foller him out through some trees, step for step!'

Stella pushed at the screen. 'What you doin here?' she said.

Crouched beside Jacko, wheedling into his ear, Mary looked up and grinned. 'Looky now here!' she crowed. 'Come on, gal, come out to see me! Been twice a coon's age since the last.'

Stella opened her hand and the fly flew off, swallowed by darkness. 'What you want?' she said.

'Nare thing but lay these two eyes on yo face,' came the answer. 'And talk to this sweet boy right here.'

'Jacko. Go in the house. Go on.'

'Aw Munner . . .'

The tiny old woman unfolded. Except for a new cap, she looked exactly the same as she had that far day in the barn. She had not aged. 'Who Jacko?'

'That's me,' Jacko said.

She extended a claw. 'Well this Little Brown Mary,' she said. 'How you come by a name such as that?'

'Well my name is Jack Otis Bates,' he announced, 'but if you say it quick like, it's Jacko.'

'Ain that a pure wonderment,' Mary said, creaking down beside his ear. 'I ain cotton to Otis, but Jack be all right. Yo name is yo name, what I thank.'

Stella had used all her patience to keep from assaulting the sheriff, or cursing him, or breaking down. Now she was out. 'Boy, you're gone.' She bent to him.

He squirmed away from her grip. 'Munner, don't!'

'Come on, gal, leave that boy be. Ain no harm. Just talkin. Just passin some time.'

'Not tonight,' Stella said. 'Jacko, you straighten up.'

'I *won't*.' He slapped at her hand.

She popped him. 'Don't you sass me, boy. I will tear your hide up!'

'Munner, puh-leeese, she was tellin a story –'

She jerked him up hard by his arms, carried him into the parlor, and set him down. 'You'll wait right here,' she said. 'Don't you dare move a hair. I'll be back for you directly.'

She went back to the porch. Brown Mary was halfway down the steps, trying to sneak off. 'Stop,' Stella ordered.

Mary turned, her hands raised in surrender. 'Here me.'

'What you doin here?'

'You ast it once,' Mary said. 'Don't be meanin to bring you no pain, gal. Just wondrin how you been gettin along.'

In the old yellow eyes Stella thought she recognized a flash of something like fear. 'We been fine till tonight,' she said. 'Howcome you come here tonight, after all of these years?'

'Seen sump,' said Mary. 'Seen what hap back down the road.'

'Then you know we aint got time for your tales,' Stella said. 'Seems like ever time you come around, something bad happens.'

'Look on it how like I do,' Mary said, coming back up the steps. 'Seem to me like the bad stay right with you most time, matter not who stop by.'

A wild sob rose deep inside the house.

'What was that story you was tellin?' Stella said.

'Ain no story,' said Mary.

'Who was it you said run out from that house, all on fire?'

'You'd like to seen him yoself, but you's standin, and watchin ol house finish burn,' Mary said, in her whistly voice. 'But I saw, and then's when I say, "Mary honey, that boy be the one Mistah Devil come see!"'

'Don't talk to me, woman,' Stella flared. 'Don't set here tonight of all nights, like you know. Cause you don't. Don't nobody know what went on besides me.'

'And maybe one more you din see . . .' Mary grinned wide, and then winked, just as slow.

Suddenly, Stella felt a light come to her mind's darkest corner. 'You mean – you saw?'

'Hooo yes ma'am, and I tellin, I seen a lots in my years, but nare like that night. One time, seen two big babes born the same time to one woman, near split her in halfuns. And seen an ol gal name Big Sally one time –'

Stella grabbed the bones of Mary's shoulders. 'But you saw!' she gasped. 'You stood and watched it! You watched us all burn!'

'Now, petunia, now lissen, just cool yo sweet head.' She was backing away. 'Ol Mary din come till too late. Till the time you was draggin yo mama, old house done already sick of the burnin.

Nothin for me but just watch, time I come. You got nothin on me.'

'But you *saw* . . .'

'You say right.'

'Munner?' Jacko's voice came through a near window screen. 'I'm sorry. I'll be good, I promise. I want to hear the story.'

Stella crossed, and slapped hard at the window. 'Hush your mouth!' The slap struck his nose, which he'd pressed to the screen. She heard him tumbling back.

'Now see, you got him all wrought up –' But when she turned back, she was speaking to empty dark air. She peered out, but Mary had vanished. She might not have been there at all. Stella had wanted to hear that particular tale.

Jacko spoke timidly, well back from the window. 'Munner? My nose itches. Somebody's comin.'

'No, boy. She's gone. Now you hush.'

'Huh-uh, somebody else,' Jacko said.

Then, too close behind Stella, a footstep. She whirled. Joe Espy stood at the head of the steps. 'Who you talkin to?' he demanded.

'Why – to my boy,' she said. 'Why'd you come back here? You go on away.'

'The doctor –'

'Gone,' Stella said. The sheriff's face was too dark to read, but she felt him trembling. 'You did it. Now go. We don't need you here.'

'He run under my horse.' He stepped close. 'And not me.'

Stella shrank from him. He was tall, and even as thin as he was, his height made him seem powerful. She saw the shotgun in his hand. 'Guess you shot that poor horse, hadn't you?' she said. 'Seems like you hurt things to cover your own self –'

'Shut up, little girl. I don't want no more talk. Run on in. Tell his wife I got somethin to say. I'll wait here. Go on.'

Stella slid her hand to the door catch. 'She's in there with him,' she said. 'I aint gone bother her now. Not for you.'

He reached with his free hand, and enclosed her throat – not choking tight, but a warm sweating threat. 'Do like I told you,' he said.

She pulled from his hand. Her hate roared inside her, sending a fine ash up into her mouth as she fled down the hall. 'Miz Dannelly,' she called, tapping, 'I'm awful sorry. I got to come in.'

One lamp cast the room in dim empty shadows. They lay as she'd left them – the doctor reclined, Everne by his side. They might have been sleeping. 'Oh my dear,' Everne murmured, '*please* go away.'

'I would . . . Oh I'm sorry. The sheriff's out there with his gun. He says he's got to see you.'

'A gun?' Everne said. 'What is the call for a gun?'

'I don't know.'

Everne closed her eyes, and drew in a breath that said everything sad. 'I'll come,' she said, rolling onto her side.

Stella crept to the parlor. She would not face the sheriff again. 'Shh, Jacko, don't make a sound.' She joined him at the window. 'Now hush, please just hush,' she whispered. They heard footsteps pass, then turn at the edge of the porch and come back. The door squealed.

Everne's voice: 'Joe.'

'Good evenin, Miz Danly.'

'What do you want with me?' She sounded cold.

The sheriff cleared his throat. 'I'm sorry . . .' His voice went high, like a boy's. 'I'm sorry,' he said again, bringing it down.

'This is no time for condolences,' said Everne.

'I know,' he said. 'I'll be quick. I don't know what you heard –'

'Sheriff, I'd just as soon you went on home.'

'Let me talk,' he said. 'It won't take long. Just, it aint like you think, no matter what she said. That horse was crazy, plumb out of its mind –'

'What in heaven? What horse?'

'Well mine,' Joe said. 'The one that done it.'

'But I thought it was *you* that hit him.' Her voice was so cool.

Stella felt the shock of his gasp. 'Well hell no,' he sputtered. 'She say that? I aint hit him –'

'Joe Espy, you go. This is no night for your wicked lies. If you weren't the sheriff I'd have you arrested.'

'No now, you stop, you got to hear me! This aint no lie! My

horse got funny on me – now please listen. Whenever I come around here, he goes wild! It's that boy. And that girl. Now I swear it, it's them. It aint me. That goddamn horse . . . as soon as I catch up to it, I'll kill it, I swear. It's a curse on it, spooked it. A curse –'

Stella heard Everne's coolness heating to rage. 'I said go. *Go!* Get off of my porch!'

'. . . all this sickness, it's him, it's his doin! He got it first! That sister of his spreads her lies, and she'll turn folks against me, but you got to listen –'

'Joe.'

'It's the work of a devil – now, ma'am, now you hear it! This is for your own good. You got him livin right here in your house! It's him that done it, not me!'

A sob, bitter and strange. Everne's words curdled: 'I said for you to go on now, just get on away –' and a scuffle of feet, a hard smack! Stella leaned close to the window and saw Joe Espy escaping the porch. The door squealed. Everne ran back to the doctor's room, crying.

'Munner?' His voice was so small.

'Oh, what.'

'What happened?'

'Doctor's real sick. She's upset.'

'But she hit the sherf, Munner, and you said the doctor was gone.'

'It's your bedtime.'

'But who was he sayin all them things about? Was it us?'

'Jacko . . .'

'But, Munner, I'm scared!'

'Boy.' Stella grasped his arm. 'You no more scared than I am. And what of, I aint got a notion. Nothin can happen that's worse than already.'

'The wild Injuns could get us,' he said. 'Or a bear, maybe.'

'There aint no Injuns, or bears.'

'We might could get burned in a fire again –'

'Hush your mouth.'

'They might come after us.'

'Who? You shut up.'

'Him. The sherf,' said Jacko. 'Or somebody.'

She stooped to lift him.

'Munner, the doctor's dead, aint he?'

She paused. 'Yes.'

'Howcome?'

'I don't know.'

'Was he dead when you brung him?'

'No.'

'Did you look at him while he was dyin?'

'Boy, you stop. Time for bed.'

'I aint sleepy.'

Suddenly, Stella was as weary of him as she was of the rest of the world. 'Suit yourself, then,' she said. 'Stay where you are. Stay there all night. I don't care.' She went across, to the door.

'Munner, here – take me.' He raised his arms, which were bent at the wrists from pushing across floors. She knew that none of today was his fault; the sorrow and hatred and death came from elsewhere.

She took him up, groaned as she lifted. One knee went out, touched the floor of the porch. She could not believe how much Jacko weighed now.

TWENTY-TWO

CHILDREN'S FEVER,
PHYSICIAN DEATH,
ADD TO COUNTY WOES.

Wide-Spread Tale of Illness
Which Renders Limb Useless,
May Be Spread Through Milk.

DEATH OF R. B. DANNELLY
DOUBLY TRAGIC
IN VIEW OF THESE EVENTS.

87 Cases Reported In County,
17 Fatal, Quarantine Set.

DOCTOR KILLED BY HORSE
WHILE PERFORMING
HIS OFFICIAL DUTY.

The distressing disposition of recent tragic events has posed troubling questions, and at such times as these we are called upon, as citizens of an orderly and clean County, or else as something beneath that worthy ideal. Those who regard these matters as frivolous or unimportant, should take themselves to realize, that these occurrences merit sound judgment in all affairs.

The most unfortunate events, befalling the children of this County, have been with us for the most part some times, despite those in the Town of Camellia who would have it they are of recent development, or derive from the acts of some individual.

Randolph Bester Dannelly, aged 56, late of the surround of Camellia, was a native of Marengo County. He attended the

University of Alabama, trained in his profession at Mobile City Hospital, attaining high honor in that education. Serving for thirty-one years as Physician, County Health Officer, and Trustee of Commerce Bank. He further distinguished himself with publication in the American Journal of Medicine, and by steady attendance with his family at the First Baptist Church of Camellia.

That church is to be the scene on Thursday following of the solemn ceremony remarking his passage. Pallbearers were not announced as of our closing time. The Rev Arnold S. Carmichael is to officiate.

Surviving are the widow; a sister, Mrs Florentine Oakley of Daphne; a niece, Miss Emmeline Hartwell, of Macon, Georgia; and several nephews, of the North.

The late Doctor visited the offices of this newspaper on the 14th of this month, the date before that of his passing, while performing the duties required by his office as County Health Officer. He informed the citizens of Camellia and the surround of the Quarentine necessitated by the onset of a Children's Fever, of which he has seen cases for several years, with the onswell most recently.

This Fever has caused the deaths of seventeen children, and the sickening of several many more. The cause of this disease is unknown, nor cure. The Doctor wished to assure citizens, however, that he earnestly wished them to adhere to the measures of the Quarentine, and not communicate with other homes, unless in case of emergency.

The Doctor's untimely passage poses the aforementioned questions, namely, Who will further administer the Quarentine, and secondly, who will treat the Ill, of whom many remain?

Some have given the cause of transmission of Fevers to milk from infected cows who spread the pestilence. Milk is to be avoided until this is proven.

Mayor Frederick Gossage wishes to inform all citizens that he is most grieviously concerned with the situation, and will do all within his powers to see that it is controlled. The Town Council did not meet last Monday, but will meet again the 27th.

There is no cause for undue alarm, but only a careful reflection on the contributions all citizens can make toward maintaining order and good relations.

After the late Doctor had departed Camellia past spreading notice of the Quarentine, he travelled toward his home when he came upon Sheriff Joseph A. Espy, who was laboring to bring his animal under control. While they attempted to calm the beast, the Doctor's injury was sustained, and he was taken to his residence, where he passed in company with his widow.

Two orphans residing in the home of the late Doctor, Estelle and J. B. Bates, will continue to reside with the widow.

Further tribute will appear within this edition.

They rocked in peace on the shady back porch. Stella looked up from the *Gleam*. 'Look here, he put Jacko's name wrong – JB, he's got it – and some more besides that,' she said.

Everne glanced away from the wooden lap desk and accepted the paper. 'Where is he mentioned?' she said. Through bifocals, her eyes displayed a calm pain.

'Down at the end there, right next to my name.'

'Ah, I see it now. Well, dear, you know Pal has problems with spelling. Bester – the doctor warned me to look up that word on the sign, and sure enough, Pal put an *e* for *a*. Never mind, dear.' She handed it back.

'Those things he put in there are lies,' Stella said. She kept an eye on Jacko, down at the porch's far end. He was learning to push on his scooter. 'Joe Espy wasn't controllin that horse any more than I was. I saw him –'

'That's enough now.' Everne dipped the nib in the blue-black ink bottle, and set to her writing again.

Since Monday, Stella had bitten her tongue so often that she was almost afraid to speak. 'Who's this one to?' she said.

'Emmy,' said Everne. 'It's so hard to find the right words.'

Aurelia filled the door. 'Beg pard, Miz, but Miz Middleton here and won't leave.'

Everne kept her eyes down on her letter. 'What do you mean?'

'Say she aint goin, not till she see you with her own two eyes.'

'What did you tell her, Aurelia?'

'Same as I tole to the rest. Quawtine still goin, you aint takin guest.'

'That's good. And be sure to say thank you.'

'I done did all that already, Miz. She just set down up there, say she aint leavin.'

Everne glanced up with a sigh: 'Lordy lord, some people . . .'

'She say she see for herself you aint took sick.'

Everne nudged the bifocals down to the tip of her nose. 'Just tell her I am, then. I've got a sick headache. I'll see her tomorrow in church.' Aurelia lumbered off. Everne leaned down for the signature, then her eyes wandered to Stella. 'He'd never approve it, a funeral. Not with this quarantine on.'

She had proved herself stronger than Stella had ever imagined – stronger, in her quietude, than even the doctor. She refused to see the people who came to gaze into the velvet-lined box in the parlor. She sent Aurelia to the door, to take the platters of food and make apologies.

Until now, Stella had rarely felt anything more than plain gratitude toward Everne, but the sorrow changed that. She thought back to a time when the terrible knock came at her own door – how long she'd wandered unhealed after that. She found herself admiring the way Everne hid the scar of her grief with a bandage of perfect calm.

After the first night, the weeping, Everne traded grief for her rocker, the lap desk, the pen. Maybe it happens when you get older, Stella thought – you can write, you can turn away callers. You don't give up your life to the pain. 'I think you're doin real fine,' she said.

'Thank you, child.' Everne spattered the ink with white sand from a saltshaker, and pulled a clean page from the desk. 'Now for poor Florie,' she said. Her pen found the top of the sheet.

Stella flipped on through pages of minuscule legal notices and advertisements for farms up for sale. On the last page, she saw a border of black.

R. B. DANNELLY R.I.P.

As a most fitting memorial to the late Dr R. B. Dannelly, we here print the last of his esteemed series of poetry, most of which appeared first in these pages. Delivered to our hand not three weeks ago, it reveals the true Godly nature of this man, truly missed.

A SONG FOR ONE
WHO WILL NOT HEAR

The wonders of the world are myriad!
No less a baby's cry than any orchestra, full-blown,
No less a ray of sun than all of light that ever shone.

The pleasures of the world are swift and sad!
A sweetness followed always by a taste of bitter pain,
A final car, eternal black, behind the whitest train.

The troubles of the world might drive us mad!
Our love-filled hearts so empty when a burst of needing
    comes,
Our peaceful ears unlist'ning for the sound of warring
    drums.

And so are we to find a finer world?
O, is this globe the only place to be?
Will we to heaven's rapture soon be hurled,
Or are we doomed to this mortality?

The questions of the world must make us glad!
Their answers, if discovered, would destroy the mystery,
The knowing would mean less than never knowing, finally.

Stella could feel his words striking like dangerous bells in some deep place. She swallowed, and started again at the top. Her eyes flew to *The pleasures* . . . no. But yes, *sweetness*, and pain *swift and sad* . . . so empty when the burst comes – needing, and rapture, and doom. The words sent a clamoring message. It seemed to come straight from his heart to hers!

She felt her lips moving as she read the last line, again, again: *knowing would mean less* . . .

Finally.

'Rabbit run over your grave, dear?' Everne stared with worrying eyes.

Stella collected herself. 'This poem,' she stammered. 'It's from him, did you see? Oh it makes me so sad – to not know what he was trying to say.'

'Let me see.' Everne's eyes ran fast down the page. 'Why, Bester,' she said, almost to herself. Her eyes filled. 'How sweet . . . oh bless me, it's too awful sweet. A poem. A poem for me.'

TWENTY-THREE

The day aged, and with it the sear of the sun. The men sealed the shed's doors and windows, but a hard shaft broke through to cast a glowing light ring on the hat of the tallest man. They all sweated through their shirts.

'Who the hell called this here meetin?' a voice said. 'It's hotter than forty hells in here.'

'Well let's get it started and done.'

'Well who the hell called this –'

'I did.' This voice brought a silence. 'Yall know why. You know it won't wait. And Fred'll be here if his little girl –'

'Whoa now. No names.'

'What the hell,' came the start of an argument. 'My goddamn hands are full now. I feel bad for Fred, but I don't see how-come –'

'My friend, your hand aint no fuller than any of ourn. That's howcome we're here. There's bad trouble. It aint enough with the chillun fell sick, without some kind of locust come down and some wild kind of spookin.'

'You said it.'

'. . . and you just plan to set on your ass, take your lickin, and not do a thing.'

'Watch out now.'

'Naw now, you watch out. You listen. I know what it is. There's been signs from the first, and now look where it's come. Half the chillun in the county took fever, damn bugs eatin cotton from off the stalk, women won't talk –'

'And all the damn critters gone wild –'

'Hey now, leave off my horse,' said the powerful voice. 'As soon as I find it, it's dead. Goddamn.'

'Oh he aint all,' came another voice. 'There been cows givin bad milk. Dogs a fightin. Why, most folks with half sense done left town already.'

'All of that may be the truth,' said a new voice, 'but I don't see howcome we sposed to just set in this barn and burn up, count of that.'

'Just hold on, and I'll tell you why. I aint even got to the niggers yet. Goddamn. You heard what they done down in Dead Fall?'

That brought dark murmurs, a shifting of feet.

'The way I heard it, ten niggers got tired of their work and they laid down, they laid in the *cotton* row now, and they all up and died, just like that on the spot. Goddamn *died*. Now what you say about that?'

'That aint how I heard it,' someone else challenged. 'I got some cousins from down near that way. They said they was seven, not ten. And they didn't just lay down to die. These boys took em to the highway bridge and shot em to hear em fall in. That other's the word they put out.'

Dissent sprang up. 'Now where you hear that?' someone said. An argument raced through the men, who hurled curses and shouts at each other under the tin roof. At last one yelled louder than the rest to shut up, and they did. 'Goddamn bunch of talky women,' he said. 'I got to know who's up to this thing.'

'What thing, Joe?'

'No names, now! We swore!'

'Well whatever. We got good folks that is scared of a curse.'

'Aw now, you talkin like hoodoo.'

'You don't say it's hoodoo, not when it's a nigger. Goddamn. What yall want from me?'

'Hell, this aint a nigger, it's only a boy.'

'There is niggers mixed up in it too. And besides, he aint just any old boy, let me tell you.'

'You want us to hang a boy? Damn, Joe –'

'Damn it, yall quit with the names! Might be somebody listnin!'

'Well shit, I don't care where we hang em or what. We got to do somethin, else who the hell's gonna do it? You know what we swore.'

'I just swore to niggers. I didn't swear this.'

'Now you're talkin,' the tallest man said. 'Turn your feathers and run.'

'This aint no way to do nothin . . .'

'What you got planned for that girl?' said another.

'What girl?'

'Yalla-head girl with big dinners,' came his answer. 'You think she just set there and let you snatch him?'

'I'm workin on that.'

'Still don't see why you called us today –'

'Hell, man, this aint for waitin. Come on! We know where he's at, now how long's it take you to look at a hot horseshoe?'

'I can't do nothin tonight, anyways,' one man said. 'We got prayer meetin.'

'Some things come first,' said the leader.

'But –'

'It's not till tomorrow, anyhow. We meet east of town, and we head on in. All them folks around, we'll get him without a peep. That girl won't know till too late.'

'Well, what time?'

'Twelve sharp. Meet out by Kline's.'

'If that's all, I'm gone.'

'Hey, what about Fred?'

'Goddamn it, Martin, no names!'

'I'll pass the word on to him.'

They made noises of leaving. When they came out into the spray of the waning afternoon, they became other men under trees, swapping stories and prices, untying their horses, asking after wives and children.

TWENTY-FOUR

The townspeople who knew how to write stooped in the vestibule to sign the church register: Vaughn May, J. E. May, Abbie Gossage, children Gossage, Hubert Ryals, Edna Hobart, Cecil Dannelly no relation, Zollie Herlong, Pal Herlong, Luther Herlong, Early Fail, Mae Emma Reynolds, Ruby Mae Taylor, Emma Lee Taylor, Kitty L. Taylor, Maude Fail, Polly M. Hartselle, Sara Liz. Hartselle, J. E. Gingles, Jessie Gingles, Bessie Gingles, Miss Belle Gingles, Mrs J. Espy, Espy children, Missouri Hammonds, Claude Gillion, Owen Gillion, Ola Reynolds, and on.

Stella bent to write Stella and Jack O. Bates. They were late. Their names were last. Aurelia had nagged to leave Jacko home, since she was well and could watch him, and since she could not bear to watch the good doctor buried in dirt.

Jacko refused to be carried, so he had always stayed home while they went to church. The doctor respected this, and did not insist. But Jacko had mastered his scooter the very first day – he played with it, rolled without stopping. He seemed born to it.

Stella tried seeing the world through his eyes: people coming and going like fireflies, every day a starting over. He should witness all this, so that he would remember when the time came to know. When she told him he could go, a hungry excitement came over his face. He tossed the whole night, so eager for sunrise that he did not wet the bed once.

He trembled now, nervous and thrilled into silence, sitting erect on his rolling platform. He was so clean that his skin still looked wet: his gawky ears covered with combed-down curls, his face pink from the scrubbing, his legs hidden by his best denim dress.

The church doors swelled with a fresh gust of music – the pump organ's dry whining wheeze. A voice called out: 'Rise my soul, and stretch they wings,' and then perilous harmonies rose: 'Thy bet - ter por - tion trace . . . rise from all ter - res - tral things to heav', thy native plaaaaace.'

Jacko's eyes blazed alarm. 'What's that noise!'

'They're just singin, now you hush,' Stella said.

'. . . haste away to seats pre - pared a - bove.' Caller and singers paused, took in deep breaths, and launched a vivid new verse.

Stella leaned on the door. Music rushed out. Jacko opened his mouth at the hugeness of sound. The sound set the blue windows to shivering, then went on up into the vault. The tune repeated itself, but the words changed with every verse. '. . . and earth ex - changed for heaaaaaven.'

With one last flourish of organ, they sang the amen. Their chorus left fog in the air.

Jacko clapped his hands. 'Go on and sing some more songs!' he cried.

Some people snickered. Some coughed. Others turned with a popping of neckbones. In every pew, children sank down so no one would think they were guilty.

Stella watched the eyes wander back to her – familiar and strange eyes and three rows of Negroes. Jacko came just up to her knee. Her hand was braced on his head. Her leg supported the door. She crouched down, feeling the heat of those eyes.

His wheels thundered on the doorsill and hit the plank floor with a burst like a rock hurled from heaven. Find the first empty seat, sit down, sit down! Her face flooded warm. She worked up a smile that seemed proper for church.

As she pushed him up the polished aisle, she saw the reflection and then the thing itself: the stark unpolished box at the altar, supported by a stand of black curvy iron. A bouquet of dried flowers mounded its lid, and the round moonlike face of the Preacher Carmichael floated above his massive songbook. 'Come in,' he called, 'room at the front. All of God's children are welcome.'

Jacko's wheels roared. The organ began to breathe chords, and Stella gave thanks for the organist.

At last, in the third pew from the front, a lady scooted to make room – Miss Sara Hartselle, praise God, beaming as if it were Easter Sunday and she had a new hat. Stella pulled Jacko into the pew, returning the smile. She pinched his arm to the bone. 'Don't you open your mouth,' she whispered, setting her lips together. His eyes went wide. He opened his mouth, but she looked at him sideways. He hushed.

The preacher boomed: 'Why should I be affrighted at pestilence and war, page one thirty-two.' All eyes swept up to him.

Trying to lighten the flush of her face, Stella suddenly realized she was slumped down in their tallness. Everyone else had stood up for the hymn. Miss Sara smiled and winked as Stella stood, murmuring nonsense words soft with the music.

Two rows ahead, swathed in black, Everne Dannelly sat in a pew by herself.

The hymn flowed ceaselessly until the amen. The preacher reached into his coat for his sermon. This funeral filled up his church for the first time since Easter two years ago, and it suited him fine, thank you Lord. If the death of a good man brings people to church, maybe calling him home was a worthy mistake.

'There is nothing we can say about our lives,' he began, 'unless we also talk about the end of them. All our lives are just trips on a map. There are different roads we all travel, but they all come out in the same place. And we have a name for that last destination: call it death.'

Preacher Carmichael's usual funeral sermon was no more than bones – to spare the families, who did not hear, anyway. And he shared the fear of all preachers: which pale fraudulent preacher would mumble too long over his own body, when the day came?

For Dannelly, though, for a church stuffed with people, the preacher had written a solid oration. He hoped they would open their dulled ears to hear.

'Down here on this earth,' he announced, 'we all live out our lives. Every day, we're hit with mysteries, and some rare days, we get a miracle. We like to think they're the same. Still, if it seems like a miracle, well we pray it'll happen to us. And if it's a mystery, we pray it happens to somebody else.'

A few amens arose and died quickly among the dark faces in back. The white portion of the congregation looked up in puzzlement: the preacher was truly preaching, and he seemed to expect them to listen.

'We ought not be here in this church today, yall know that?' He eyed the frontmost pews. Eyes came up. 'We're all under quarantine, supposed to be home, according to those yellow signs. But just look at us, disobeying the last wish of the man we have come here to bury.'

He let his voice drop, so the people leaned forward. 'More of you here in this church than on any Sunday in my memory. Guess we decided that this was a good man. A man better than his own wish. I guess that's the way we've paid honor to him . . .

'Or else it's the way we've tried measuring out this mystery.'

He cleared his throat, checked his notes. 'If you all were to wake up tomorrow morning and see that the pigs in your pigpen had all sprouted out wings and took flight, why I reckon you'd call it a miracle. Right? Wouldn't that be some to see? You'd run to your neighbor's and drag him back with you as quick as you could, so you'd know you weren't out of your head.'

His dire tone dared someone to smile.

'And then you'd sit down, set to thinking. You'd think on that miracle, wonder it out. Your own home miracle, aimed straight at you. You'd wonder what it could mean, what you'd learn from a pig that had wings. And whoa, they'd be flying. I promise. Like birds.

'Now then. Some folks would take it to mean they had God as their personal buddy, so close he made miracles right in their yard. And they'd start in to selling admissions. They'd put it out in the newspaper. They'd tell all their kinfolks to come for a look, free of charge.

'And some others would run off, as frightened as Adam the morning he found the door locked to the garden. They'd blame the devil, or ghosts, or something.

'And some folks would pick up their hoe and do their best to ignore the whole thing. They'd go right to work till the pigs had all come down, and it all was back like before.' He paused for breath. He saw no wandering eyes. He picked the moment to issue his charge.

'But maybe, if you just read in the Bible, if you put good sense on the shelf, if you thought and thought on it as hard as you could, you would figure it out. Maybe sneak right up to it. Maybe. Don't know. You might decide what happened wasn't a miracle. No sir. Cause you couldn't read nothing from it.

'You'd decide miracles are like signs that God puts out by the roadside, and if nobody reads them, or they can't be read, they aren't miracles after all.

'So then maybe you'd figure out that what you had in your yard was a mystery. You'd trip and fall on that word. Mystery. Puzzlement. Great big sign, nobody can read. Pigs can't fly, but if they could, what's it mean? Not a thing. It don't mean a thing. It's a question you don't even need to be asking.

'Like when we wonder howcome we were born. We think it's a miracle, cause we can't remember it. We've got it over and done with. We think we know all about it, but we don't. No more than we know of dying. Dying's a mystery, a big fat question, just a hanging there. We know we'll all get it asked, and we'll find out the answer, but we don't like to think on that.'

In the back, some eyes had gone glazy; the preacher wondered if he might be going too slow. 'Before us, my friends – and I'm winding it up – before us we think we've been hit by a mystery. A big road sign without any words on it anywhere. This good man dying, this doctor, this man with so much of his goodness still in him. A man of faith to his wife, and to all of us here in this town.'

A ruffle of sadness rose in the first pew.

'And faithful to Jesus, as well, every week. A man who could heal – now yall tell me why God would take such a man from us, with so much illness still abounding? A man we need here, right here this summer, right here – we wonder: what job does God have in heaven that's more important? A man in good health – why take him from our midst? And then we ask: if God takes him, when will he take me?'

In the right bank of pews, at the back, a distraction: a child who could not stop coughing. His honk was deeper than a cough should go.

The preacher continued over the noise. 'More than most passings, this poses a question. If we call it anything, it's a mystery. But I propose to you now that we have us a *miracle*. Yessir, a bonafide miracle, right here in Camellia, Alabama. Like I said, being born is a miracle – and this is a miracle that's an answer to that. Both mean something, but what? God leaves us to decide.'

The hacking grew louder, until the boy was nearly choking. At last the mother stood, bustled him out, leaving the door swinging, murmurs. Some heads turned to whisper. Some looked back. Carmichael felt their attention take flight, led away by the plague of all preachers, the children. He found his place, and went on.

'There have been signs by our roads lately – signs, or omens, or auguries, visitations, prophecies. Call em what you please, I've heard em all. This good doctor we bury today, well he tried as hard as anyone to read those signs.'

From the pews at the far left, a sad sigh, then the voice of the woman who made it. 'Come on,' she said to her pew, 'let's go home.' She glanced apology up to the pulpit, then led her little girl back to the door. The child held a hand to her face, flushed and pink. Her legs seemed fluid, unsteady. More parishioners turned.

'The doctor knew there's a spirit afoot here,' the preacher thundered, making his words matter one last time, 'and my friends, I'm not talking the spirit of God. I'm not talking a spirit that makes pigs to fly. It's a spirit of sickness, I tell you – a sickness at home, in our cotton, our poor empty pockets, in the children that's sick when they ought to be well. And our church, when it's empty and ought to be full.

'But why? Why us? Why Camellia? Folks, I been prayin on it, and I can tell you why. It don't come from any one place, or any one person, or God, or a demon. It comes from inside us, every last one of us. The way we act toward each other. The way we pray, and the way we don't pray near enough. We play like we know the answers to questions that haven't got answers and, Lord, ought not even be asked!'

He surveyed the stolid faces, seeking out the fervent. His eyes met two blue eyes, without shyness, reverence, or hesitation. The boy stared as if he'd heard every nuance of meaning, and was building a detailed rebuttal. The preacher's face darkened; he put on the glower he used to transfix children who talked during prayers. This boy stared up, unmoved. The orphan. The doctor had mentioned him. This was why Dannelly had left him at home all these Sundays, despite his own faithful attendance. The boy brought a feeling in with him, new air: a cool sort of challenge, an independence.

'The Lord uses mysteries for his own reasons, and we'll never know what they are. He glues us to him with questions: Why this? Why that? What makes the sun come up in the morning?' His hand made a sweeping gesture that took in the unvarnished coffin. 'If he gives us miracles like this one here, why we're likely to just walk away and quit asking. But, friends, we are meant to keep asking. It's part of his plan. He knows the one thing that keeps a man going is the hope that one day he'll get answers to things he can't know.

'So take heart. A good man has followed the road signs to heaven. He's sleeping there now. We'll get to go, if we keep on with asking. As long as we don't get our wheels off the road. Now let us pray . . .'

It was done. The finish was weak, but the rest was fine stuff. The preacher recited the Lord's Prayer, then turned to Miss Bessie, whose feet began kneading the pedals: 'Amazing Grace.' The stern row of men all in black left the wall, rubbing hands, coming up to the front. When they reached the box, one leaned down to the widow with a whisper.

Before they could lift their burden, a moan came up – yet another child's mother, in back, to the right. 'Darlin, what is it?' she cried. 'Oh God Jesus, the fever!' She snatched her boy and pushed out. People cleared a path. 'It is! Oh Lord help us God Jesus, the fever!' Her screaming trailed behind her, all the way out. Miss Bessie's feet stopped. The silence seemed loud, but then everyone scrambled up, talking and looking around them for something – the face of a demon? The fever itself?

At the preacher's frantic wave, Miss Bessie pumped earnestly, sounding a hymn, double time. 'Praise the Lord,' shouted Carmichael. 'Let us move to the churchyard.' But it was like a schoolteacher who hollers stop! as her children fly out into summer.

His eyes came down to the box – a good man to bury, in all this madness, he thought – then drifted back to the strange eyes of the boy, watching him still: something in his eyes, something peaceful, unsettling, knowing.

The congregation wanted out. The pallbearers shouldered the casket down the jammed aisle. Stella just sat in the uproar, thinking how the preacher's words echoed the doctor's poem, and made sense of her own thoughts.

Miss Sara Hartselle stood up beside her, and used her shrillest voice: 'Quiet down! You all show some respect!' She tapped Stella's shoulder. 'Move him in here, where he won't get trampled.'

She was not hearing anything but what the preacher had said, clanging inside her like bells, clanging with words from the doctor's poem. The lines all made sense in an instant, like a dream puzzled out just before it is done. It fit, every word, with the questions she barely remembered asking, as a child – questions she fended away and deflected, mysteries sleeping in silence, dying in answerless sleep. Buried until this moment, this answer, this sudden terror of knowing, at last.

Every word was printed, so the whole world could see, but no one but Stella could know what it meant. The preacher seemed to tell the tale with his dark talk of mysteries.

She felt a door fall away then, and she plunged down in darkness to faces and whispers long vanished: a man at the door, her mother's smile warm, as she answers, the dim light too late from the barn, a child rubbing fog from the glass to see out. The preacher, coming in summer, leaving only dark murmurs of damnation, sin, sour hell. Mama's face turning away. Each child too soon past the child before. Jacko, the last of them, dying the day of his birth, resurrected by a man who vanished.

A doctor, who vanished.

And much later, his welcome, his arms opened wide. No surprise in his face when she brought Jacko there, as if he'd always expected them.

His kindness, beyond the common kindness of any man for any children: the kindness a father discovers for his own children: secret nickels granted for sodas; the long nights in the wood-shed, building a crib, nailing bright wheels to a board; uncountable hours massaging the white shrunken legs, rubbing the pain away.

Father. It could not be. But yes, oh it could – a real father, treasuring a secret family, and not just a stranger who came every summer, left money, left in a week. Father. Doctor.

The terrible sleep on his face in the satin-lined box, the tin-type from when he was young – the same silvery hair, and a certain strong curve of the chin, like her own . . .

In some odd secret way, Stella realized, she had spent all her years in his house listening, gathering signs, wishing this dream to come true.

Then these words, spoken from the pulpit, and his words wrapped only for her in a border of black. She never knew she had spent her life searching for her father until she found him at his funeral, and on the last page of Pal Herlong's newspaper.

She strained to remember the words from the fog when he died. She heard mumbles, a dim haze of meaningless sounds, and then real words began to emerge: *daughter*. Something like *daughter, my daughter* . . .

Oh, only her ears wishing.

But she remembered something else: a half word, a soft letting go near the end, just a sigh. She was sure. He said *stay*, or else maybe he was trying to say *Stella* . . .

William knew. Must have known. She believed it was William who woke her that time, so she would see the lamplight too late from the barn. The knowing must have burned him beyond ashes, burned him to dust. *Less than never knowing.*

Finally, a man who matched with Stella's hidden longing: a

man who gave out his own love in hiding. A fine man. That love
was his power, his weakness – the haunting, the burning, the
pull strong as gravity. Bound by the barn and their secret, the
flesh of their flesh.

But how could he stand with his daughter and not take her
into his arms and say yes you are mine, yes I am yours? Torture!
How his blood must have cried out: *Tell!*

How could her mother go down to her grave without ever a
glimmer, a hint, a whisper?

If only Stella's eyes had been open to see. She was dumb,
deaf, and blind until now, until she saw it suddenly, heard it, felt
it to her bones, and yet nothing was left except wondering,
circling, wandering back.

'Honey, bring him in like I said. He's just about to be stepped
on,' said Sara.

Stella forked her arms under Jacko's, mumbled thanks, and
retreated with him to the pew. His dress came up, revealing his
shriveled legs, slender as bones. He started hollering. Faces
turned. Way in the back, a man shouted: 'Look at that boy!
Look at him! It's that boy!'

'What is it?' said another man. Stella recognized Pal Herlong,
craning back to see who had accused. 'What is it? What's he
done?' he said.

'He brung this fever down, didn't he!' came the shout. Some
ladies made soft little cries, as if they'd been touched.

'This boy?' Herlong glanced down. 'This boy hadn't got fever?'

'He had it first! He's the one brung it down!'

'Oh, what an awful thing to say,' Miss Sara gasped. 'Oh my,
that is awful!' The faces around them were hardening, straining
to see who caused all the commotion.

Pal Herlong stuck his face into Stella's. 'This boy got a fever?'

She felt herself flush. 'Nosir,' she whispered, 'not for a long
long time.'

'Speak up, so they can hear you.'

'He hadn't had it, not since he was just a libitty baby,' Stella
said, louder. Faces fell back.

Miss Sara urged at her elbow: 'It's time, dear, let's go. Never
mind what they say.'

Stella turned to thank her, but it was not Sara Lizabeth at all, but Everne, still consumed by her veils. 'I'm sorry for all the noise we made,' Stella said. 'I thought Jacko knew how to mind.'

'I said let's just go, dear. The preacher is right. It's time for the graveside.'

Jacko sat, clutching the hem of his dress to his knees, his face shining with shame and excitement.

'Now, ladies, hurry.' The preacher, behind them. 'I think it's fixing to rain.'

The church had emptied so fast that the preacher, the widow, Stella, and Jacko were the last to enter the vestibule. His wheels rocked on the doorsill.

People wandered aimlessly through the churchyard just outside, as if looking for someone to tell them what to do. Three small groups stood apart, gathered around three small patches of grass, where the three stricken children lay – upturned pink faces, bright hot, showing fear, each attended by a mama down on her knees, and a daddy looking up at the clouds scudding, threatening, bringing damp air.

'What is happened here?' said the preacher.

'I want you to know that was the finest talk you'll ever give,' Everne said as Cleo scuffed up, with an umbrella.

One by one, wagons pulled near. The daddies swept up the sick children, and rattled away.

The sound of rain beat the rain by moments. Then it came in a visible sheet, slowing the pallbearers' halting parade to the grave. They threaded a path through the headstones. The youngest among them was old. Rain pummeled down, discoloring the wood, dislodging the bouquet. The men reached the hole, set the box down, pulled their hats low on their eyes, and stood waiting.

Most of the people fled in wagons at the first droplets, but a few mourners huddled under the eaves of the church. Everne and the preacher struck out through the downpour, hurrying, sharing the big umbrella. Stella followed them, and others went after her, and soon a small clutch of dripping heads bowed at the side of the red muddy pit. The bearers tied knots in their

ropes, lifted, strained, counterbalanced. They lowered their
burden to earth.

The preacher's right hand came up. He prayed quickly, of
ashes to ashes, and dust down to dust, but he did not mention
the rain drenching everyone, drowning his words.

Stella looked past the mourners, out into the green fringe of
woods. She tossed the bouquet she had rescued, heard its
thump on the lid of the box. She did not look down to her
father . . . She blinked: her eyes spoke lies: but no, the truth:
men appeared in the edge of those woods. Seven men. Watching
her watching them. Two horses. A wagon. Two mules. Seven
white V's of shirts, seven faces half-hidden by hatbrims, seven
pairs of black boots – seven strange sudden watchers, holding
horses, watching through rain.

No one saw them but her.

'Amen,' said the preacher. The mourners broke, and hurried
off toward shelter.

The men flicked whips at their animals. They vanished back into
the trees as suddenly as they had come. Stella shuddered. Could
they be friends, sent to guard the doctor to his last moment?

No. Friends would come close. They would make themselves
known. They would not act like ghosts.

Rain pounded her cheeks, cold as January. She raised her
skirt, and ran for the church. When she pushed through people
shaking rain from their coats like wet dogs, she found Jacko's
scooter inside, by itself.

'Jacko, where you? Answer me!'

He was nowhere. He was gone. He was gone.

Stella stood, dripping. Rich colors fell from the windows. She
felt as if her arm had been torn off, but she could see it still,
lying nearby.

'Jacko?'

Who would want her boy?

He'll take cold. If he's out in this rain. How could they take
him out in a cold rain?

The man shouting out from the back. Or the watchers.
Someone with a plan. It had to be someone who meant no good.
Jacko would not just go off.

In the vestibule, the preacher was speaking softly to Everne:
'. . . and when I was little, my daddy told me that a storm on
the day of a funeral is the tears of our Lord Jesus,' he said. 'Of
course that's not in keeping with Gospel, but . . .'

'It's a sweet thought,' said Everne, with a rustle of silk.

'Jacko's gone,' Stella said. They turned. Stella showed with
her hand the empty sanctuary where Jacko was not.

'Who?' said the preacher.

'My brother. Jack Otis. I left him in here.'

'Well surely he's round about somewhere,' said Carmichael,
stepping inside. 'I bet he just wandered away.'

'He don't walk,' Stella said. 'He don't wander.'

'Oh him . . .'

'You spose Cleo took him?' Everne offered the umbrella.
'Here, run and see.'

Stella started to open it.

'Not inside,' hissed the preacher.

She dashed out, each step exploding a puddle. Cleo sat on his
rostrum, holding the reins and ignoring how wet he was getting.

'Cleo!' she cried. 'You see somebody take my boy?'

'Sho din,' he said.

'Well get down now, and hurry. Unfasten your side. I'm gone
ride on Annette. You hurry! Somebody took him!'

But where? She had not even seen the man who accused from
the back. And the watchers had blended like deer with the
woods. Who would steal a crippled boy? And once they had him,
where would they go?

Stella wrapped her arms tight around Annette's neck, closing
her eyes to the bullets of rain. They went sprinting off – which
way? To town: check at the doctor's house first, and hope
maybe Aurelia, for some reason . . .

She glanced up. A wagon was coming toward her. Its wheels
drew straight lines in the mud. As it neared, she recognized
Fred Gossage holding the reins, but he did not seem to see her.
He sat propped on his seat like a dead man, driving and staring
blankly straight ahead.

She turned as he passed. In the flat of his wagon, a small
bundle bounced up like cordwood.

Oh Lord, and wrapped in damp quilts: his Louanne. Stella had seen enough limp bodies carried in wagon beds to last out a million lives.

Another child gone from this life and its troubles, bound down for peaceful dark earth. Children dying as fast as the holes could be dug.

It was no mystery, no miracle. It was too awful common for that. People die. They leave others behind.

It must be quiet, and dark, being dead. An end to the wondering, waiting. An end to the fear. A stealing away, to where stolen ones sleep the long sleep.

Callie, the children, the Gibsons, the doctor . . . all gone off with their secrets. And now her boy: her blood: Jacko: gone and maybe for good, and if that was true, Jacko was good as dead. If you have no one else, gone and dead are the same.

Stella gripped Annette's mane with both hands and remembered her vow to live on for all time. Maybe she'd vowed the wrong thing. Maybe the real hell was cold, cold and wet, a place nothing would burn.

TWENTY-FIVE

The storm was a war between moist warm wind swelling up from the gulf and an early surge of cool that fought down from the north. The innermost leaves of trees shuddered and quaked: collision and battle, advance and retreat. Flashes of lightning froze things in their places, and thunder boomed louder than cannonfire. At last the cooler wind won, and swept through, bringing word of a change. The rain steamed from trees, cloaking the ground in a fog, softening rawer red edges of fields. Barn swallows plunged through dense clouds of wet insects, eating the spoils of the storm. Beneath the pale mist, in a tiny house nearly swallowed by vines, Little Brown Mary was choosing a story.

'Lessee which one it could be that you ain heard fore now,' she said, sending a fine belch of smoke. 'Way I am, tunia, no need to make one up. All I gots to do is just thank back. Sweet Lawd . . . the thangs I done that I can remember. And hooo, all the thangs I forgot.' She winked, but Jacko just studied her with one cold eye.

'Give on!' she cried. 'I know which one it is! I could tell you bout this big ol gal I known. Come from up Dead Fall. A big gal, hooo yeah. Gal could pick up a full-grown nigger and toss him so hard he would bounce. Hooo!' She cackled. 'Big Sally her name, and I tellin you truly – big was the one thang that ol gal sho was. Like this barn, honey, but some bigger. Arm big around as a side slice pork ham. I member one time she come to my –'

'I want my Munner!' burst Jacko.

'Just hold yo britches, big snuff,' Mary said. 'I done said it already. She comin directly. Just you wait and act down some.'

'But I want her *now*!'

'Well now, did I just say she be comin, or was it a dream? She be come. You just lissen my story.'

Jacko glared up from the splintery floor. Coming with Mary had seemed such a fine idea, back at the church, when she promised him stories and sweet things and maybe a wagon he could drive himself. She'd said Stella knew all about it, and would follow behind them. It was a lie, but it sounded as real as the other things, and now Jacko was in trouble. Bad trouble. 'You told a *lie!*' he accused.

'Aw, just you got yo back up cause we left yo old rolly toy back yonder,' Mary said. 'We go back for it, soon as we get settling in.'

'I hate you.' Jacko's nose made bubbles.

'You no such a thang. You some mean kind of boy,' she told him, crouching so her eyes were level with his. 'You acted right dandy when you come along. Now let's hushup and see what I'm fixin to say. Or else, what I might show you to do . . .'

She creaked up, a snapping like twigs, and took a long draw on her pipe. Making her crusty lips into an O, she popped her jaw and shot forth a blurred cloud, which refined itself into a wide wobbly ring, flexing and drifting in air. She squinted, leaking smoke from her nose.

Jacko's eyes widened along with the ring.

'Now you thank that was some,' Mary said, 'just get set for this.' She drew twice on the pipe, working her mouth pop! pop! so a second ring followed the first, and shot through its center.

Jacko laughed. 'Do it again.'

'Like it, yassuh, boy like him some tricks. Lessee can we try for three . . .' Pop! Pop! Pop! Three perfect rings formed and floated together, dissolving.

He clapped his hands. 'Do it again!'

'Hooo, petunia, that's all for me.' Mary sank down to a wooden crate, the only furniture Jacko could see in the dark empty rooms of the house. 'This old gal gone get *high*. Sides, three times is all you ought do any trick. Three times make folk to believe you, without you wore out.'

'I know a trick,' Jacko said. 'I can do one. I seen the doctor do it.'

'What trick you got?'

'This!' Jacko produced his right hand with its palm stretched out. His thumb bent back and kept bending, until it nearly touched his wrist.

Mary tried to seem pleased. 'Now you don't need do that trick, tunia,' she said. 'They's somethin wrong about it. Look like it hurt you.'

'It don't.' Jacko happily flexed both thumbs out of joint, watching her face.

'Say yo Mistah Doctah done that way?'

'Sometimes,' said Jacko. 'But mine go back farther than his. It always made Miz Danly scream whenever I do it.'

'And no wonder howcome,' Mary said. 'A thang like that could get next to you. Stop with it, honey, you gone hurt yo bones.'

'Howcome when I do it everbody looks funny?'

'Well now, how you mean?'

'Like you looked,' Jacko said. 'Like it scareded you.' He bent the left thumb.

Mary reached out. 'I say don't do it,' she said.

'You aint bossin me,' Jacko said, jerking his hand away. 'I'll do whatever I want.'

'Hooo now, just hear that boy talk!' She tumped her pipe against her sole. 'Nawsuh, ol Mary the one come to quit all the bossin on you. Liss, I tell you howcome they look funny. I save ol Big Sally for sometimes, seem like she too big for right now. But I know some mo tale, and it's ever bit true as a stump. Happed a long time ago – hooo, child, way back befo I was born, if you can picture such thang. Befo you could find any nigger near here. Way on back in the Injun time, we talkin now.'

Jacko perked up. 'What kind of Injuns?'

'Law, ever kind. Got yo Chickershaws, Pocomos, got yo ol Libertines, got some Po-Knees mixin in. Them ol Po-Knees was round here the first, and go fightin amongst their own selves, like folks do to see who gets to stay and who gots to go on. When here come some white fallas, movin in on em. Comin on wagon, and bringin they gun. Hooo, can you think what the Injun man thunk of a stick that would kill him from outen one end?'

'But they had their bows and arrows,' Jacko said.

'Yeah, but, honey, put arrows up next to some shotgun, and you purt soon find out which you want. But now, guess on the first thang them white fallas done.'

'Killed the Injuns.'

'Not right off, swee pea. First thang was buildin some house, right there where all the Injun stay. Then turn right back and say, "Hey, Mistah Injun! We sorry to tellin you, but this here place blongs to us! Yall just gone has to move on." Now if you was a Injun boy, whad be yo answer to that?'

Jacko shook his head solemnly. 'I'd shoot em with my bows and arrows,' he said.

'Well, but firstlike, you'd pitch you a regular fit now, you take my word on it. But these was some good Injun boys. They just seddown for some thankin on it, lit some pipe up between em . . .' This reminded her to fill her own pipe with the strange bristly weed. She snapped fingers; a blue flame leaped out of her hand to the bowl.

Jacko stared. 'How you make that fire?'

'Just you do, little man. If you hush up, lissen my tale, I might show you.' She puffed, producing a cloud. 'Hooo, so them Injun boys settin and smokin, and saying, "Aw, them ol white mens, they ain mean nothin bad. They just need get some experience. They come around." And then laugh, like some joke.

'But I say some truth now: they ain a white man in this world is gone let you just set there and make a joke out of hisself. He ain gone let you laugh at him. Back then the same as today. He gone push at you, pushin and pushin, till purt soon you either do thangs like he tell you, or find you some color sides the one you is.'

Jacko squirmed, fighting impatience. 'What happened?'

'Well, ol white mens done cut down some tree now, done built some big ol fine kind of house with a porch on the front that runs all the way. And he go to set on it. When some them Injun come by, whitey say, "Now go on! Yall done trespassin me!"'

'Did they kill em then?'

'Hush up now, and I tell it. Ol Injun, he walk on off smilin,

cause Injun don't want no trouble, least not no new kind. He try
lettin it slide. But he cain. Fo too long, some them white boys
start to chunkin rocks over his way, and poppin they guns, such
as that. Injun man just keep a walkin, straight up like a pine
tree, on back to his other boys. They start talkin, a powin and
wowin, like Injuns, and soon they done figure it out. They don't
see no two ways on it. Put all them paintin and such on they
face, and all grab up some hatchet, and sharpen em down. Waits
till nightfall, till long bout this time.' She peered around spookily.
'Yassuh, just near bout like this.'

'Come on!' said Jacko. 'You teasin me! Whad they do then?'

'Well just went on a walk to some white folkses house, name
of Whatloe. Now them was the old Whatloes, good kind, not
same as the Whatloes you see these days. Mama and daddy,
some cheeruns, be settin there eatin they supper – some greens,
I rackon. Just then them fo Injun boys break the door down,
come wavin them hatchet and screamin like painted up devils,
all fired up and hot and good ready to do what they done. And
they hatch em all up, hatchin good, ceptin mama and one ol boy
child. She grab him by and fly hoop! out the back.'

Jacko's eyes glowed. 'Did they hatch em?'

'Tunia, that mama manage to get out without gettin hatch.
She run to them wood, to a hollowy log. Now I tellin, that gal
wadn't under that log much as she was crawl up inside of it.
Injun come lookin for her, they look high low and ever place
else, but they din find a hair of her. Nare single hair. And that
gal, she just laid up inside that ol log the whole night, and some
mo of the day, when it come. Tryin to keep that po baby from
makin a peep. And way I heard told, it was like that boy knew
what was up and he kep hisself still.'

'Tell me another story,' said Jacko.

'Hooo, this one ain done! Come long about noontime, next
day, ol mama go back in that house to see who she had left.
Found em all, ever one just as dead as the next, her ol husband
with bone showin out. All them po cheeruns. But she last till
she come up on her newest babe, and that's when that white
mama gone wild. All that child's hair was gone, same as the rest
of his head. Chopped off, just clean as a snake cut in two.'

'Yuck,' said Jacko.

'By time some mo folks come along, say that mama gone crazy. Ever hair on her head done turn white. She be cryin dark tears. She done left the live child out to mess on his own, say she crawl back up inside of her log. Took that dead baby on up in there with her. Took up a heap of pine needle, been stuffin em into that po baby's head, try to fill it back up.'

A cold sudden shudder seized Jacko. He looked away. 'Don't tell no more,' he whispered.

But Mary moved even closer; her voice grew soft and went straight to his ear: 'If you listenin stories, you gots to hear till they done,' she said. 'Just a touch mo to this tale. Them white folk set in to killin them Injun, and then's when they find out what good is some gun next to hatchets and arrows and such. Folks come to some place where they diffunt, they bound to get scared. Scared of the bugs and the trees, so bad skibbity they get to actin all bad. Injun be scared cause the whiteys was diffunt, and white folk be scared cause the Injun was too.'

Jacko glanced up. 'You said one of em got out without gettin hatched,' he said.

Her face broke into a pleasury smile. 'Now you thankin, swee pea,' she said. 'You some quick boy. That child done turn out like you. Got the same kind of trouble. Cause he done come through some bad, like you done, and it left him alone, just the same. And when he got growed, all them other folk say, "Hey now. He got a somethin, some kind of a power, to come through with nary a scratch. I ain got no truck with that boy." They stay shed of him cause some thangs that ain happen, not cause some that did. Same as you.'

She reached out to grip Jacko's arm with her dark withered fingers. 'You hearin me, sweetunia? You like that boy – done walk right thu some bad, so the folk think you brung it down with you. Folks, they be lookin for somethin to get scary of, and settle it mostways on you.'

Jacko pulled from her grip. 'You mean, like they look funny when I do my thumbs?' he said.

'Sho.'

'Or like when the sherf said I was howcome his old horse acted up?'

'Now you catchin!' Brown Mary grinned. 'I known you could thank it, if you was just use that fine head on yo neck. And now you thank back yonder at the churchhouse, how them cheeruns all took down with fever real quick.'

'I couldn't see,' Jacko said. 'We was sittin up front.'

'Well I seen, the way they just put it to you. And just twix us, swee pea, I spec they was right.'

Jacko stuck his lip out. 'But I din do nothin.'

'Hooo, I believe! I ain say you did. I don't spec you brung the fever down on em, but lissen: word done got out on you, boy. Them cheeruns bounden to heard it. Folks talk, and fo you can spit, they done start to believe what it is they done said. So it din take them white babes but one good study on you, till they memberin all they heard said, and like that – hooo! Fallin down sick!'

Jacko shifted his legs with his hands. 'But howcome they blame stuff on me?' he said.

'Child, you bout the most easy to blame.'

'I want my Munner,' he said.

'You gone get her, and some mo besides, now you wait.' Mary emptied her pipe, and reached into her bib. 'Look here, swee pea, you take just a taste of this here. Then we gots to be shuttin our eye. Soons we get up, why, yo gal be here.'

He eyed the tiny brown bottle. 'What is it?'

'Nare a thing but some sleep juice,' she said. 'Go on, get you some. It ain much for lookin, but hooo! take a taste. It's sweet like some candy.'

'Where'd you get it?' Jacko felt his wariness begin to crumble; he loved sweet things the best.

'Come straight from Brown Mary. I mix it up special. Petunia, look here, I'll take a taste so you see it's good.' She took a tiny swig. 'Hoo-ee! There's some goody.'

Jacko knew better. But now that he thought about it, he was thirsty. He could not remember the last time he had a drink of water. He took the bottle, examined its sugary lip, and peered in. It was brown. It looked awful. He sniffed. It smelled like something gone bad and then worse.

'Go on, you like it,' coaxed Mary. 'Go on.'

He closed his eyes, held his breath, tipped up the bottle. The first taste was oily, but then it went ting! on his tongue. She was right. It was good. He tipped it again for a real swallow.

'Hol on now, boy, what I tell you?' She reached for the bottle and stowed it away. 'Too much, you be sleepin' for good!'

'I'm hungry,' Jacko announced.

'Done et all I brung, babe, but I fetch us some while you sleep. I gots to slip out awhile, anyways, run go meet with some folks.'

'I want Munner.' His words slithered out like molasses. His tongue felt thick to his finger.

'Honey, I told it till I'm near done tellin,' she said. 'She be here, and you fine with ol Mary. Be hard to find better folks you could be with. And there's some mo niggers here roundabouts, just as good, some you ain gone find none better of. You see, come tomorrow.'

Jacko did not mean to yawn. 'What kind of niggers?' he said around it.

'The best kind.' She reached down in her gunnysack, and brought out a musty brown blanket. 'Here you some warm to wrop on you,' she said, digging again. 'And looky what I made up special for you, just some soft for yo head. I gone run meet my peoples, and then come the sunup, gone tell you the rest what you needin to know. Lay on down – thataway, yeah, gone have some sweet dreams.'

Jacko felt soft and all mushy inside. He fought to keep his eyes open. 'I want my Munner . . .'

Her words drifted down on him like leaves: 'And you get her directly,' she said, ever softer. 'Done left plenty of trail. You best get some snoozin, sweet pea, got you one big day comin. Gone learn you some trick you don't already know, less they ain one. And then we find out what kind of a witchy boy you plan to be.'

He saw the pink of her smile, then he felt his eyes fall, and nothing past that.

TWENTY-SIX

Stella dashed down the hall to the kitchen, toward the sweet miracle waiting for her at his little white table, wanting a cool drink of water. Aurelia turned in surprise from the skillet, and asked was it done that quick, where Miz, where Cleo, howcome she all wet, where the boy, why she cryin . . .

Then Stella knew Jacko was gone, truly gone, stolen by someone for some reason she could not know.

No time to answer Aurelia, or explain, or even to change to dry clothes. She flew up the hall and out, tugging Annette to the trough, pleading, 'Faster, oh hurry, drink fast!' Then a blur, hold on, hold on! Pounding hard down the empty mud road, Stella heard birdcalls too shrill to be songs – *Go back! Danger! Go back!* – a rustling of trees, of conspiracies, a thudding of hoofbeats or drums or her heart as it raced the cold fear.

A whisper told her to look, and she discovered they'd reached the last slope to the bridge before town, nearly there. Somehow the wild storm had vanished, leaving a new sky swept clean of its clouds, puddles shining like mirrors set into the road, and oh thank God, rolling fast down the opposite hill toward her, waving his hand, full of news: 'Luther!'

He strained hard at the pedals, but his wheels bogged down in mud and he tottered there, inching ahead. Stella urged with her knees. Annette did not like the clank-rattle of Luther's machine, and stopped halfway across the bridge.

His wheels spat mud as he came up, red-faced, out of breath. 'I'm so –'

'Oh Lord, Luther,' she cried, 'I'm so glad to see you here. You got to help me!'

He nodded, slapped his chestbone. The knob in his throat bobbed up and down.

'It's my boy Jacko. He's gone! You got to help find him! Somebody stole him, just now, from the church!'

'I – I been looking –' he sputtered.

'You seen him?' Her stomach clenched up like a fist.

Luther nodded.

'Oh sweet God.' Stella swayed in the woozy hot flood of relief. Oh sweet thank you, you did hear me pray, you have ears and you heard me.

'Daddy,' said Luther. 'He's – the one seen him. You got to come – come back with me.'

'Who took him? Is he hurt? Did they hurt him? If they hurt him . . .' Stella wished she could reach down his throat for the words. 'Oh please, tell me!'

'He just said to bring you,' he managed.

'Who?'

'Daddy. He knows. Said to bring you back with me or stay gone myself.'

Stella heard in his stammer the shade of another voice, louder: his father's voice, mild as milk, rising over the babble, the shouting: *This boy got a fever?* Defending. Searching the crowd for accusers.

Suddenly, she understood. Pal smelled the danger. Saw the men dressed all in dark and boots, watching. Took Jacko to save him from them. All her fears turned to vapor. 'Come on,' she said, 'climb on up. We both can ride.'

Luther blinked, and looked down at his bicycle.

'Oh now, Luther,' she said, 'please, let's hurry! You can't keep up on that thing.'

She saw hurt in his glance. 'Yes I can.'

'But the mud . . . Oh come on, we'll come back and get it soon as I see him, just see for myself he's all right.'

Luther eyed his silvery handlebars. 'Well I can't just go off and *leave* it . . .' he tried.

'Luther Herlong, you listen! I aint playin! I'm bout to go out of my head scared to death, and you worried about your durn toy! Now run hide it up under this bridge and let's go, or else tell me where, and I'm gone.'

Luther swallowed. 'Well I guess just for a while,' he said,

glancing up at the mare. 'But I swear I'd beat this old nag, hard as you've run her.'

'Hurry!' She held Annette steady as he rolled the bicycle over the bridge and down an embankment. Someday she'd tell him how silly he looked on the thing, at his age, so tall his knees stuck out to both sides. The news he brought made such sense, so far gone from her fears, that Stella could not quite believe it. She slid up to make room for him.

Annette groaned under the new weight. 'Ride,' Luther said, settling. He held on lightly to Stella's arms with large warm hands. He did not feel as bony as he looked.

'Which way?' Stella said.

'Town.'

'But where? Where'd yall take him?'

'We didn't,' said Luther.

'Well who, then?'

'I don't know for sure. Daddy does.'

'Luther, good night!' She twisted back. 'You'd think that havin your own kin just stolen aint nothin to worry about. I know you aint one for talkin, but you got to start. Tell me what happened.'

'Only thing I know is I got back home from the churchhouse, and Daddy came back, and he told me to find you and bring you back.'

Stella found soft between the mare's ribs, and kicked, and wished they were Luther's ribs instead. Luther wriggled back to keep from bouncing too close as Annette jolted ahead.

The houses of town slid by, shut up and silent. No dogs barked. No one was out in the yards. Not a soul, just a buzz of insects the whole way up to the square and down Front Street. Gold light showered down, polished clean by the storm.

Stella remembered the ride with the doctor, when she placed the yellow marks on all these doors and imagined a silence like this. Now it was deadness more dead than she'd thought, every windowshade pulled, everyone gone from Camellia or else huddled in steamy dark parlors, while their dogs lay panting for cool on the hearths.

Luther stayed quiet too, scanning the crepe myrtles as if he expected an ambush.

The Front Street stores were chained shut, although most windows still had Open signs. The screen door at Planter's Mercantile hung half off its hinges. Gadney's Hardware was black to its bowels; in the dark glass, Stella saw her own face – weary, much older since morning, when she brushed her hair and put on the dress.

'Here.' The first word from Luther since out by the bridge. She slid down after him, and tied Annette while he fumbled with keys. He opened a tall skinny door. She pushed past and ran up the narrow stairs to the frosted-glass door that revealed only the shadows inside. 'Jacko?' she called. 'Boy, you there?'

'We must of beat Daddy back,' Luther said, at her side.

Stella followed him into a stale grayish room with a maze of machines and great spills of newspaper, an ink smell just sweeter than paint. It looked like a place where men come for dark work.

'Sit down.' His voice rang. 'Here, I'll make you a place.' He bustled in, moving stacks of paper from a green swivel chair, settling against a machine that was taller than he was. She noticed how handy his gangly arms would be here, to reach things.

'But you said he was here,' Stella said. 'And Jacko.'

'You sit here.' He patted the chair. 'I'll show you our shop.'

'I can see it. You aint answered me. Where are they?'

'He'll be here. He just said wait. You want somethin to drink? What you want? Want a dope? We got dopes, but they're hot. They're just as good hot.'

'I don't want a thing except what I come for,' Stella said. The chair squealed in pain when she sat.

Luther looked to the door, as if he could make his father appear. 'I ought to start up the press,' he said. 'Then you could see how it –'

'Luther, howcome your daddy puts lies in that paper?'

'What you mean?' He blinked twice. 'He don't put lies.'

'In that paper he did,' she said. 'That stuff from Joe Espy, where he was sayin about when the doctor . . . where he said he was tryin to calm his horse down. That's all lies.'

'No it aint,' Luther stammered. 'Cause – cause I heard him say it. The sheriff, I mean.'

'Well then, you heard him lie. That horse wasn't bad, or else he made it bad, cause he had it tied up to a fence and was beatin the poor thing to death, Luther! I saw it! Doctor went over to try and stop Joe Espy, not his horse. If he said all that, he's tryin to make his damn self look good –'

Blood colored Luther's face. 'Lady ought not to cuss,' he said. 'You wait and ask Daddy. He'll be here.' He studied his hands. 'You mean he just had it tied up to beat it?'

'As plain as you set there now, Luther, I swear it. I thought Joe Espy was the one who took Jacko, until I saw you at the bridge.'

'Well why would he beat him like that?'

'Aw Luther, where have you been? The whole town's gone crazy, and Joe Espy's leadin the way. He's scared somebody'll blame him for the doctor, and somebody ought to, but he turns it right back on Jacko – says Jacko spooked his horse. He's a damn liar. And your daddy passed his lies right along.'

She saw Luther wince as if her words pinched. He edged away from the hulking machine. 'Wait and ask Daddy,' he said.

Stella stood. 'I aint waitin,' she said. 'I've waited enough. I'll go find him. You don't know nothin without him, anyway.'

'He's tryin to help.'

She put her hand on the cold marble doorknob. 'Luther, I'm sorry, I can't just set here and yack with you till nightfall. I preciate you comin to find me and all, but I got to go find him myself.' She swung the door out. 'Where'd you see him last?'

'You can't go,' Luther said. His anger disappeared. Stella saw fear in his eyes. 'Please don't. Just sit, he'll be here any minute. I'll get you a Nehi, or anything. Just please. He made me swear –'

Below, Stella heard the door scrunch. Light flooded up. Pal Herlong wedged sideways through the door, clumping up toward her, as wide as the stairs. 'Well, I see the boy brought you,' he called up.

His bulk edged Stella back into the room. 'Lord, Mister Herlong,' she said, 'I am sure glad it's you. I was comin to find you. Luther says you have my boy.'

Pal stood huffing in the door. He pulled out a red handkerchief, mopped his face, blew his nose. Stella saw Luther shrink back, and she saw the resemblance – just take Luther, widen him out, make him shorter, give him a belly and a ripe smell of hair tonic, and they would be just alike.

'Well I'm thanking you,' Pal said. 'We're right proud having you visit. And I just want you to know I'm as sorry as one man can be. For your tragedy, I mean to say. Bester Dannelly was one of the finest men I ever knew – correction; ever knew or shall know – and I mean that, bar none.' He ambled past her to the swivel chair, and stood studying it. His face darkened. He turned to Luther. 'Boy,' he intoned.

Luther's head turned. He shuddered.

'Boy,' Pal thundered, 'what have I told you about this particular piece of furniture?'

'She was the one, Daddy,' came a squeak.

'Ah well, in that case it's all right, I suppose.' Pal lowered himself; the chair took his weight without protest. When he turned to Stella, his face had assumed a kind smile. 'Now then, where was I? Oh yes, your tragic loss . . . Such a fine man! And a poet to boot! As the good pastor said, we needed Dannelly more than a man is most usually needed. This strange illness frightening everyone, a general quarantine, and now we have no physician. We'll find one, sometime – but we needed him. And right now. Doctors coming along today simply aren't –'

'Mister Herlong,' Stella broke in, 'Luther told me that you know where my –'

His plump hand rose up. 'Let me finish, young lady,' he said. 'I was trying to say, and it does take a scrivener longer to say it, that Bester Dannelly spoke of you to me quite often. Almost like blood kin. He thought the world of you.'

'Well I thank you,' Stella said, 'but my boy –'

'And I know he'd approve someone lifting a hand in protection of you. I know it's the thing he'd have wanted.'

Stella knew why Luther never spoke more than a few words. His father took up all the air in the room. 'Mister Herlong,' she said, 'I'll tell you the truth. I'm here because Luther said you knew who took my boy. Now –'

'Luther, what kind of fyce dog did you bring back with you?' Pal said pleasantly. 'I ought to be proud of you.'

'Just did like you said –'

'Well now, did you explain to her that I've offered to help?'

She tried again: 'Please, Mister Her –'

'And did you explain that I know where her . . . brother is?'

Luther nodded, up and down.

'Well then, tell me and I'll just go get him,' said Stella. She felt her skin tighten. Something was wrong.

Pal matched up his fingers, and studied the pattern they made. 'Weeeeelll,' he said, 'he's in trouble.'

'What trouble?' He was keeping her here. She knew it. She looked, and found only one way out: the door by his chair.

'Well that's the thing I'm trying to ascertain. I don't know who has him now – not for certain – but I know there's a whole bunch of folks looking for him.'

'That's why I got to go,' Stella said.

Pal smiled. 'We both want the exact same thing,' he said. 'Trouble is, it's not that simple. That boy of yours, my dear girl, he is the cause for some talk in this town. For someone his size, he has stirred up more trouble. You saw what happened today. At a funeral! God in his heaven, what next? Well at any rate, some people – foolish people, I'll grant you – they've settled on him. As the cause of our troubles. And they came to that church today, and they had in mind something that they thought would finish our troubles. They wanted your boy.'

'Who did?'

'Some people who mean well, but who act rather . . . hastily,' Herlong said.

Stella started across to the door. 'Well shoot,' she said, 'you don't know any more than I do.'

'Before they could get to him,' Pal said, 'he was already gotten.'

Stella halted, her hand again on the knob. 'But by who?'

'Ah now, that's where the real trouble starts,' Herlong said. 'It was minor until she arrived. Seems your boy's been kidnapped before his kidnappers could take him, and he's mixed up with a . . . well with a colored witch woman. An old old old woman, and more of her kind.'

Of course! Little Brown Mary! Stella said her name, and then wished she could swallow it back.

'Ah, you know her too, then,' he said, his eyes narrowing. 'Then you're mixed up in it too, I suppose.'

'Mixed up in what? She's just a funny old woman.'

Pal matched her stare. 'No,' he said, 'that woman's a great deal more than what she seems. She's a world of trouble, all by herself. Stirs it up. Lives on it, eats it for supper. My granddaddy came up against her one time. She outfoxed him. Back then, folks called her an agitator, but today we don't use all those long pretty words.'

'You can't mean Mary,' said Stella. Her mind was whirling, searching the two brief encounters for clues. 'She's got to be a hundred, at least. She acts peculiar, but she's just a funny old –'

'Oh no, she's more.' Pal smiled up, restraining his belly with soft fingers. 'You'll learn that looks can deceive, my dear girl. When I was younger than you, by a lot, she used to lead the hoodoo in the quarter. Friday nights, late, so you'd wake up to the sound of them, chanting spells and playing their songs.' He stroked his throat. 'The coloreds all called her Hoomama. There were at least three uproars that were traced back directly to her. Back then was when they had all their uprisings and haints – way back then, not now. We don't need any of it. Got problems enough as it is. Your funny old woman is up to her tricks again, got all the colored to talking their hoodoo. Now me, all this talk, I don't believe in it. But I know plenty of folks who believe, and I tell you, they aren't going to stand for more trouble than what we have now. Those boys I mentioned. They have short tempers and not too much sense. I'll have my hands full if I'm going to get your boy back without someone being hurt in the process.'

'Well howcome we settin around talkin?' Stella said. 'Let's go get him.' She turned the knob.

'It's near dark,' Pal said sharply. 'I'll wait until morning.'

'But what if the other ones get to him first?' She opened the door.

'Come away from there,' Pal said coolly. 'You will stay here. This job's not fit for a lady.'

'Oh no sir,' Stella said, placing her foot on the landing. 'Not while my boy's out there somewhere, oh no sir, I aint –'

For a fat man, Pal Herlong moved fast. Before she could shut

the door, his hand was blocking it, his other hand like a vise on
her arm.

'You let me go!'

'No now, missy, I said this was man's work. You'll stay right
here. Luther will watch out after you.'

'No I won't –'

'Oh yes, you most certainly will.' With two fingers, he pulled
her back in. She tried slapping his hand away, but he just smiled
like an indulgent father. 'Come on and sit down. We're all on
your side. No one wants anyone hurt.'

The fingers paralyzed her. He led her to a tall hanging cabinet.
'You can't keep me here,' she protested.

'Luther, come here,' he said.

Luther looked up from the floor. Stella swore she heard his
teeth chattering as he scuffed over.

Pal said, 'Son, you know the sixteen-gauge.'

'Yessir.'

'Know how it's used.'

'Yessir.'

'Hadn't forgot.'

'Nosir, Daddy,' said Luther.

'All right then.' He reached in and brought out a long blue-
barreled shotgun. 'And here's four shells. I want this thing
loaded. I want you to stay put right here with this gun and her,
and that's all.'

'Now, but, Daddy –'

Herlong cut his eyes to Stella. 'I don't like it either,' he said,
'but she doesn't know these boys like I do. If she was to take a
mind to go against em, why there's no telling what would
happen.'

Luther bit his lip, nodding. Stella wanted to hate him, but she
just scorned his obedience: oh you fool, you long skinny fool.
He's outsmarted us both. Not a traitor, just a little boy, scared
of your daddy.

'And one more thing. If I come back, tonight or next Easter,
and you and this girl aren't right here where I'm leaving you . . .
well, son, I'll make you wish you had some other daddy. You
hear me?'

'Yessir.'

'And you be a gentleman . . .'

'Good gravy, Daddy, I will.'

'All right then.' He guided Stella back to the green chair. She sat to keep him from pushing her down. He leaned close. His eyes were still friendly. 'You can believe me or not, I don't care. I'm trying to help. If it weren't for me, we'd be writing an obituary right now for that Jacko of yours.'

'Don't you hurt him!' she spat, wrenching away from his hand.

'I'm only trying to keep him from it,' said Herlong. He fixed his son with one eyebrow, squeezed through the translucent door, and shot the bolt from outside.

TWENTY-SEVEN

Jacko heard someone say his name: 'Jack Otis.' He strained to wake up, but his eyes refused. He could just hear their murmurs, as if he were sleeping in one house and they spoke his name in another, nearby. A man's voice, deep as a low organ note: 'Look like he dead.'

'Hooo, he the livest one here. Just I give him a potion. He right excitable.'

And a high voice, a woman: 'Aw, gone and wake him up, Hoomama. Give him a dose of some else. Make him do us a trick.'

He felt their eyes watching him, and he longed to awaken, but a glue seemed to seal his eyes shut.

'Don't look nothin too bad bout his thumb,' the man rumbled.

'Not when he sleepin, but hooo! just hol on till he bendin em where you can see. Make you shake, when they bend like them legs.'

'Them some legs,' the high woman agreed.

'Both em bend?'

'What, the leg?'

'No, his thumb.'

'Sho. Now din I say I find us a witchy boy? Din I speak truth when I did? Hooo. Niggers hear we got this boy they done heard all about, they gone come from some miles to sign up with us.'

Jacko felt the warm throb of sleep juice, pulsing him down to the white misty place.

'Don't he look sweet when he sleep.' The woman's trill reminded him of a bird.

'He look right puny to me,' said the deep man.

'Now hear me say it, this boy plenty big for what we wants. Come mornin, I learn him some trick, and some thangs he can

say when they see him. And then hol on, Mistah Devil, here
come some new band! We wait a long enough time to rise up.'

Jacko could not resist it, and he gave up trying. He slid back
down. A dream fell after.

TWENTY-EIGHT

Darkness spread over the room, and its spreading seemed to be the force that held Stella. At any instant she could grab the barrel, twist it away, hit Luther hard with the stock, and escape. But she could see nothing except the ghost white of newsprint everywhere, and a vertical glint of the moon on the gun, and she stayed.

He was invisible. She wished to hate him. At this moment, she hated everyone in the world, and Luther with a gun at her neck.

'I never thought he would do like this,' he said, over and over. 'You got to believe me.'

A boy afraid of a father: it made Stella sad.

'He must know the right thing to do,' Luther said. 'He just wants to stop trouble.'

'Don't stop it by holdin a person in jail,' she said into the dark.

'Well now, you heard him. He says you'd get hurt.'

'I saw him, Luther! He talks like my Jacko's done broken the law. I think he's one of em. I know he is.'

'Sometimes they know the right thing,' Luther said, 'and we just got to trust em.'

'Oh you be quiet. I swear, I think any old bug knows as much as you do. You didn't know he would do it, any more than me. He pulled one over on you too, Luther. We both got ourselves made a fool.'

'He knows the right thing to do,' Luther said.

'You sure do look funny, tryin to act like a man when your daddy's gone,' Stella told him.

'Watch out.' The gun shifted.

'Luther, go put that thing up. You don't want it.'

'I can't.' He propped his feet on the desk.

'Your daddy's gone, Luther. It's down to just you and me. Howcome you won't help me now?'

'But he'll be back,' came the whisper.

'Well I never had me a daddy,' said Stella, 'but life of me I don't see how you can take keepin on as his little old boy.'

'I can do anything I want to do,' he announced.

'Well go on then, let's see.'

'Well I'm tryin. You just can't grow up when you tell yourself to.'

Just a big helpless baby. She knew he could never hurt her. He sat with fingertips just off the gun, like he feared it as much as his father. In the blue moonlight, she saw the rim of his face, and a stalk of his hair sticking up. She felt a flowing between them – a sharing, a moment when each thought of nothing except the invisible eyes of the other. A prickling, cold, like white ice.

'Luther,' she said, 'seems like we could be friends. You and me. I need me a friend so bad, Luther, you just don't know how bad I do.'

His words all left him.

'You're the first boy I ever talked to,' she said. 'About the first anyone. That night we set in the swing. It was nice. You were tellin me things. I thought you liked me that night.'

'I do,' he said.

'Oh, and I sure like you, Luther,' she said. Saying it made it come true. She felt his eyes coming forward toward her, seeing, as if hers were the first face he had ever seen.

Stella shuddered. 'Put down the gun,' she said.

He cocked it, took out the shell, laid it back on the desk jointed open. His face in darkness was stubble and shadow. She learned it, so she would remember. 'I liked you a long time,' he said. 'I saw you at the school. I don't like talkin, but you listen real good.'

Without knowing for sure she would do it, Stella stood up, walked to his chair, leaned down, and kissed him. It lasted three heartbeats.

He broke away, his eyes melting. He brought a hand up to her shoulder, but it hovered without touching. His kiss lasted longer. 'I never did that,' he said.

'Lord, and neither did I,' Stella said. 'But I think I like it. You did it like you knew how.'

Both his hands hovered now. She smelled sweat and ink. His lips this time were smooth warm.

'I aint no little old boy,' Luther said.

'No.' Stella pulled away. 'You're sweet, but you're too awful shy,' she said. 'And you do whatever he says to do. But when I get my brother back, you and me can be friends. If you want to.'

'I can't let you go,' he said. The tremor had moved to his voice. 'He would kill me. You heard him. If he comes back and finds you gone, and me sittin here . . .'

Stella saw his new feeling lose its ground to the usual fear. His eyes smoldered with doubt.

'We could both go,' she said.

'No, but somebody's got to wait here for Daddy. He might have already got him! How bout you stay here, while I go look for him. If you stayed, he wouldn't kill me.'

'I aint waitin, and that's all there is,' Stella said. 'I aint waitin. He's had enough time to go to Montgomery City and back. Now I'm goin lookin. And you can come with me, or else you can not. I don't care.' She lifted the gun. It was cold and twice as heavy as it looked. 'I'm gone take this. I might need it tonight.' She slid the shell in, clicked the stock shut.

He had not moved since the last kiss. 'Please,' he said. 'He'll kill me. Or else you might shoot yourself.'

'No I won't.' She found the safety.

'Come on, Stella, please. Come on. I'll be in the worst kind of trouble you ever saw.'

'Well I'm already there.' She went to the door, and he let her. She turned the knob, then remembered the click when Pal Herlong departed.

'You can't just go.'

'Yes I can,' Stella said. 'And you know I can.'

'What am I sposed to tell him? That I just let you go?'

'You just tell your daddy that I took his gun and went out to find Jacko. And tell him you let me go, but that it wasn't for good. Tell him you plan to come find me.' She slipped past him, went to the window, and tugged at it. 'Luther, I'm just about scared to death, leavin like this. I'd rather stay here. I don't want to know what'll happen out there. But I got no choice. What all I said before – well I still mean it. But you got to stay here, and I got to go.'

The window gave. The roof touched under her foot.

'I'll come out as quick as I can,' he called, but he stayed standing beside the black hulking machine.

A white moon lit roofs marching both ways down backs of the stores along Front Street. Beyond that was good dark, the kind that soaks down in the trees. A warm breeze brought a faint smell of bread baking. Suppertime. Stella kept her balance with the gunstock to the edge, dropped it down, heard a swish! Then, remembering William's descent, she swung down from the gutter and dropped to the earth. She found the shotgun in a forest of weeds. A rat rattled by.

Stella crept up the alley and into the empty dark street. Annette's tether swung from the post beside Gadney's. Pal must have taken her.

Well, she would have to walk. She skimmed through yards, ducking under giant camellias, restless and washed by the wind. The night was too hot to have peace. Only the moon looked cool. Stella was careful to hold the gun out in front of her. The bushes might be full of eyes.

She would go to the place where she met Brown Mary, though Mary could be anywhere. It would take all night to walk, but she felt as if she was awake forever, set on finding him, setting it right. She wished for just one good thing to happen.

The next time she saw Luther Herlong, he would not choose to wait there for his father. She had enough of strange murmurs, terror in the road. It was time for some good things. She crossed the bridge, looked to the young moon hung high in the top of trees. She felt a welcome from the woods.

TWENTY-NINE

The dream came down storming on Jacko. Brilliant green things did wild dances in front of his eyes. A black cloud swept the world, then a light like the sun rinsed the hills to green shimmering. He dreamed a thunderstorm, down to its bolts and explosions; a green funnel spun away from it, unfolded its wings and took flight as a large sparkly bird with green feathers of glass. It came for Jacko with emerald claws, picked him up, gently flew him away, so high he could smell the cool clouds drifting by. Then it let go and he fell, down through air, his legs tumbling in the wind. He started to cry, and that brought him from sleep.

He felt something curled up against him – a warm, snoring something. Rubbing sleep from his eyes, he sat up. It seemed a lifetime ago the bad dream began, and before that, strange voices . . . He could not remember. He picked little threads of the blanket from his dress and socks, and stared down at Little Brown Mary.

She was so old she might have been dead, except for the eerie soft whistle she made. Jacko shivered. She wanted to keep him here. He had to get away. Get back to Munner. Munner would whip him. He knew it. But still he had to get back.

Green vines were so thick at the windows that only a few morning rays slipped between. The blanket, the tiny white pillow he'd slept on, two logs by the fireplace, the crate, and the wallpaper peeling in curls – nothing else in the room.

The windows were too high to reach, and all broken to daggers. Mary lay between Jacko and the door. He remembered imagining the house Munner told about, the one that burned down around them. This was the same kind of house. Maybe Jacko could start a fire here, and get away.

He thought of the magical fire Mary brought from her hand.
Maybe she just thought a fire, and it happened.

Maybe he could. Just by thinking. One time she told him he
might could do things that way. Maybe just think a fire, and it
would start.

He looked for something to burn. He poked at the little pillow
she'd brought out from her gunnysack, a white flourbag stuffed
with bristly straw. His fingers loosened the knot – it was not
straw, but pine needles inside. So dry they might burn.

He pulled himself slow, so as not to make noise, across the
rough floor to the hearth. The needles fell from the sack in a
shower of dust.

Something about the way Mary did with her hand, rubbing
fingers close in to her palm. A snap. He never could quite see
how she did it. He snapped his fingers. No fire came out. He
thought double hard about fire, and snapped, and twice more,
but no fire sprang up.

Maybe thinking was not good enough for this trick.

But this is a good trick, Jacko remembered, good when you
want to make people look funny at you. He held his hands out
and flexed both his thumbs, so the little worms of muscle ran
down his wrists.

Nobody else could do it but the doctor, and his didn't bend
near as far. Jacko liked the looks on the faces, the changes in
eyes.

Now he decided Brown Mary would not hear a thing but the
racket of her own sleeping, so he dragged around her, just a bit
at a time, right past her nose to the door. Mary wheezed on,
content. When he pushed, the door creaked. He nudged again:
creak. After each nudge he looked back, but her hooo! went on
in its rhythm.

Slow, just as slow as he could, he eased the door shut. He
was out on the porch, shady bright in the tangle of covering
vines. Jacko had never been anywhere except the doctor's, and
into Camellia sometimes on a Saturday. Now he was so far away
that he knew he would never find home by himself.

Taking care of the rotten spots in the planks, he got down
the porch steps and out into mud. For a while he sat, blinking,

savoring his escape, then he pulled across into high weeds, slapping bugs as they bit. It was good to be out. The sun felt like milk. He reached the first root of a big old oak tree, and sat up to breathe and find out where he was. Mud dried to a crust on his skin. His shoulders felt strong. He wished for his scooter. Then he could roll off, and find out the way, and find Munner, and something to eat. Instead he was here in weeds up to his eyes.

It scared Jacko to think how scared Munner would be. He was sure she would do something he would deserve as soon as she got over the scared part. He would deserve it but he was sure it would be awful, whatever she did.

He could go someplace where Munner might find him. Or stay with Brown Mary and find out about witchy boys. He did not know if he wanted to be one. He was not sure what one was. The spooky way she talked about them made him want to know.

The oak tree was halfway across the weed patch to a road. Looking back, he could barely make out the house for all the wild vines. It looked eaten alive. Only the steps showed in front, and a spot of cracked paint here and there.

Just past the root of his tree, in a tiny new creekbed designed in the sand by the rain, Jacko saw something: a flash: just a half-buried glittering, sparkling at him.

A treasure! Washed up for him! Instantly that thought brought his other treasure to mind, the one in his pocket right now. The treasure he never dared take out, for fear someone would see it and know. Munner would know. She would tell from his eyes.

But this might be better treasure!

When he dragged near it, Jacko could see way down the road. No one coming. He dug at the thing with one hand. Sand stuck to it like a wrapping, and he lifted it. A cannonball. He brushed the sand with his sleeve, and the shine brightened. No, it was glass.

A bright ball of green shiny glass, the size of a peach and three times as heavy. Green in most places, but with bright blue, red, and purple swirling in its middle. He rubbed and rubbed at it, put it to his ear. He thought he could hear a high train whistle singing to him, from way deep down. He grinned. This was the best thing he'd ever found.

He heard the crack of a branch just behind him. 'Whoo! Look out there, sister,' a voice cried, 'you bout landed on him!'

Jacko slipped the treasure under the hem of his dress. A shriek split the air. 'Ooh, oh, Lawda mercy, Bro Prentiss!'

Jacko turned. Two large brown people hopped back, as if he were a snake.

Dozens of hoops and brass bracelets jangled when the woman jumped. She wore a bright yellow cloth in her hair, and a look that said she was the boss. A sparkly chain hung from one ear. 'How you get way out here, you – boy!'

Her squeal was high as a bird. It came back from a dream to Jacko. 'I come out all by myself,' he told her.

The man was as wide as the woman, or wider. His suit was yellow, except the bottoms of the britches, which dragged past his shoes. His face was shiny, a glaze of light sweat. He came up warily, leaning down, placing his hands on his knees. 'Where old Hoomama at,' he rumbled, 'since you out by yoself?'

'I reckon still sleepin,' said Jacko. 'I come out here all by myself and she never woke up.'

'Hm,' the woman said. 'Probly tasted a taste of that sleep juice herself.'

'Boy, what's yo name?' The man squinted at him.

'Jacko,' he said. 'Jacko Bates.'

'Aint he talk good,' cried the jingly woman.

Jacko said: 'Yall got to tell me yours, since I told mine.'

She came back a few steps toward him. 'My name Retha,' she said, 'and this here Brother Prentiss. We already know who you was.'

The man squatted, inspecting Jacko like some kind of cow he was planning to buy. 'How old you is, boy?' he said.

'Eight,' Jacko said. 'How bout you?'

The man grinned. 'Shee – well some mo than eight,' he said. 'Show us yo thumbs. Show us what is that thing you can do.'

'Howcome yall heard about that?' Jacko said.

'Hoomama,' Retha said. 'We know a heap about you. Hoomama, she say you do spooky like. Say you done touch by the fire. And makin all kind of critters to actin up strange.'

'I aint done nothin,' he said, 'but I can do this.' He put out his hands, and popped the joints. By straining, he reached almost all the way to his wrists.

'Law,' said Brother Prentiss, 'quit that.'

'Amen,' said Retha. 'She told us, but not nare like that. And just see how his legs do, Bro, shrunk down so tiny and white, aint it some.'

Jacko tugged at his dress. 'You quit lookin,' he said.

'Oooh, baby, now don't take me bad. I aint mind them legs nare a bit. Just them thumbs. Ain much care to see them. Well look who alive,' Retha said. They all turned. Little Brown Mary ambled out of the vines down the steps, slowly, one step at a time. 'What's the matter,' Retha called, 'you done down in yo back? You movin too slow!'

'Cain get too weary,' said Prentiss. 'Big happnins tonight.'

She squatted and stretched, shook out her arms and legs, yawned twice, shuffling over. 'Hooo, cheeruns, looky how young massuh here can take off when he sets out to go! An ol Mary done slep thu it all.'

'You bout to get old,' Retha said, giving Mary a hug.

Brown Mary let out a cough and a cackle. 'Bout to? Hooo. Law now, suster, you quit yo bad talk. If these po ol bones ain old yet, tell me when is it gone be.'

'Shoo,' said the brother. 'You younger than us put together, way you get about.'

'Ain gettin too good yet today,' Mary said. 'Sweet tunia, bout fright me to death! What you doin out here?'

'I'm hungry,' said Jacko. 'I aint had nothin to eat for a week.'

'Sho you did, boy, you right fat in the face as it is,' Mary said. 'You could stand some not eatin. But I be rassle us some, here directly.'

'And you said Munner'd be here. In the mornin. And now it's mornin. And she still aint here.'

'Ol boy got a mouth on him too,' observed Prentiss.

'Ain he, though.' Mary nodded. 'He too good at askin what most folk won't answer. You wait for tonight, and see don't all

the cheeruns be listnin at him. When I shown him what all he
gone say.'

'I want my Munner,' said Jacko.

Retha peered down. 'Say who?'

'Sweet-face white gal,' Mary said. 'This boy's suster. She
posed to come out here to us, but some's holdin her up. I
rackoned her quicker than this. Say now, Bro, why you wear
yo fine preachah suit here first off this mornin? Still a long ways
tills meetin time.'

'What kind of a meetin?' said Jacko.

'A big kind,' said Mary.

Brother Prentiss groaned, rose to his feet. 'Hey Hoomama,'
he said, 'we got to find us some new place.' His hands made
round balls in his pockets.

'Now hol on, Bro Prentiss, we already done spread the word,
ain much time left to switch.'

'But we brung some news. Some whole lot of soury talk on
a whole lot of tongues.'

Brown Mary's face lost its drowse all at once. 'What you
hearin?'

'Just some thangs we aint want to hear,' Retha said. Jacko
marveled again at the trill in her voice. 'Color folk hearin what
white peoples say. And most all the white people rile cause
some sign done been nail up on most all their door. Got em all
talkin wild.'

'Honey, what kind of wild?' Mary said.

Retha glanced at the brother, who coughed in his throat.
'Same old kind as the last,' he said. 'Same as the last before
that. Aint heard who, nor how many, or who they out after. Just
heard the same as before: Yall watch out. Some bad on its way.'

'I wanna go,' Jacko said. He felt left out. All this strange talk,
and not a word more about him. 'I wanna be a witch boy.'

Retha stared down, then threw back her head in a high soaring
laugh. 'Hoomama,' she cried, 'you was right what you say! He
don't look no more than a nothin, but hear what come out! I aint
believin it.'

'Ol boy done give us a fright with he thumbs,' said the brother.

Jacko's hand came out. All three of them reached to prevent

it. 'Hooo, slow up now, big man,' said Mary. 'Already shown em to us. We *convince*. Ought not be doin that trick but when you just cain hep it.'

Jacko pulled his hands back. 'You can't stop me, unless I want to,' he said.

'Well then, petunia, I wish you'd start wantin. Just somethin about it makes all my ol neckhairs sit up. You gots to save it. Be plenty of folk want to see, then come time for yo trick.' Mary steadied herself on his shoulder. 'This some sly boy,' she announced. 'Known some trick I ain seen. We gone show it tonight, Bro, gone show it off, suster, gone raise up a band for this boy!'

'Amen,' both of them said.

Mary sat hunched on her knees beside Jacko. 'You gots to hep us,' she said. 'Been a whole mess of folk done been lissen at me talk so long until most ain got hearin ears left. I preach it, been preachin some preachin, I say, tellin how they gone join up with Mary, gone lead em on out for some milk and some honey.'

'Amen!'

'But now, hooo, come a nightfall, gone be some new ears! Honey, ain mo than two folk twix here and some else that ain hearin the tale of some dead-legged boy! Been come thu some fire since near day you drop down, and been left with the power.' Mary's yellow eyes came alive with the word. Jacko sat mesmerized. He followed her shaky finger as it pointed off into woods. 'Massuh, you look. See where? If we could look thu them tree, be a hill.'

'I don't see nothin,' said Jacko.

'Yeah, sho you don't,' Mary said, 'but now tend like you see some ol hill, big ol lines of some tree standin on it. Right up yonder, petunia, a house was. And now it aint. Cause the fire reach out for it, burn all but you, it done touch you and suck out some life juice and put in some power.' She folded her arms.

'I aint done nothin,' Jacko said, absently gazing off into deep woods. He tried to picture the hill past the trees, and tried to match it with stories Munner told.

Mary sighed. 'Hooo, ain nothin now cept we here burnin

time,' she said, turning. 'Brother, I know a spot. Petunia, stay put right here.' The brother and Retha followed her back to the porch, and stood inside its wall of vines.

Jacko turned away, reached quick up his dress, and tucked his new treasure deep in his breast pocket. It made a lump anyone could see. Maybe if he hunched forward just a little, and played like his back hurt . . .

Brown Mary returned. 'Tunia,' she crowed, 'some the matter with you? Bent up like ol snappy turtle. Give on.'

He craned around. 'I'm *hungry*,' he whined. 'My stomach hurts, and I got to pee, and I'm thirsty. And you're bein *mean*.'

'Hooo, honey, try not to die. Mary hear you! Runnin off now cause you is. Gots some thankin, though, first. How you pull yo own self all from inside to out here?'

'A big green bird come,' Jacko said, 'and he got hold of me, and then – then he flew me all in the air, and he dropped me down here. While you was asleep.'

'I sho wishin you'd shook me,' Mary cackled, 'with all that to see.'

'It all happened at once,' he said.

'Honey, gone fly myself off for a piece with my cheerun, fetch you some eat. Sho be hatin to leave you to see for yoself,' she said. 'Stay where you at, and soon be some folk come here to find you. The kind you ain like to get found. Else come hop on my back, let me tote you in where it's cool. Yo suster the only one knows where you at.' Brown Mary reached down.

Jacko lifted his arms, but struggled to turn so she would not see the lump on his chest. His words bounced as she lugged him through weeds. 'Wait,' he said. 'Wait!' Then he felt warm, and the wet.

'Hooo, mammy, look out!' Mary cried, looking down at the yellowish trickle. She held him way out and ran all the way to the porch, dancing to keep her feet out of the stream.

Jacko reddened as she held him there, in the air, waiting until it was all out. 'I din mean to,' he said. 'But I told you.'

'Sho did, sweet petunia, sho did,' she cackled. 'And this ol gal, honey, come next time you speak, this gal be plannin to hear.'

THIRTY

The road was near infinite dark, sudden ditches. Stella kept losing her way. The moon played games, hiding in clouds. The miles stretched forever out through the night. Weird birds hollered and mocked. A breeze came and stirred the deep leaves. The trees dripped all night, trembling, dripping false rain.

If only the sun would come up, she would know where she was and how much more to go.

When her ears caught a warning, Stella hid down in a ditch. A wagon passed by, a large figure slumped at the reins. She swallowed a cry – a fool once, maybe, but not again. She could not trust a soul, not tonight, not a stranger on a road through a city of trees, so late that the stars fled the sky.

She kept walking, counting her steps until she lost count. She could feel her feet crying, and she sank to a stump near the road. Down at the root, she discovered a hollowed-out place that might have been carved for her shoes. She tucked them there, then memorized the stump with her hands, so she could find it again in the dark.

The cool mud was a balm for her toes. She kept to the road but her mind stumbled off to the doctor, her father too late, the father she knew she deserved . . . so real to her now that he seemed to be leading the way.

At last, in the places above where the trees did not meet, she saw pink. The world lightened. Leaves began greening again. Birds hushed and flew to the business of morning.

No more than a mile at the most to the last rising hill, to the orchard, the barn. The road took the long way, but Stella cut across a pasture to meet it again at the creek.

She knew this earth by heart: how the road doubled back on itself, straightened, then gently inclined to the rim of the hill, where the ranks of pecan trees marched through an early gold mist. Stella ran. She did not feel the pain in her feet. She ran to the shade and the mist and at last to the rope that would open the door to the barn, if she could just summon the strength to pull down.

On its own, the door swung in to dark and hard quiet, the old smell of hay, a black circle – cinders, ashes, a fire of the past – and way deep in a corner, an object so densely embroidered in spiderwebs that she did not see its four wheels until she was beside it.

At her touch, a piece of the shroud fell away; in its place, she heard squabbling: It's my turn now, Foster. Mama, tell Foster it's my turn! I been the durn pony for you, now come on! *Maama!* The little wagon belonged to the twins, but Stella could not recall who bought it, or why. There was never a pony.

The webs clung to her hands like invisible glue. She wandered back into the light, sinking down in the doorway.

Through the night, as she counted her steps, Stella had reached this door a thousand times, pulled down on the rope, and pushed in. Every time she'd found Jacko inside, with Little Brown Mary, and safe. Now she could not think of anything to do except squeeze her cold toes. She wanted to cry, but the dry sobs stuck in her throat.

Then a hot sweet meat smell from outside. Stella's stomach turned. She stood to trace the aroma past the giant pecan, to a pale green jungle of slender reeds shooting up where the house should have been. From the lone chimneytop poking higher than the growth came a fragrant blue smoke, caught on a breeze and brought over to Stella.

Someone in Mama's kitchen! Stella did not resist the lure of the smell. As she came up, she saw the tall reeds had joints – green fishing poles, growing precisely within the lost walls of the house. The stalks rustled when she parted them.

A white shirt. A long leggity crouch, like Luther – but it was not. Bones, not much more, enough flesh just to hold him together. A rag of a shirt showed his ribs, and his face was too awful and skinny, grown over with scraggle.

Stella knew him before thinking.

He is gone with the rest of them, gone and not crouching down by the hearth . . . the same kind of skinny, same thatch of blond hair, with his back to her, guarding the fire.

Stella laid the shotgun down, willed a breath, whispered his name.

He turned.

It is. Oh it is.

He watched her. He did not stand or blink. With two fingers, he kept twirling a spit. Five charred pink animals, impaled along it, dripped their juices down into the fire.

His stare burned his eyes. 'Brother,' she said, 'brother. What in the world . . .'

'Sister,' he said.

He was everyone dead, come to life, all wild in his eyes. Tiny red scratches up and down his face. In that instant, Stella was little again, in a tree, hauling boards up and down with a rope, following William's directions.

She heard her own voice from a distance: 'Your breakfast is burnin.'

'They taste better burnt,' William said. As if he had not stopped screaming since that night, the edges were stripped from his voice.

She could not think what to say. William was so long dead. This man crouching by Mama's fireplace was not him, not except in the eyes. 'Brother,' she said, 'now you listen. You tell me just where in the hell you have been.'

He did not blink. 'I thought sure you were dead,' he said. 'I thought for sure.'

'William, listen to me now, you come on now, you got to tell me. You know you do, now damn you, William . . .'

He tasted a dribble of juice on his finger. 'No need for blasphemin,' he said. 'I'll tell you. I been to hell. I thought yall was all dead. Yall went up, but not me. I went down.'

'Oh now shut up your mouth. You aint got me believin that mess,' Stella flared. 'I aint no little girl anymore, like I was the last time I saw you. You been right here on this earth somewhere all this time, same as me. You went off someplace and you never come back.'

'I come back,' William said.

'Well I reckon you did. It took seven long years, but sure enough, here you are. Seven years, brother. I kept up a count.'

'You aint tellin me nothin,' he said. 'I aint never quit knowin. I thought for sure you was dead.'

'But where, brother? Where in the hell!' It was almost a plea now, a whisper.

He closed his eyes. 'Oh Lord,' he croaked, 'Lord God, I pray you to come down and drive out her demons.'

'Brother, you answer me . . .'

One of his squirrels came apart and fell to the fire.

William glared up at the sky. Stella saw the mad shine, like a wax on his eyes, and she knew he was mad, pure and cold – beyond madness. 'My God,' she said, 'you gone out of your head.'

His hands came up to his face as it fell. 'I pray you, and pray you to hear me now, Father, I'm prayin for her and me both. Beseechin you, please, just to have some mercy on two souls that are all rotted over from sin –'

Stella touched his hand.

William jerked back. 'Don't touch me. You swear on your soul you won't . . . swear you won't touch me.' When he raised up the spit, all the meat dropped to the fire. He let out a howl, brandished the stick like a sword, and raged circles in the bamboo, kicking white sand on the hearth.

His fury crested, and died; from his throat came a sob, and then sobbing. He sank to the ground, put his head on his knees, and wept until his throat would make no more sounds. They sat quietly. Stella did not reach to him. She said, 'Tell me.'

The clock sounds. A table heavy with food and the elbows of children, the wavering candles. Two boys return from a tantrum. Chatter begins again. Those two stay quiet. Little fat hands make a mush in a plate.

A brown sack – no, two sacks, begging under a chair, full of oranges and presents from Kline's. He resists. Not quite yet. Someone is gone from the table. Someone has gone up the hall.

Someone else goes to the sideboard, and brings out a twig from the drawer. Mister toe!

Then a hug, then a kiss, then a scream that dies ringing.

Someone is trying to stand from a chair. But children keep giggling, sucking on spoons.

He is up. He is screaming don't move not an inch not a one of you now, and they cower, they hush, their large eyes watch as he runs to the hall, where fire spills out of a door.

He fights his way through to a garden of flame. Her room. The large square of fire is her bed. Her curtains are dancing. The frames on her pictures are burning.

Someone screams.

Cradle has fallen, one end in the hearth, blooming savage and red. It has toppled the trunk at the foot of the bed. In a spill of bright burning quilts, something refuses to burn.

A paperboard box lying smothered, unburning, in fire.

Someone is burning. He feels his whole body afire, his hands and his pants. He touches his face and feels jelly. His eyes are melting. Strong suckers of flame are attaching themselves.

He snatches the box and floats out from the garden, down the long hall, past the large eyes and the door, and then suddenly out into blackness so cold that it scalds him.

All night running, and part of the day, running nowhere and everywhere, until he collapses. When he awakens, the gray box is locked in his arms.

He breaks the string, lifts the lid. A crackle of white tissue paper, and then.

Ten fingers. He counts them. Ten little toes. White and so tiny, and too awful clean. Minuscule twisted white legs. But something is missing. Above where its eye ought to be, something has caved in the head.

Her careful knot in the string.

A chant swells up to a horror that bursts in his head, trickling down slowly, infecting him.

He feels the new skin on his arms and all over, too pink tender painful to touch. He learns to make fires and sleep in the branches of trees, to sneak up on squirrels and strangle them, strip off their hides and impale them on sticks over fires.

He sweats the evil out into his clothes. He tastes the old sweet dark sin of his mother, the light too late in the barn, the whispers. Did she burn for a taste of the sweet?

He scoops out a hole for the box.

A voice speaks into his ear. It says go, but don't run, go the long way through woods and the towns and the woods, and then someone is standing beside a depot with a sign that says BELZONI MISS.

A fat man comes over. A smile and a word and a promise of something to eat. William asks about preachers who died. The fat man takes him to a tree, with a gray wooden cross.

Someone is down on his knees, asking why, but the earth at the tree remains silent.

The fat man says: It was a mighty good sermon. Only a preacher knows another preacher. Right at the end, he fell down. It was over and done with that quick. We all of us buried him here. But come on with me, boy. I show you the way.

The fat man prays. He teaches William to pray. William does nothing but pray, in a mutter, or loud, in the bed in the fat man's dark kitchen. Lord God Almighty, only me here all sore and afraid, and in need of your mercy, now listen, just hear what I say, use mercy on me, all the mercy there is. Amen. Amen.

Someone is preaching. A tent sweats, and listeners. Someone stands with a story – a table, the candles, the oranges, presents. Then the almighty fire.

One day the fat man says: Now is the time for you, boy. Used up the room at the inn. No more you could learn, not from me. You got to go back, got to spread the Lord out to your folks. Come back sometimes, if you can.

Someone is walking again in the trees. Praying and building small fires. The flames point the way to the garden.

Stella saw clouds in his eyes. 'I had dreams too,' she whispered. 'I did, brother, bad dreams. For the longest time after, I swear it, real bad. I dreamed that they all were alive and not dead, brother, I heard em talkin just real as could be. I heard Charlie Boot –'

'Wasn't no dream,' William said.

'There's nothin else it could be! This is wild talk, William, crazy talk. And you makin it up. Say what you want to about your mama, but my mama never killed none of her babies. She aint your mama no more. Not since you went. I'm the one put her up on the wagon while you run off and hid.'

William coughed in his knee, then he reached out to rub a leaf between his fingers. 'Look how these canes are growin,' he said. 'Look how straight. See how they only grow right where the house used to be? I been prayin on it for three nights. They're the work of the Lord. He was makin a mark. He saw down. He saw sin, and he sent down his fire. And he planted these here where it burned. She knew what she did, sister, she tied it up in a box and she saved it. She knew what it was. She knew she was bounden to burn.'

He shielded his face from Stella's hand. 'Well tell me!' she cried. 'Tell me who was it out in the barn that you seen, you so powerful sure. Tell me what was his name.'

'I never saw him,' said William, poking the coals with his boot. 'I went all the way to Belzoni to find him, to look for somebody who knew. He was bound to have known. She was his wife, holy God! He had nothin to say to me, not even dead. And now the Lord brought me back. And the Lord says it don't make no difference who, it's sinnin that counts, and just about the time I get settled on it, I found out.'

'Oh please hush,' Stella cried. 'You said plenty enough. You got no right to talk. You run off and left all us to burn.'

'That's what I did,' he said. 'That's my cross. Sister, I never thought you got out. If I'd thought you did, ever, I'd come back.'

'I got out, yeah, but I got bad burned,' Stella cried. 'Me and Jacko! We both got out but we aint spent not a minute where we hadn't burned.'

He looked up in shock. 'You and who?'

'Jacko,' said Stella. 'Jack Otis. Your brother. Mama saved him. She died saving him.'

William sprang to his feet. 'It can't be,' he shouted. 'No! It's a lie!'

'But it's true . . .'

'No! You tell lies of the devil!'

Stella dodged his wild fist, scrambled up, and ran back through the reeds for the gun. It was cold in her hands. 'Come ahead on,' she warned, 'come on and hit me. I swear, I know how to shoot it, and I sure aint afraid to, not a bit. You been dead so long it won't hurt me to kill you again.'

William watched the end of the gun. 'But it can't,' he said, 'it can't be. It was *him*. It was him that tumped over. His crib in the fire. He couldn't of ever got out.'

'But he did.' Stella lowered the barrel. 'And he's out here somewhere. And the whole world is out here lookin for him, and that's why I'm here. And you got to help me. You're still my brother, and his brother too. There's so awful damn much you don't know.'

'You should pray,' William said. 'You could learn how to pray.' He got down on his knees.

Stella did not hear him. She studied him, trying to find the William who must be there somewhere, behind those hard glassy eyes. Was this the same boy she built treehouses with, or could years have turned him into somebody else? The weird heat of his praying made Stella remember the Preacher. God lived like a fatal disease in the blood of the Bateses.

Maybe if she told William all the years since that night, if she told him of Jacko and Gibson, and who their real father was, really . . . if she could convince him what happened and what never did, it might cure him. She had to try. Whoever he was now, he was her brother once. Stella could not walk away.

THIRTY-ONE

A butterfly traveled the breeze, struggling, dancing, working its wings. Jacko watched as it sank to a leaf on the vine nearest him. When he brought his hand cupped to catch it, it flew aimlessly off.

Jacko shivered. Only a last beam or two of the sun still penetrated the green hidden cage of the porch. He was lonesome and hungry again. Brown Mary left him here on the porch of the empty house, all by himself, and the jelly biscuit was gone. He heard treefrogs tuning up. He did not want to hear how they would sound way out here in the night. The wind died. Night-bugs began landing on his arms. Jacko crushed them, and waited.

He wished himself home, but the wish did not take him. He wished to his stomach for Munner, but she did not come. And for Little Brown Mary, who promised to be back by now. No one listened to his wishes.

Or else someone listened, but gave him no answer.

Maybe because of Jacko. The bad things he did. The treasures stuffed down in his pocket – one he had stolen, and one he found in the sand. Maybe they brought all this terrible empty alone.

He took out the heavy glass ball, raised it to his ear, but its whistle was dim. He fished again for the stolen treasure, in its bit of white dirty rag.

Jacko was scared to look at it. It was too pretty to see, a fine coin of bright gold, with a lady on one side, a bird on the other. He found it way way at the back of a drawer, that night in the doctor's study. Then he heard someone coming and tucked it away, and pulled out to the hall, and the doctor tripped over his legs.

The shining gold lady called out to him all through the night.

The next morning, when the house was empty, he went back –
but only to look one more time, just to look.

It felt good and heavy and warm in his hand.

It went straight down into his pocket.

And then the horse kicked. The doctor fell dead. The sheriff
said Jacko was why.

Then at the church someone yelled it was him, it was him, it
was all Jacko's fault, everything!

Maybe because he was a thief. He balanced the coin on the
green glossy sphere. It slid off, teetered on its edge, went
rolling away. Jacko lunged, smacked it down with his hand just
an inch from the edge of the porch.

Maybe he could undo all the bad things, if he unstole it. But
he was so far from its drawer in the doctor's study.

He flung it away. It struck a vine, bounced, and rolled lazily
back to his feet.

It belonged to the doctor. The doctor was dead.

He stared at it, wished at it, hard as he could. He said now
laymedownasleep, and again. He prayed godisgreatgodisgood
letusthankhimforourfoodamen. He pictured the low drawer,
open. With his eyes shut, he could see the gold lady sparkling,
way way at the back. Put it back, put it back like before.

He looked. The gold lady smiled up at him, sparkling.

Maybe wishing would not put things back, or maybe there
was a secret to it – some trick he could learn from Brown Mary.

Jacko wadded the gold lady up in the rag, and put her down
deep in his pocket.

Then, from the other treasure, he heard the faint whistling
sound. It seemed to come from inside, from the spirals of red.

Jacko lifted the green crystal into the last shaft of sunlight.
One side glazed over, a dazzling white.

His nose itched suddenly: somebody coming! A loud noise,
ba-ra-a-a-ack, like a stick dragged along a slat fence. Jacko hid
the magical ball just in time.

A familiar hooo! and a fussing, and ba-ra-a-a-ack, then a frantic
clatter as Little Brown Mary came onto the porch, tugging a
rope in her hand. Something resisted, then stumbled up the last
step: a creature as big as a dog, but too shaggy and thin. Jacko's

legs felt the quiver of its sharp hooves scrabbling, striking the porch.

'Get on, you poface ol raggedy thang,' Mary crowed as she tightened the noose on its neck. The thing waved its funny white beard, showed its teeth, and bleated an indignant answer. Jacko remembered a night of bad dreams like this – scary beasts, sharp yellow teeth.

'Witchy boy?' Mary called. 'Speak up, petunia, cain hol on to him and be lookin for you the same time.'

'What is that thing?'

Mary turned to his voice. 'Now I see you,' she said. 'Thought you done tuck off again, but you ain. I be glad.'

'What is that thing?' said Jacko.

'Less I blind in both eyes, he a goat,' Mary said. 'What he look like to you?'

The goat skittered around her in circles, winding the rope on her knees.

'Get it away,' Jacko said. 'I don't like it.'

'Swee tunia, this goat ain for likin or not. He gone still be a goat, either way.' She ran a hand down its knobby backbone, and wriggled the rope down her shins. 'This yo suprise,' she said. 'Law, ain no guess what I gone thu to get him. You ought to be proud, if you was to find out.'

The goat applied teeth to a vine.

'Take it away,' Jacko said. 'Why'd you bring it?'

'Honey, done brung him to you. Ol Mary too powful old to be totin you, big as you is. We gone get that ol wagon up yonder, gone hitch this here animule up in a lickety split. You be ridin up high back of him, like some king!'

'It's gonna bite me,' Jacko said doubtfully.

'He only just bite what he eat,' she said. 'You ain look too tasty to him.'

'But what if it –'

'Babe, just you wait till you settin up sassy, done drivin yo own self wherever you go. He gone be yo locomotion. You see.'

'That thing's gone pull me around?'

'Hooo, well I rackon, less you plan to cook him up for supper,' Mary cackled. She stooped, and took Jacko up onto her hip.

'Child, wrop yo arms bout my neck, but now watch how them sharp little fingers. They sho flat dig in. Bout to tear my po head off my neck, way you dug em last night.'

'Where we goin?' said Jacko. 'You put me down. You said Munner would be here by now. Watch out!' He batted the curious snout away from his feet. 'Stop! Oooh! Get it away!'

Mary tied the rope to her wrist, slung the gunnysack over one arm, and adjusted the burden of Jacko. 'Law,' she said, 'hang on, petunia. Just one mo fast ride fo we rollin.' She went hustling quick down the steps, dragging the goat through high weeds by its rope.

They went across the road, up a darkening path. His legs dangled and bumped, but he clung to her neck. 'I wanna be a nigger,' he said, admiring the curly white hairs in her chin.

Mary cackled over her shoulder. 'Well, from here you mo pink than a nigger,' she said, 'but you could be one in yo heart.'

'Are all niggers witchy boys too?'

'Hush yo talk with that "nigger," petunia. Ain nobody told you bout nigger?'

'No! Tell me!'

Her knees could not stand to the load. She set Jacko down on a moist mossy hummock beneath a great chestnut tree, where the path forked. A bush bloomed with bright yellow flowers. Jacko watched her eyes scan the woods, as if she could tell gnats from air. 'Honey, big meetin tonight, and a whole much of niggers gone hear what you say. If you calls em nigger, why, they ain much gone like it.'

'Can I do my trick?' he said, wiggling a thumb.

'Little man,' she said, bending through the wires, 'you can do all yo tricks, and some mo.'

'*Then* do I get to be nigger?' Jacko said.

She straightened, hiking her overalls. 'Niggers and witchy boy's two diffunt things,' she said. 'Both of em somethin you is or you aint, but they diffunt. I tell you bout niggers, petunia. Bout my ol Paw – now there you had you a nigger – some way long back slavery time. Back when the sun din stay up long as it does these day. Niggers all slavin for white.

'My daddy slavin for some whitey man name of Singleton.

Mama, all of us cheeruns be slave. Then's when the fightin an all such start up. Where we live, we din hear so much of it, but this Muster Singleton do. Head up to Montgomery City, gone join up some Grays. Grays done get started up there. Now them Grays was one mean ol bunch of white boys, I be tellin. Us posed to be scared of the Blue, but saw nare not one of em, not the whole fightin time.

'This Singleton, he left my ol Paw and all us to run look after he place. Left his wife and his cheerun there too. Tuck off fightin.

'My ol Paw, he din put much stock in no war. Say it only make the bad things to worst. He kep up that place for that whitey, the same. Well, honey, some them Grays hear bout a nigger be runnin a white place all by he lonesome. Say he get fat on a white falla's hog. So they come out to stop by, long one evenin. Come sangin a song, a right drunky like tune, I can hear em now, sangin . . .'

Her eyes drifted off.

'Say, "Come out, you nigger boy, show yo black face." Ol Paw had all us to down and get quiet like. I seen them Gray thu a hole in the wall. Ain nothin Gray about em, what I saw. Just white. Ol Paw went out there, I can hear him, say, "Please, suh, what trouble," say, "Please, suh," and bowin down low to them drunkety mens.

'One tell him, "Nigger, we fightin to save yo black butt." Then's when they start in on kickin. All us in there, crowd down together like bugs, like to die just to hear, way he holler, be beggin, "Oh please, suh, oh please, suh," and hearin em kick.'

Her voice trailed away to a whisper. Jacko saw the gleamy sad look in her eyes. 'Law, we hear some rib pop.' She sighed, blinked, looked up. 'Well what would you do if you could, swee petunia? We run, what we did. So hard I was pickin the trash out my hair for a month of Saddays. They catch up right to us, some hoss they was ride . . . took Mama down for some waggle, shot all the brothah, tuck one look at me and run off. Guess I's too homely for mens, even then. Then's when I find out bout homely, petunia, bout how special you is sometimes, if you is.'

'Then what happened?' said Jacko.

'They gone off. Went on up to the fight. My ol Paw weren't nare but some fun for them Gray boys. They just come to practice the fight.'

Jacko pulled in his legs. 'Well who won?'

'Well they did, petunia, them Blue,' Mary said. 'Come in and done some to hep, for a time, but a white folks, they white just the same, nare what coat they got on. They din care for it much down here. Rackon was too awful hot. Purt soon they packin bag, and a hightailin home . . .

'Then's when I learn they is two kind of a nigger, babe. One kind get down and say "suh," and it get em not one thing but kicked in the rib, kick to death. And other kind learn him some tricks. So that's me. I decide you could fight without gun. But it too awful hard by yoself. Gots to get together, make up a band. Been tryin to make up a band since then, babe. Folks done hear me so much they plumb wo out. Hooo, but I thank they lissen at you.'

Jacko jutted his thumb out. 'I bet I can scare em, too,' he said.

That set Mary to laughing, wiping her eyes. 'You talkin bout twice of yo size,' she said.

THIRTY-TWO

Ben cut the oaks with his cousin Lafayette when they were young and dreamed of wives they would have. They dug the mud for caulking, set the logs in, lugged in red stones for the pilings. Whiskey lit the nights they spent carving the corner notches.

At one end of a fallow cornfield, they built Ben's house, and then another exactly the same at the far end, so that one day their children could come meet in the middle of the field, to play.

Each house had a door in front and a window in back, a stoop of pine boards, and a chimney of logs.

Together, they tacked the last scrap of tarpaper onto Lafayette's roof. The next day, Lafayette said his chest hurt him some. Two days past that, he was dead.

To honor his memory, Ben stayed alone and took care of the houses. He cut enough firewood for both, so he could walk across the field some nights, build a fire, and listen to Lafayette's room.

Now he sat on his own bed, holding the doorflap open in hope of a breeze. He had a jug of corn whiskey, a three-legged stool, a ladderback chair, a slopjar and a pail, a spitcan the color of fish. A squirrel gun hanging on hooks. A blurry tintype of Lafayette.

He breathed hard at the memory of a sunrise, a ruin still smoking. The girl lived through that, and the spooky-leg boy, with his eyes that seemed old as the trees.

And now they were back.

Ben reached for his jug. If you were cold, whiskey would warm you, and if you were hot it would make you feel cool.

When he heard the noise just outside, he thought it was only another sound from his head – whispers, a feeling of danger returning, glimpses of strange fleeting figures in woods. But then the noise came again, a horse sound, and Ben stood up tall as his door to see who.

In the hot glare of noon, he could dimly make out a skittery horse and a man on it – a white man, holding a long black shotgun. 'Your name Ben?'

Ben did not move. If he reached up for his own gun, just over the doorway, he would be a clean quick blast.

The thin man swung down from his horse. 'You want to step out here a minute, please, Ben,' he said, speaking too loud, as if he assumed Ben was deaf. 'I aint come out here for trouble.'

Ben did not answer.

'Don't know who I am, do you, boy, but I wager you heard of the sheriff. I'm him. Name is Espy. Now step on outside.'

Ben could not move.

'Boy, what you lookin so flippidy? You aint been breakin no law now, have you? Already said I aint come here for trouble.' He led his horse to the stoop. The eyes of his shotgun stared up. 'Shit, I aint messin with you. You too big. You got a trough on this place?'

'Nosuh,' said Ben. 'Got a well.' Ben had never talked to the law in his life, but he knew to say sir and to keep his eyes down. 'Got a bucket inside.'

'Well go on.'

Inside, Ben tried to imagine what he might have done. He could not think of anything. He went out with the pail.

The law stood fanning his face with his hat. 'Go on,' he said, waving the gun. When Ben started around to the well, the law walked beside him. 'Fine house,' he said, 'for a nigger house. This whole house is yours?'

'Yessuh. I build it myself.'

'Who owns the land that it sets on?'

'Welsuh, I rackon I do.' Ben tied the rope to the pail and let go: a far splash.

'You got a paper to show that?' said Joe Espy.

'Well nosuh, don't member no paper. Muss Bates, she say I could stay here on it.'

'Miz Bates? Which Bates? Only Bates I recall was the one

that burned up in that house right up yonder. Long time since that happened. Seem to me nothin been probated on it. Seem like it's bound to be county propty, by now.'

Hand over hand, Ben hauled on the rope. 'Welsuh, been livin right here all along.'

'Well now, that don't tell me that it's yours. If somebody was to ask, they might find out you livin on propty belongs to the county. Reckon they would, brother Ben?'

'I don't rightly know, suh.' Ben trailed after the sheriff, who seemed to know the way. 'Muss Callie, she always say I could stay here long as I needin to.'

Joe Espy set down the can. 'If she aint wrote it down somewhere on paper, it comes out just a dead woman's word,' he said. 'Let me ask you. You look after the place, so you know there's a barn still up there. If anybody'd been up in that barn, why you'd know it, wouldn't you.'

'Welsuh, done brung them cow down for the summer, ain been by up yonder since then.' Ben hoped his lie did not show in his face.

'Aint seen nobody, then – hmmm,' said the sheriff. 'Aint seen no kind of little old nigger, like the one yall call Hoomama? Sure hate to find out that you did, and then lied to me, boy.'

'Nosuh,' Ben lied again, softer. 'Aint been back up yonder.'

'Aint heard talk of no trouble tonight? I done heard ever nigger in this county whisperin behind my back.'

Under the sweat of his fear, Ben felt a vague relief: the law was not out after him.

He'd had only a glimpse of the stooped-over figure, but he knew her instantly. Old witchy Mary. Come back for trouble, just like the law said. Watch out. A boy on her back, with some white little legs.

'If you was to hear some this talk, why you'd tell me about it, now wouldn't you, boy.'

'Yassuh, sho would, if I did.' Ben wondered what terrible thing they had done.

Joe Espy stopped fanning, and settled his hat on his shiny bald head. 'Hot,' he said. 'Bout near hotter than hell, aint it, Ben?'

'Yassuh,' said Ben, 'sho is.'

'Seem like to you it's bout hotter than it's ever been? Does to me. Seem like hot as it is, like some things might just catch up on fire. Seem that hot to you, Ben?'

'Welsuh,' said Ben, 'sho is hot.'

The horse wore the pail on its nose like a mask. Joe Espy pried it away with his foot. 'Lord, and it would be a shame if some house was to burn, just cause whoever lived there was tellin a lie.'

'I aint now, please, suh –'

'But if somebody was to find out where some trouble was fixin to start, and come tell me, why things might just start to cool off around here.'

Ben's eyes came up. 'What you ax me to do, please, suh?'

'Not a damn thing, Ben, not one goddamn thing, and don't you forget that. Alls I said was how pure goddamn hot it is. Heat must not get to you like it does me.' With a grunt, he climbed up to his saddle. 'I reckon you hear what I say. Go on back to your house. It's a mighty fine house, like I say.'

Ben's heart kept banging long after the law was gone over the field, out of sight down the road. He sweated his only good shirt, standing still.

He had smelled trouble. It hung with that old witchy mama, and that little boy.

He sat on the bed with his jug.

Not half a mile from here, resting beneath a big chestnut tree, up to some kind of no good – the old Hoomama chattering to the shrunk-leg spooky boy.

Just a glimpse of them sent Ben fleeing home, to his jug and his fear. When the law rode up, he was still breathing hard.

Then he lied to save them. Lied to the law. He did not know why. Maybe he just wanted to save someone, once in his life. Maybe it just happened to settle on them.

He took a hot swallow.

Tonight his house would burn. He lied to the law, and the law promised fire.

He began to be cool. There was only a swallow or two, not enough to save. He finished it off. He was no longer shaking. If anything happened, there was always the house just across the cornfield. He could always live there. Lafayette would not mind.

THIRTY-THREE

Boxes. Not enough boxes. Leavings and dyings and white shrunken legs, yellow eyes in a barn, dogs and horses gone wild and the looks in some eyes, rumors, plagues of the children, more boxes, more legs, a dark house in town with its parlor displayed on brown grass in the yard. A horse rearing and bringing back down. Rain on a box, seven watchers beyond.

When William started up weeping or praying, Stella would wait, longing to touch him but waiting, until the only sound was the whisper of wind through the fishing-pole canes. The sun passed over, slid down through the leaves. William did not look up from his knees until one whole side of the sky turned to gold and began fading down, turning red. 'Sister,' he said, 'sister, listen to me. Now that's all. I aint hearin no more. I been hearin all day.'

'I aint through,' Stella said. 'That aint all.'

'Yes it is.' He stood. His knees popped. 'It's enough.'

'You can't say cause you don't know it all,' she said, rising.

William turned away. 'Oh Lord, this is only me here prayin . . .'

'Go on!' Stella cried. 'Pray on! Pray till you're blue in the face! You can't help but hear me!'

William hushed.

'Now, brother, now listen,' she said to his back. 'You got so awful burned that you still aint healed. You got it twisted all up. It was her. It was Mama out there in the barn that night you showed me the light, and all those other nights you say you saw it. And you and me known all along that it wasn't the preacher out there with her, we known it, and never did say it, not once. But it was our mama now, William, our very own mama! It wasn't some bad woman! Don't you see? Don't you even remember her? Think who it was. It was Mama. If she hadn't ever loved somebody sometime, brother, you and me would of never been born! There'd of never been Charlie Boot or Foster or Imogene or the baby. You talk like . . . like she was some kind of a – whore! Like she'd kill her own –'

'Oh Lord, strike the foul words from this –'

'Hush! You hush it!' Stella seized him. He did not pull away. He let her turn him around. 'It's just me here you talkin to, brother. Just me. Nobody else listnin. You aint prayin at all. You just talkin to ghosts.'

William's voice was just air. 'It aint ghost, it's the Lord. It was sin in the eyes of the Lord.'

'No, William, this is Stella! Your sister! And your mama, your very own mama, your brothers and sisters . . .'

Wind brushed the leaves aside, bringing in dark. It washed through Stella, through the sweet fragile picture she'd drawn stroke by stroke, through the years – embellishing, brushing it warmer and warmer, until it was nothing but warm: Mama smiling, the barn and the pea patch, the smell of the babies, and biscuit. The last stroke, so new it was not yet dry, filling the space where a father should be. The wind stirred the colors.

'William, we always did wish for a daddy. You went all that way, just to find him, but that wasn't him in that grave. He was here all the time. I been livin right there in his house, never knowin it was. Not till now. It's the doctor. It's him. I found out too late.'

For a moment, the sound of it made it so true.

William shrugged from her hands, staring at her like a stranger, while she told him everything. 'You don't know,' he said at last, 'you never went out to see. You was always asleep when he came, cept that once. You never did see who it was. And you never once heard what they did.'

Stella shuddered. 'Be quiet.'

'You're all rotten from her sin, it's in both our blood. You the one makin ghost. It aint him. You think maybe if it was somebody from town, some fine rich somebody, then her sin don't count and that fire caught up on its own in her room. But it wasn't nobody fine, sister. Just a man from down the hill. From the closest place. Could have been anybody – could have been Ben, all I know. Or ten men, or a hundred, and he was just the one I saw.'

'No!' The scorching wind of his eyes blew through her skin, and the delicate picture vanished like smoke. 'It's a lie!' Stella ran. She left the gun. She broke from the tangly reeds into dusk, carried out under the giant trees by the blast from his lies. As she passed, the barn door swung out, caught her foot, sent her sprawling.

A hoarse whisper from inside. 'Who that?'

Stella screamed, scrambling up. Someone dark, tall, peering around the door. 'No!' she cried again, then, 'You let me go!' But the hand was too large and too quick on her arm. He breathed a familiar whiskey.

'Mistella?'

'No! You let me go!' She would flee, to the farthest far place, where nobody told evil lies or hid out in dark barns. But then she saw that the big fingers were Ben's.

'Hol on, Mistella,' he whispered. 'Aint hurt you.'

'Ben!' His other hand steadied her. He held her out from him. 'Oh Ben, help me!'

'Come to hep now,' he said. 'Don't you cry. Ain no time.'

'Ben, I've lost my boy! You got to help me –'

'Who that?' He looked beyond her, to William standing in silence.

'It's me, Ben, it's William. I'm Callie Bates' boy. You remember.'

Ben looked slowly from him to the girl in his hands, and then back. 'You aint done it,' he said. 'You dead.'

'I come back.'

Ben did not seem surprised. 'Yall gots to git,' he said. 'White mens come lookin for you.'

'You seen my boy, Ben?'

'Thought he be headin up here, last I seen. Come to warn em. That Hoomama plannin some troubles tonight, pose to hap up here. Them white mens comin. Bad troubles. I tol em old Hoomama ain here, be down to yonder, where Muss Gibson house use to was.'

'But we been waitin all day, Ben! They aint come! Have you seen my Jacko?'

'We gots to git,' Ben said.

As if to answer him, a brilliant sun erupted in woods down the hill. A tremendous concussion rolled up toward them, freeing leaves from the trees as it came.

'Lawdy lawd lawd,' breathed Ben. 'Too late. A somethin done blown.'

'Where can we go?' Stella cried.

'We can wind up in heaven,' said William. 'Let's pray.'

THIRTY-FOUR

The men rode together for sport: to dream up infractions of Negroes, and then track them down; to speechify, terrify, ride like white thunder. Sometimes they used tar and henfeathers and fear. If the crime seemed enough, they used ropes and bloodhounds and shotguns and a more powerful fear. They cut eyeholes in bedsheets, made torches from pine knots, and rode off at dusk. They told their wives nothing.

The day was long gone, but its heat lingered, killing their talk. They rode toward a fat moon, brilliant and hot as the fire streaming from their hands. The terrible glistening thunder of horses rose over a dark cottonfield, savage whipstrokes, and from all throats a weird piercing howl.

The first rider swept past the little gray house, jerked his horse up – a wild scramble of hooves – then he hurled his fire hard through the window. Pounding close behind him, another – a slow looping arc to the roof, and a third through the door. They pulled up, to trade fire for new torches and watch the flames grow in the house.

One more pass. Three fires sailed in. One caught up at the edge of the doorflap, which burned away to reveal swelling illumination inside. The house gave in swiftly. Tongues licked and leaped from the floor. Tendrils dripped from the roof. There was nothing inside but the fire.

The first rider's eyes shone through raggedy holes, then drifted across to the field's other end. He snatched the hood from his head. 'Jesus goddamn, we done burned the wrong house.' He pointed. They all turned to see. Everyone cursed, it seemed even the horses.

'Well whose the hell house did we burn?'

'I don't know. Jesus Christ.' The horses jostled. 'It don't

matter. We'll just burn em both. Hie now, giddon now, let's go!'

Two men tottered up, cheering, sharing a mule. 'Hoo-ee, Cuz,' yelled one, 'look at her burn!'

'But the nigger aint home,' said the other.

'Yonder's the one we wanted,' said the leader. 'Come on!'

They rode for it, flailing and raising their cry, drawing splinters from saddlebags, touching torchpoints. Their attack was identical – first strike the window, then one to the roof, and then one through the door, to make sure. One pass was plenty; this house had fuel inside – a mattress, a chair, a jug that went thoomp! as it burst. The men backed their horses. Fire spread in a pool on the roof. The log chimney tottered, disintegrated. They stayed just beyond the heat's reach.

'Aint a nigger home in this county tonight!' came a cry as the mule straggled up.

The sheriff struggled with his skittery horse. 'Shit!' he cried. 'Ho hey, come on!'

One of the men on the mule told a joke, and the other laughed so hard he nearly fell off. He weaved upright, bringing a flask from his pocket, raising it in a salute to the dazzling inferno. 'Come on out, nigger!' he roared. 'Give us a taste of some nigger barbecue!'

The other one laughed so hard he did not see the arm flicking out. The flask flew from his hand to the dirt. Both men dove after it. Their skulls cracked hard. The flask dribbled out its last, just as hands seized it.

'Aw now, come on now, who'd go do a fool thing like that!' They blinked up, still dazed in their sheets.

'Yall are drunk.' The leader's voice glittered with fury. 'Get your ass up and go. We got no need for a pair of damn drunks.'

'That you, Joe?' said the brave one. 'We aint drunk, Joe, we just havin some fun.'

'*Fun.*' It came out a curse.

Other riders arrived: 'What's goin on, Joe?'

'Hey, no names!'

'Well what the hell, nobody out here but us, and we know who the hell we are . . .'

'Yeah, we a bunch of fools that's wasted a night just to burn down a couple of nigger shacks. Thout even a nigger inside. I say let's all just go home.'

'We aint done yet,' Joe Espy said. 'We just warmin up. That old Hoomama's set up a fight. Hear niggers talkin, she's got ever black face in the county het up to burn down the town and run wild on the rest.'

'I aint just –'

Then the tarpaper roof dissolved to tatters and fell in. New air rushed into the fire: bright thunder: detonation: a cloud of pure exploding fire.

The walls opened out like petals, crushing the mule and two men.

The horses squealed, stumbling back.

Something immense and on fire sailed toward the sheriff. It looked like a man. Espy flung his arm over his face, pitched off, screaming, 'Holy sh –'

'Jesus God, I been burned!'

'No you aint! Just your sheet –'

'Come away, Fred, get up now and run!'

One man staggered blindly after the others, entangled in fire, sobbing and fighting to unwrap himself from the bedsheet. Strong arms threw him down. 'Roll, man! Go on!' cried the sheriff. 'Just roll on over!'

'Jesus Lord God, I been burned!'

'No you aint, Aubrey, you shut your damn yap and come help me.' Joe stood over the burning man, wanting to grab him, but his hands would not touch the fire. 'Roll over, Hobart! Oh goddamn, goddamn, I can't put him out . . .'

A fog of black sweet stinging smoke wafted in, choking all the fire in an instant. Coughing, colliding, all shouting at once: 'I can't see! Oh Lord God, I gone blind!'

'No, it's the smoke! Come this way!'

The sheriff found an opening in the dense wall of smoke and fled through, into night air infested with stars. He whirled. The cloud covered half of the field and was still swelling fast. He moved just ahead of it, led by the moon and the dying dim fire of the first house.

His hands searched the air for oaths. 'Damn,' he yelled. 'Damn damn it damn. I aint goddamn believin it.'

'Joe.' Behind him, a Martin escaped. Joe Espy was not sure which one it was. There were three just alike. 'Joe, it's me. It's all right. What the hell . . . Jesus God, Joe, what blew?'

Another man emerged in blackface. 'Yall got out!'

Words came from their feet, from a cotton row, from the man who had stumbled out burning. 'Am I dead?'

'Well hell no,' said the sheriff. 'Get up.'

'I can't,' he said. 'I'm dead.'

The sheriff nudged the man's ribs with his toe. 'Get up, Hobart,' he said. 'You aint dead.'

'That aint Hobart,' a voice said: the deputy. 'The wall fell in on both Hobarts.'

The sheriff stared down. 'Well then, who the hell is this here?' This nudge brought a groan.

'Let me be.' He did not lift his face.

'Joe, he aint one of us,' Martin said. 'He's too big.'

The man groaned again, and rolled over. They could not tell who: just the wisps of a burned away beard, and white eyes, and black smoke.

'Mister, who the hell are you?'

'Name's Gibson,' he said. 'Or it was, but it aint nothing now. That was back when I still was alive.'

'Where you from?' said Joe Espy. 'What the sam hell you doin out here?'

'I'm *from* here.' A deep growl from his chest. 'But I went and come back. And then somethin blew up.'

'What you mean?' Joe Espy's eyes narrowed. 'Whad you put in that house?'

'Powder,' Gibson said, struggling to sit. 'A whole brand-new keg. And a full jug of kerosene too. I was spreadin it out, and then all kind of fire come in, and it blew. It blew right where I was. Bam. It was loud. And the next thing I know, I aint dead . . .' He rubbed his eyes.

'You come to blow up that shack?' said the deputy. The man nodded. 'Hell, we come out to burn it.'

'Burnin don't work, not out here,' Gibson said, grunting to

his feet. The men could see smoke still drifting from his skin. 'Plenty of burnin been already tried.'

'What the hell business you had with that nigger?'

'Not just him,' Gibson said. 'Whole heap more than just him. The whole place. From the top of that hill down to where my old house . . .' He looked up. 'It's all bad. Ever last inch. How yall know we aint dead and just thinkin we not?'

'Cause we aint,' Martin said.

'If we aint, I'm the same as that boy now,' Gibson said. 'I ought to be dead but I aint.'

Behind them, the mass of smoke began to rise. Nothing was there anymore, not a flicker of fire, only splinters of wood where the house used to be. Only smoldering dirt, and the smell.

'I tell yall,' Joe Espy said, 'I bet that nigger is laughin the laugh of his life, long bout now. And I hope he laughs while he can. We got fire. Any yall seen my horse?'

'Yonder,' the deputy said.

The men felt the heat of the earth through their boots as they followed the sheriff. 'Yall move it,' he said. 'I got an idea. Aubrey. The three of you go on out yonder, all way round that hill. Set your fires in a line. It's dry. Wind's kickin up. We'll go this way and meet you.'

'Joe . . .'

'If it looks like id burn, burn it,' the sheriff said. 'Now go on.'

'I done told you,' said Gibson. 'Burnin's been tried here already.'

Joe Espy smiled. 'There's more kinds of fire than one.'

THIRTY-FIVE

A snake rattle punctured the air: shik a shik a shik a shik shik! A wild chant, a hundred wild singers and shouters, their harmonies rising, colliding, slithering out through the cracks in the barn. A glow, like a new moon held captive inside: shik a shik shik!

Jacko sat hidden in a thicket of fishing poles, watching dark somebodies steal across the yard and into the barn. The canes sprang back up from his hand. Already, more people than the barn would hold, and more coming, alone and in quick little groups.

'Hooo, whad I tell you?' Brown Mary leaned down, with a grin and a flash of her tooth. 'You hear? Hear em shout! Liss em sang! And they sangin for us! Now you member yo trick, swee petunia?'

Jacko wiggled his thumb.

'And now how bout yo words?'

'I think so . . .' He peered out through the fishing poles. 'All them came here for just us?'

'For you, witchy boy,' Mary said. 'You gone see. Tell us yo words now, one mo last time.'

'I know em,' Jacko said. 'I know em good.' The reins tugged his hand. 'Woof's ready too.'

'Say who?'

'Woof,' Jacko said. 'That's his name.'

Mary whistled, down low. 'Like to be the fust goat called that,' she said. 'Leastways, you won't get confuse.'

'I like it,' said Jacko. He put out his lip.

'Well that's who he gone be, then,' said Mary. 'Mistah Ornery Woof, like you say.'

A soft bleating, in answer.

'Petunia, you stay put here with yo Mistah Woof while I run
on to tell em you comin,' she said. 'Gone rise up tonight! Got
us fine kind of band, hooo! Ain never could done it without
witchy boy!'

'Somebody's comin,' said Jacko.

'Babe, most all is done here.'

Jacko pinched his nose. 'I mean somebody else,' he said.

'Well ain them white mens.' She started out through the
thicket of reeds. 'Bro Prentiss done fox them boys up. Spread
the wrong word. Sent em a invotation to the wrong place.' She
strutted off, outlined in light from the barn. 'You come on when
I give a hoot.'

Jacko struggled to remember all the words Mary had taught
him, the way to make fire with his hand – a cotton boll dampened
with lamp oil, a tiny white wick in his fingers, a flintstone and
flint. He rubbed two fingers down into his palm. A blue flame!
Easy magic, once you knew how.

He was not sure he knew all the words. There were too
many. Brown Mary said to just play like he knew, and he'd
know, or they'd all think he did, anyway. Jacko was not sure
what a witchy boy was, but he tried to think like one.

From his pocket, a sly silver whistly sound. He touched the
lump. Maybe he was wrong about it. Maybe it brought him good
luck and not bad. Maybe it was why he was almost a witchy
boy, with a whole band of brown mamas and daddies to love him
and bring him cool drinks.

He scratched. His nose had itched since the sun went down,
but this was a new kind of itch.

He wished Munner could see him now, driving. She would be
proud.

An Amen! swirled out from the barn, and the door opened,
flooding the yard with warm light. Brown Mary's shadow
stretched over the yard, beckoning to him with both arms.

Jacko clicked his tongue, and lifted the reins. 'Go, Woof!' he
cried. The goat moved ahead. The fishing poles fell down to
clear out a path.

The whole choir fell silent, except for a high shrieking trill,
like a bird: 'Oo ooh take it take it!'

Jacko peered past Brown Mary, into the golden fog of smoke and brown people stomping and wheeling and shouting hot joy. 'Sweep me, hoo Lawdy, come sweep us away!' Mary cried, clapping time to the beat. She turned back to the mist of their noise. 'Cheeruns! Hear me, I say! Got a witchy boy ready to rise!'

In a breath, the barn hushed. Shik shik sh – Brother Prentiss lowered the round rattly thing in his hand. All eyes turned to the door.

As Jacko glided in, he could see all the people – old brown men, hats in one hand and lanterns in the other, tall ones, fat ones, short skinny ones, brown babies cradled in arms. Retha waved from their midst.

Jacko waved back and sat tall. 'Go on, Woof, don't be scared.' The goat lifted its beard, let out a trumpety fanfare, ba-raaaaaat! and marched in. The people fell back to the walls.

Jacko felt their astonished eyes washing him and the goat, the white shroud of spiderwebs on the wagon. No one breathed.

'Cheeruns,' said Mary, one claw on his shoulder, 'all yall done liss what I say. Now just look what I brung.'

'Sweet Jesus,' a voice said. 'Sweet God.'

'He drivin that thing like a chariot hoss!'

'Do like she say –'

'Oh dear Law –'

'See his legs!'

'Brothern suster!' Brown Mary announced. 'Yall gone sang him a song?'

'Oh yeah, Mama!'

'Well sang it then, cheeruns, give on! Bro Prentiss, give shake to yo sweet tambourine!'

The brother obliged. A great song sprang up, and it sent a warm fever of pleasure through Jacko. After the song, Mary would say her speech, and then he would say his, and then the lights would go out. And then, Jacko's trick.

Each singer sang a different song, but they blended together like voices of birds in the trees. A man to one side squeezed a box, and its stale honk kept time to the shik a shik shik!

Suddenly, Jacko did not know his words.

How did it start? If he could just remember that . . .

The box wheezed its last. All throats opened and exhaled a long note; some people babbled on after the end.

'Sang more more!' Jacko cried. Woof stamped and bucked.

'Fo we sang again,' Mary said, 'less us lissen a minute.'

'Say it, Hoomama!' said someone in back.

'Make him show us!'

'Show you what, Brother Arant?' Brown Mary squinted into the crowd. 'You see him. What else you want see?'

'What you say he can do,' said the cool hidden voice.

'Oo weee, Devil Doubt, now jump up and run out!' She pointed a finger. 'Ain been believe without seen you a trick? Now yall hear me. I been preachin so long, but yall still ain believe. Oh now, yall believe in ol Hoomama, blieve, say, "Ol Hoomama, she got the power, wo yeah!" But liss when yo Hoomama tell you. This boy got it *twice*. Great Law lookin down, he lookin on all our po tribilations!'

'Amen! Tell it, Mama!'

'He done seed how the Hoomama bout to be old, be too old to lead all of the cheeruns to rise! Done sent us a boy now, this boy with some legs, and the power! Done touch that ol boy with some fire. Done suck out he life juice, done send him to spreadin the punishinment. This boy spread it, cheeruns, he live thu it all. Come to show all us how to spread, come to show us we gots to rise up!'

'Whooo! Praise the Law!'

'Done rode in a chariot, done tame the dumb beast, Bro Arant, what mo you want? Now he ast yall to sang! Will you sang?'

And they all cried yes, yes, and they sprang up again in their glorious song. Jacko beat time on his feet.

THIRTY-SIX

Fire in these woods! Ben again! Stella plunged after him through the creek. Her life had come circling back like a dog to its tail, circling fire back to fire, again Ben! from the years, shouting danger, and William! now raving and mad as the Preacher – dead, gone, and buried, and never their father, because William said . . . oh, but none of it mattered now, not who she was, not who created her, not what evil might have burned in the past, because a great fireball rose up and vanished in smoke, and now loud shouts and hoofbeats, the flicker of torches approaching through trees.

For someone so slow, Ben moved fast. 'Ben! Slow down! I can't keep –'

'Hush, Miz, giddown now . . .' They hid in a dense thorny bush. She felt the rumbling up through her knees. Horses flashed by on the path, so close she felt spatters of mud on her face. Maybe three horses, or five. Stella kept her head down.

An argument, saddle to saddle: 'Goddamn nigger doublecrost us –'

'Not for long –'

'We gone take care of him . . .'

The thunder went on up the hill. 'Ben!' Stella whispered. 'Where's my brother?'

'Posed to be down at Muss Gibson . . .'

'No, I mean William. He aint behind us.'

'He done lost us,' said Ben, springing out of the bush. 'Ain no time, Miz. We gots to git on.'

Let William go. He was already gone seven years, in her mind. To come back with his wild visions, to slander her warm colored picture with his ugly one – it seemed a worse crime than his leaving.

Her foot struck a slippery place and she slid, crying out, down from darkness and into the shimmer of moonlight, a muddy road. Ben raced ahead, and Stella followed him across a yard once so green and neat-trimmed, to a tangle of vines where a white house should be.

'Ben! They aint here! Oh they're gone!' She heard his footsteps echo through the house, hollow as her steps on the day she found Gibson gone and nothing inside.

'Somethin bad,' he murmured, towering over her. 'Tol em to stay from up yonder, cause there's where them law headin. Tol em to move it down here. Somethin bad . . .'

Stella went to the porch. 'Look, Ben,' she said, 'hurry, look.' She smelled him beside her. 'Aint that fire?'

'That my house,' Ben said, oddly resigned. 'That where we heard the boom.' Stella followed his finger to a dim glow through the trees to the east.

'No, Ben, *look*!' She pulled his hand to point out west. 'See up yonder? That's my mama's place! That's where we just come from, Ben, that's my home!'

In daylight, the woods would have obscured it, but she could see it plainly now, in the dark: a glittering necklace of fire, alive, sparkling, a chain of bright fire, draping the dome of the hill in a circle, beginning to close.

'Come on, Ben!' She was down the steps, halfway across the yard, before she knew he was not following. She turned back. 'You comin?'

Ben took two steps down, and stopped.

'I can't blame you for not,' Stella called. 'But I got to find Jacko.' There was no time to convince him, or thank him. He was done. This was her fire to fight. Stella ran.

THIRTY-SEVEN

'My name is Jack Otis Bates.' To his own ears, he sounded too loud. His words seemed to roll off their faces, like sweat.

Little Brown Mary leaned down. 'Give on, tunia,' she whispered.

'I can't,' Jacko said. 'I forget.'

'Make him show us, Hoomama.' The doubter was still at the back. All the passion of their singing had fallen to silence when Jacko raised his hand. Sister Retha wiped her face with a bright red kerchief, and smiled.

'Gots a few word, Bro Arant, and then come the trick.' Mary detached a web from Jacko's nose, where he had rubbed it. 'Just start with yo name,' she said softly.

'My name is Jack Otis Bates,' he began again, 'or else Jacko. That's what my Munner calls me.'

A cough, in a hand. A brown lady told a wriggling girl to be still.

Jacko looked up. It all seemed so easy. *Just think like you know* . . .

'And then you was born,' Mary prompted.

'And then I was born . . . and then . . . then I was borneded again, in a fire!' He saw Mary nod. Hundreds of hot eyes on him. '. . . and touched by the fire, but I was too little, but I think . . . I got touched by the fire?'

She grinned. 'Hooo now, cheeruns, been touch by the fire! Give on, witchy boy!'

'And it touched me,' he said, growing bolder, 'and I think it took all the juice out of my legs.'

'Sweet do Jesus,' said Retha. 'Do Lawd.'

'And then's when my legs wouldn't walk,' Jacko said, 'and that's howcome . . .' He paused. 'That's howcome . . .'

'He say that's howcome the fever,' said Brown Mary, squeezing his shoulder. 'That's howcome all kind of some white cheer-

uns, black cheeruns both done be strick down with it. Done
been touch in the legs, just as same as this boy.'

'Yeah, now I member,' said Jacko. 'All that's the howcome
part. And then I say, now I got saveded out of the fire, so I
could come back and tell yall what it was. I come to keep you
from gettin burned up.'

'That just hoodoo talk,' said the deep voice in back.

The goat looked around to see who. The brown sea of faces
looked too, and began muttering, turning, all eyes at once, to
the doubter. Their hands passed him down the wall, opened the
door, pushed him out. Someone slammed it behind him.

'Now Judas, he gone,' Mary hollered. 'Who goin on with him?'

No one said a word. They all looked at Jacko. He lifted both
hands, turned the palms out in front of him.

'Not yet, tunia . . .'

Jacko grinned, shut his eyes, and bent both thumbs back, just
as far as they would. He heard someone say, 'Law.' He opened
his eyes, bent them more, strained and gritted his teeth, until
the thumbnails reached all the way back to his wrists.

The tambourine crashed to the ground. 'Make him quit it,
Hoomama!'

Mary grabbed his thumbs, one each in a hand, and gently
moved them back to their usual place. 'Sweetie,' she said, 'you
done spent all yo trick fo we done.'

'That's just one trick,' Jacko said.

'But you still got some mo yet to say!' Mary turned to the
awed silent band. 'This boy come here to tell all yall cheeruns
the time come to rise! Got to rise! And it's risin tonight!'

'That's the part I forgot,' Jacko said.

'Say he touch by some fire, but been save for tonight. Save
to lead all yall out –'

'Say to rise!' Shik-shhhh, Brother Prentiss retrieving his
tambourine. 'Amen, Mama, and we ready to rise!'

'I can do it,' said Jacko. He straightened. 'I member it now.
Say you niggers all been put down –'

'Sooooo,' Retha breathed.

'Give on, swee petunia, just watch what I told you and not,'
Mary said.

'I mean come to tell all you brown folks that the time comes tonight. And I . . . I'm own hep you. I'm own bring down the power, to keep yall – to hep yall to rise!' That was all. He was through. He sank down in the webs.

Mary showed her tooth, and flung her hands up. 'Hear it said!' she cried. 'Hear it! The time come to rise!' Her feet danced a quick little jig. 'Got us all here, cheeruns! Got us a big enough band, now yall ready to rise?'

And they all roared together they were, oh they were.

Mary bent to Jacko's ear. 'You done it, big man! Hooo, din I tell you!'

Jacko clapped his hands. The string of the fire trick dangled from one sleeve. The flint flew away, to the floor.

'Cheeruns! Liss up to me!' The din lessened, but babies cried, startled awake. 'We all set! Got white mens a comin. They be late. They be late, but they come. These some boys we been troublin with all our life. And they daddies was troublin, fo them, and the granddaddies troublin, them Gray! The troublin go all the way back!'

The infants wailed high, in alarm. The goat shifted and bucked. 'Be still, Woof.' Jacko tugged the reins, scratching his nose. 'Mary, somebody's comin . . .'

'Hear the witchy boy speak!' Mary pranced in a circle, cackling high. 'Hooo, they comin, he say, say they near to most here! Got to rise!'

Mary's face met the door as it swung. She tumbled to the ground. William staggered in, snagged his foot on Mary's leg, and hit down on one knee. His eyes came up.

'Rise up!' Retha screamed, and the band surged around him, attacking with feet and the swell of their shouts.

'Get his head!'

'God Lord Jesus, gone rise!'

'Get his neck!'

Jacko watched Brown Mary climb up, shaking her head, then she tore into the mob with both hands, shouting. Her cry mixed with the grunts and the popping of ribs. She threw back her head, opened her mouth, and let fly a sound that bashed all the noise like frail glass: 'Hoooooooooooooo!'

She yanked arms away. 'I say *Hooo*! Stop it! Git! Go on, git back!'

She pulled the last hand off the man on the ground. 'Cheeruns, yall risin good, but you risin too soon!' she announced. 'This ain a one of them mens. This a stranger.'

The crowd shuffled back. William lifted his face. 'Oh my God,' he groaned. 'Dear blessed Jesus.'

Mary touched him with her wrinkly hand. 'White boy,' she said, 'is you broke? Is you been broke for good?'

'This is me,' William croaked. 'Lord, this is only me, William.' He pulled his legs up to his chest. 'Lord, I know you aint hearin, cause it's just me prayin, and with all my sins, Lord, I aint deservin you listenin . . .'

'What he sayin,' said someone in front.

'He aint sayin,' said Mary, 'he prayin.'

'Honey,' said Retha, 'way he come in that door, he be lucky to still have the air. Sweet Lawd.'

'Hear me, Lord, cause you got to, just this once.' William got to his knees. 'I come all this way, Lord, you brung me back, and I'm here, and I'm prayin it now. Bring down your fire again, Lord, bring it down on this place –'

'Who you, boy?' Mary tapped on his arm. 'You done eat up with it. What's yo name?'

'Lord, you brung it here once, you set fire to the sin, but there's some left that didn't catch up! Lord, have mercy! Have mercy and bring down your fire!'

A scream: hands on ears: Sister Retha. 'Sweet oh sweet Jesus! Oh Jesus, fire! Oh sweet Jesus heavenly fire!' She fell in a swoon.

Jacko shut his eyes tight, yanked back hard on the reins, felt the goat lurch ahead through the forest of legs.

'Lissen, cheeruns!' Brown Mary leaped on a haybale, but her cries drowned in the vast flood of terrified sounds, the wild panic that set the roof buzzing. Everyone saw through the cracks in the walls.

Someone's hand pulled the rope on the door.

A violent heat burst in.

Jacko looked to a world made of fire.

THIRTY-EIGHT

Stella stumbled on, sucked in by the wind of fire. The hill wore fire up to the necks of its trees, in a wavering chain that grew into a fence then a wall then a cloud, roaring, gobbling air as its food, until it was a giant mountain of fire. Peaks of flame leaped. Naked trees waded along the crest, holding out their skinny limbs.

Stella passed through a curtain of vapor to the outermost circle of fire. Her feet did not burn on the scorched smoking earth. Her heart beat *No, faster! Run fast!* In the firelight, all the little pine trees looked too green to burn, but all wore torches in their tops.

Within the borders of her mama's yard, set by the fallen barbed wire, a sheer blinding wall, red, and yellow, and orange, so bright Stella saw it through closed eyes. She was no longer afraid of fire. She put a hand into the wall of it. She felt a chill.

The wall split. Something stuck out its head, and ran through on four feet. A goat pulling something.

A wagon.

White spiderwebs.

Jacko.

Clearing a path with his wagon for Negroes who spilled out behind him, stooped down in the fireless tunnel. They uttered cries, kissed the ground, fled down the hill.

'Jacko!' she called.

He stopped the goat with the reins. Hysterical people flowed around him, and ran.

Jacko looked back. 'Munner!' he crowed. 'Munner, look! See! I'm drivin'!'

Stella froze. The fire felt cold on her hand. She smelled her clothes smoldering.

'Munner, look, look at me drive! Go on, Woof!' He snapped hard. The goat put down its head, and went clanking away.

'Jacko, wait!'

Little Brown Mary dashed last from the flames, slapping out tiny blazes on her overalls. The black tunnel swelled shut behind her. 'Hooo babe!' she hollered. 'Touch by the flame!' She called to her fleeing congregation: 'Come back, cheeruns, we ready to rise!' But no one heard her over the vast roar.

Jacko drove the goat in wide loops, shouting joy.

'Boy, you stop that! You come here to me.'

'White gal, you let the boy drive, seen he brung us all out thu some bad kind of bad.'

Stella whirled. 'You! Oh, I knew it was you all the time!'

'Sho now, gal,' Mary said, 'it was me seen some troublin all set to fall down on this child. So I toted him off just in time.'

'*You.*' Stella put a hand up to the glare. 'Jacko! Stop it! You hear me, boy?'

Jacko heeded the tone of her voice, and pulled up. She examined him in the firelight. He looked fine: just his hair was messed up. He looked fine. 'Boy,' she said, 'listen to me. Turn your face here to me.'

'Munner, don't,' Jacko said.

'No I mean it, boy, look here to me. You ever run off like that . . . you ever run off from me again that way, just go off without – look here, Jack Otis – without even goodbye . . . well. I make you wish you was somebody you aint.'

'Munner –'

'After all that's gone on, Jacko. And what do you do but the foolheaded thing? Howcome didn't you yell for me? Howcome you took off that way?'

His face fell. 'But she said you was comin,' he whined.

'Who you listen to, boy? Her or me? Who raised you? Her or me? They aint no excuses this time, Jacko.'

'Gal, you ought not lay all it on him,' said Brown Mary. 'Lay some on me. I take it. I meant you no sorra. I left you a trail.'

'What trail?'

'Child, his rollidy thing. Had my writin boy write it down on a note, stuck up under them wheel. Thought for sho you would see.'

'It's still there,' Stella said. 'Where I left it.'

The fire sank down to the size of the hill, turning deep red, beginning to die. 'Munner, you ought to of seen,' Jacko said. 'I membered all the words. You ought to seen me do my trick.'

'Jacko, hush —'

'Now, gal, pay you some heed what he say,' Mary said. 'This boy make the fire stand aside. Just you ax him the way, he gone cut you some road with them goat!'

Jacko snapped fingers. No fire came out. He had dropped the trick back in the barn. 'Munner, I know what's wrong,' he said.

'What?'

'I know what's wrong. It was somethin I took,' Jacko said. 'It was bad.' Reaching down in his pocket, he brought out the white rag and unwrapped the shiny gold lady inside.

'I can't see.' The light was fast fading. 'What is it?'

'It's somethin I took,' Jacko said, 'but I din mean to, Munner. I meant just to look and to put it right back. If we just put it back, it'll all be all right. Munner, please put it back . . .'

Stella weighed the cool coin in her palm. 'Jacko, where'd you get this?'

He winced. 'From his drawer. From the doctor. I saw it, but I meant to just look —'

'And you stole it.' She glared down at him. 'You liked it. You stole it from him. And he's dead now, aint he, boy, he's dead!' The coin fluttered up, twinkling, sailing into the fire.

'Munner, I took somethin else too,' Jacko said. He avoided her eyes. His fingers found the lump in its ratty white cloth. 'See what I found.'

He revealed the plump ball of green glass.

Colors swirled in its heart.

'Jacko Bates,' she said, 'where in this world did you . . .'

'Down yonder,' he said.

Stella clutched at his elbow. 'It was her favorite thing,' she gasped. 'Where on earth? Tell me, boy.'

'Down yonder,' he said, 'by that house where the stuff all

growed up. She left me there, Munner. I found it. Munner, she left me there all by mysellllf . . .'

'Jacko, you hush your mouth.' Down at Gibson's!

The crystal transfixed them. They watched the fire die in its curve. Callie's favorite thing. From the sideboard to Gibson, to Jacko's small hand. 'I found it,' he said, drawing back. 'It's mine.'

'Boy, you give it to me –'

Torches approached. Jacko slid the treasure under his dress. The men cantered up, bearing fires and shotguns. 'Don't move.' A rumble. 'Stay right where you are.'

'Come away from there!' cried the next rider, jostling his horse. 'You're burnin! You're burnin!'

'Git up, Woof!' Jacko tugged, and hard, and then harder. The goat did not budge. It seemed to recognize the black eyes of the guns.

Charred strips of cotton trailed down from their saddles. Stella saw through the black soot and beards, to their faces – the sheriff, his deputy grinning, and a man who could not be.

But he was.

Stella knew by the diamond eye of his horse, the spine bowed by the years of his weight, and then she knew the black flash of his eyes, his hair blown wild, his beard burned away, his quick tongue on his lips.

'Mister Gibson,' she said, 'you come back.'

He climbed down heavily, keeping his aim on Stella, his eyes out into the hot red. 'I said stay where you are,' he said. He pinched the knot on his saddlehorn. A body crashed down. It was Ben, with ropes around his throat, arms, and ankles. He flopped like a fish in the dirt.

'Looka here,' said Joe Espy. 'Look what he caught.'

The fire made Stella strong. 'Let him go,' she said. Gibson flinched at the power of her voice. 'There's not one of you fit to kill him.'

A pecan tree sent its biggest limb crashing down.

'Mister Gibson,' said Stella, 'I heard you was my daddy.'

His eyes tore away from the flames. They found her. Deep fire.

'That what you heard,' Gibson said.

She silenced Jacko with a hand. 'Is it true? It can't be . . .'

'Come away,' said the sheriff. 'Man, come away from the heat.'

Gibson's eyes said it was true. 'Who told you?'

Joe Espy coughed. 'Aubrey, watch out, the nigger aint dead.'

The deputy swung down, rope coiled in his fist. He bent over Ben.

'Tight,' said Joe Espy. 'You make sure.'

Stella made a shield of her arms for Jacko. The spiderwebs clung to her skin. 'Mister Gibson, it was William who figured it out. I didn't believe it. I still don't. But you aint said no to me yet.'

'William who?' Gibson rumbled.

'William Bates, my brother. He's gone crazy from wonderin who, Mister Gibson. He thinks it was you used to come to our barn. Said you was friends with my mama. I don't want to think it, now please, Mister Gibson, just tell me you aint.'

'Where'd he go?' He spun down from his horse. 'He got out?'

'Boy got out from the first burnin,' said Little Brown Mary. 'But he stood still for this one. He shoutin. He prayin to burn.'

The sheriff poked her ribs with his gun. 'You shut up.'

'He still in there? Yall just leave him?' Gibson's eyes were bright wild.

The deputy lifted Ben's head with a rope. 'You gone burn,' he warned.

Gibson straightened his shoulders. He braced for the heat. 'Fire can't catch me,' he said. 'I never been burned. I come back to finish it now, and I'm gone.'

He set up a cry, lunged away, and the cry drifted after.

'Wait!' Stella reached out. 'Daddy, wait!'

'I'm burnin for you, Stella,' he said, and went charging in. A fresh sweep of wind whipped the embers. He seemed to lose his way, then found it again, stumbled on, burning, toward the barn, through the door, then the tin roof fell in and the fire consumed him. His strange cry dissolved in the flames.

'Whoa!' Joe Espy tried to fall off his horse, but he could not. It went storming in, bucking, straight into the fire. The deputy's horse thundered after. The horses galloped through fire to the largest pecan, stood up, screamed, shucked their riders, glanced down once with the whites of their eyes, and came down.

The wind died.

Sparks curled spiraling down, like stars freed from the sky. Stella felt something wet on her cheek. She held out her hand. A drop struck there, then another. The rain slashed down hissing, and rising as steam from the fire.

Jacko clapped his hands.

THIRTY-NINE

Rain and wet smoke and the last of bright fire, wild dancing, the bones bumping bones. If Stella could find a place out of the rain, she could dream a new dance for herself, without bones.

'Gal, just leave him,' said Little Brown Mary. 'Ain time nor the shovel to bury em all.'

'But we can't leave him out in the rain.'

'He all right.' Mary slipped the noose up over his head. 'Found him some quiet.' Ben's eyes watched them both without blinking. 'Got some mo to worry about. Like yo boy. I done wrong bout his kind of power.'

'You the one who told him all them things, you showed him the tricks . . .'

'Honey.' She whistled out, low. 'He done tricks I ain taught. He gone out on his own.'

Stella shivered. She could not remember a time without rain. 'Jacko aint but a boy,' she said, 'or least not till you put all them wild ideas in his head.'

'Hooo, gal, and ought not to done it,' Brown Mary said. 'Ought to smelt bad round that boy. But I din. And now all the troublin's on you.' She was rubbing the talking blood back to her arms. 'Ain a thang of yo doin, babe. It's yo blood. It go all the way back. Yo po mama, she wrop up in troublin –'

'Oh please don't,' Stella said. 'Don't you start in on her too. William was crazy with lies about her.'

'Nare a lie,' Mary said, 'cep she wadn't no bad gal. I know her a long time fo you come, child. Brung all yall babes to this world, cept that boy ridin yonder. You got to thank like she was. Had nare mama nor daddy, nobody but ol Little Mary. She just a little ol gal, not as big as you now. Honey, she take her a smile where she get it. She don't know howcome to not. This boy come up a smilin. A right good old boy. She tatch up to him quicklike, and fo you can say spit, she swoll up with babe. But you see, he done already married.'

'You mean . . . you mean Mister Gibson?'

'Hooo, yeah, but fo he was ever a mistah. He weren't but a boy with the wrong kind of eyes. He hep me bring down that child. He saw them legs, sweet petunia, same as me. Saw the wrong way they was.' She took a breath.

'And so we done what we did. Him and me. Saw they wadn't no good use in heppin that po child to live, so we both of us hep it to not.'

'A baby, with bad legs. William said –'

'Hooo, child, they was. And some wrong in her head, after that. She ought done what I say, dig some grave, but she kep it. Like it was a charm from some bad. And kep onto him. She been too powful tatched. I give her a charm, babe, I give it to break that ol spell, but she turn soury on me. She run me on off. Like I was the cause of that old sorra, gal, just cause I was there to see it.' Mary reached out and took Stella's arm as if she meant to hold on forever.

'Gal, yo mama no bad gal,' she said. 'Nor yo Mistah Gibson. Nor yo doctah man. Only yo boy. All the bad get collect up in him, honey, he got it all. He done touch by the fire, like I say. He done keepin the troublin alive.'

'Sounds like everbody done somethin wrong except him,' Stella said. 'But he always gets blamed.'

Jacko drove the goat over. 'Munner, watch! Munner, see, I can drive with one hand!'

Mary's eyes found the crystal. 'Petunia,' she said, 'what you got?'

Jacko's eyes flashed. 'It's mine. You keep away.'

'Hooo now, big man, don't get rile. Show ol Mary what is.'

'No!' He jerked away, clattering. The goat sang. Mary chased him, and snatched the green ball from his hand. Even in moonlight it glowed, swirly green.

'Tunia, I got it now, I see where come the power. This the same witchy ball I give yo mama.'

'Give it back!' Jacko snarled. 'Give it back. It's mine!' He held up his hands, flexing both his thumbs, looking for fear in Brown Mary's face.

'Ain scare me now, boy, I got it,' she said, dancing out of his reach.

'Give it here,' Jacko warned.

'This the thang, gal,' Mary said. 'He cain do nare a trick, now it's mine.'

The crystal took on a weird glow in her hand. Green fire burst inside. She flung it away, put her hand to her mouth, howling. The crystal lazily rolled to the ground beside Jacko. He leaned from the wagon and retrieved it.

Mary stared down, sucking on her fingers. 'Gal, make him give it to you.'

Stella held out her hand. 'Jacko, give it to me.'

'No!'

'I'll whup you, I swear . . .'

'Oh no you won't,' he said. 'You aint *never* gone whoop me.'

She saw someone new, not her innocent boy. He looked the same, but his eyes burned a new way.

'Here,' he said. The crystal was dark. He put it in her hand. 'Hold it up to your ear, Munner. It makes a sound. It'll sing you to sleep.' He patted his knees. 'You can rest here, Munner. I'll stay up while you rest.'

She sank to the wagon, her legs dangling over the side. Little Brown Mary had slipped away, somehow. Stella's ears caught all the sounds of the woods – liquid patter on leaves, and a damp hum of insects, some far yelping treefrogs, and a whistling hooo! . . .

And the dark.

FORTY

Pile troublin on troublin, up higher and higher, till purt soon the lightnin got no choice but to strike. Once it struck, lightnin strikin to stay. Hooooooo, gal, done stir up one troublin too much. Done stir up a band, yassuh, stir em up good. Got some shrink-legged boy got em all to believin and sangin, and ready to rise like I say. Got em all set to spread trouble. Mm-hmm. Done spread. Spread Bro Prentiss, po Retha, the rest of em, out thu some wood. Spread a smile on some God-crazy white-boy face, spread him out flat, so he pray for some fire. Spread all my cheeruns to run back to home.

Ain gone make up no band, not in this lifetime. Made up just one band too many. Mm-*hmmmm*.

Ought to not let out a cat from his bag. Got the power, that right, but some mo kind of power.

Old kind of eye, when they set in to lyin. To showin things ain never hap. Comes a time then to shut em. Just stop em from seein. Go back where you come.

Sometimes, old libitty snake run by next to yo feet, little brown snake, same brown as the dust. If you stop to look down to him, at them sparkly eyes, he might get to seem like not the bad kind of snake. Them ol shiny eyes, teasy like, baby snake eyes. Might pick him up like he some kind of playpurty. Might take him off with you. Teach him some snaky-like trick.

But a snake be a snake, matter not what you think. Snake cain be nare who he aint. He gone bite. Them po white gal, she blind to him. She cain see snake for them eyes.

Hoooooo, for the troublin.

FORTY-ONE

Stella opened her eyes to a hard morning light, in the bed of a trundling wagon. She was afraid to speak. Someone's lap held her head in the bed of a trundling wagon. When the wheels struck a rut, she heard something rattle beside her – a beat-up red bicycle, inches away, with a silvery bell, shattered spokes, wheels twisted so they would never roll.

'Daddy. Slow down. She's awake.' Stella felt his warm breath on her ear. 'Lay still,' he said.

'She all right?' came a shout from the front of the wagon. Pal Herlong.

'I don't know. She looks scared. It's all right.'

Stella whispered, 'Where are we?'

'We're almost to town,' Luther said. 'We'll be home anytime. You just stay like you are.'

'Luther . . .'

'He got mad, like I said, when he come back and you were gone.' Luther spoke low. 'He busted my bike. But I busted up somethin of his . . .'

'What you telling her, boy?'

'Nothin, Daddy.' A whisper: 'I'll tell you later.' He smoothed down her hair.

'Where's my boy?' Stella lifted her head.

'He's up there.' He motioned to the front. 'In his little wagon. I think he's asleep, but that goat knows the way. I never seen a goat like that.'

The wheels drummed on the planks of the bridge. 'Luther, what did you see out there?'

'I'm not sure,' he said. 'Burned trees.'

'What else?'

'Go to sleep,' he said. 'That's all buried.'

'You buried em all?' Stella said. 'By yourself?'
'Me and Daddy. But now it's all done.'
'I had a bad dream,' Stella said.

FORTY-TWO

UNUSUAL WEATHER
IN COUNTY.

*Seven Stricken Children
Have Recovered, New Dr
Says, Cause For Hope.*

QUARENTINE MAY BE LIFTED

Some Merchants To Re-Open.

*While attending the ceremony marking the passage of the late
Dr R. B. Dannelly, some citizens may have observed the sudden
illness of several children of the town of Camellia. Dr Orville
Pardue of Dead Fall, Visiting Physician, wished to inform
citizens of the marked improvement in those conditions, and in
those of several others stricken in the surround. The infants
have shown signs of recovery, giving cause for new hope.*

*The Quarentine imposed by this disease may be lifted in some
days, he said further, and milk is no longer under suspicion as
the agent of the disease, if gathered in sanitary fashion.*

*The particular affliction is most properly called Infantile
Paralysis, according to most recent scientific terms, and is not
said communicable in usual ways.*

*The late Physician had been in contact with others of his
profession before his passage. The information intended for him
was reviewed by Pardue.*

*Although some new instances have been noted, they are fewer
in number and degree than in the weeks prior.*

Several merchants of Front Street, when questioned, planned to resume commerce at such time as the Quarentine is lifted and normal order restored.

County Peace Officer Joseph Arthell Espy, aged 43, was a native of Belk County. He was elected as Sheriff on three occasions. Surviving are the widow; a brother, Amon Buford Espy; and three children, Junie Sylvia Espy, Elwanda Mavis Espy, and Joseph A. Espy, Jr.

Deputy County Peace Officer Aubrey L. Lomax, aged 34, was a native of Coffee County. Surviving are an aunt, Miss Minnie L. Eubanks.

John Francis Gibson, aged 58, late of the Pigeon Creek Community, was a native of Belk County. Surviving is the widow.

Malcolm Lester Martin, aged 39, late of the Pine Hill Community, was a native of Belk County. Surviving are the widow; seven brothers, DeWayne, Bud, Jimmie, Sam, Jervis, Frank, and Bill S. Martin; and two daughters, Kitty Martin and Maude Martin.

Duncan DeWitt Hobart, aged 51, late of the Pine Hill Community, was a native of Belk County. Surviving are the widow, and eleven children.

Frederick B. Gossage, aged 47, was Mayor of Camellia, owner of Gossage Lumber Co., and a member of the First Baptist Church of Camellia. Surviving are the widow, and seven children.

Two others died in the occurrence of this unusual storm, but could not be identified.

An undisclosed number of Negroes had assembled unlawfully near the Pigeon Creek community. The deceased were performing official duty as Peace Officers.

Services were performed at the site.

Acting Mayor Herman L. Middleton wishes to inform the citizenry that steps leading to appointment of Peace Officers, and placement of a new Physician, are well underway.

1918

FORTY-THREE

More time than fits in a clock, since his fingers. Since she kissed his fingernails one at a time in the dark.

He combed his hair to one side, just for her.

She touched his soft hair for him.

And if he never comes again . . . this is enough.

But he will come again.

A dozen times she heard his bicycle bell at the bend where the doctor – but it was just her ears wishing, a branch rubbing the screen at the parlor window.

He said he would come, and she prayed it – to him, not to God. God can send me to hell if he wants. God never gave me a kiss.

But *he* did. And Jacko sometimes, when he wants to play sweet. And Mama. Stella wondered if Mama burned this way. Down deep in the middle. If she handed the burning down.

Then the tap of the toe of his boot on the porch. She drank the sound. Blood warmed her hands. At the door, his glad eyes.

'Hush. Be quiet,' she said.

'Hey.'

'Oh Lord.'

'What?'

'You came,' she said. 'Oh I'm so glad.'

'Give me a kiss.'

'You first.'

'Well . . .'

A kiss, to the cold of her bones.

'Oh Lord, I reckon,' she said.

'What?'

'I just reckon.' She turned. 'They're asleep. Let's go walkin.'

He took her arm at the elbow. She smelled his Ivory soap

and some kind of hair oil, and another smell, rich like the earth after rain. The night had a moon and a mild breeze, caressing.

She thought: The night has a moon, and he has a good heart. I'll watch his heart like I watch to the moon.

'Give you a penny,' he said.

'Bet you would, if you had one.'

'I'm the one sposed to be quiet.'

'Just thinkin.'

'Bout what?' Luther said.

'You.'

'But what? Tell me.'

'I can't,' said Stella.

'Why?'

'I aint as good as you, talkin,' she said.

They broke from the trees. The moon wore a pale halo.

'Don't.'

'Don't what?'

'Don't look at me that way. I feel like you're looking inside me. Like you'd swallow me up.'

'If I could.' He closed his eyes. Stella could see him complete, to the shapes of the bones in his face. And she knew. Mama said *you'll know* and now she did. She spoke with lips but no voice.

Strange, every part of it, the way it felt. Like watching herself all on fire.

'You like that?' he breathed.

'What?'

'This.' Again.

'You silly,' she said. 'Let's sit down.'

'Are you happy?'

She nodded.

'You promise?'

'Listen at you with your sweet talk . . .' she teased him.

'Sweet gal. Wait. Let me spread out my coat.'

A stand of willows on the rise of a hill. Somehow Luther had discovered the place Stella went when she needed to cry. Then a kiss, and then he said, 'We ought to get married.' Like that. Just that fast.

'Oh now, Luther,' she said.

'But I mean it. I want to. I always did, from that very first time I saw you. I carried a telegram all the way out to your mama. I remember your hair . . . just it went down your back, all the way.'

Silence. A flush.

'What you think?' he said.

'I don't know.' She looked out into the dark. 'I don't know if I can.'

'Look at you,' Luther said. 'Why, you're crying.'

'I aint.' She put her hand up.

'Then what is this, then?' He kissed it away. 'I thought you loved me.'

'I just hadn't thought about it, is all,' she said.

'Never?'

'I mean, not . . . I can't say for sure. Not for good.'

Some kind of a dove made a sad note, far off. Stella thought: I don't love anyone, not even him. I don't know how anymore. That part of me died, or I killed it myself. The part that knew how. I built a high wall around it, and now comes this long-legged boy, climbing over.

'Say you want to,' he said.

She wondered if she would ever be healed.

'Say it.'

She wanted to, oh Lord, so bad. 'Well, it's just – I don't know. If I can or not.'

'What?'

'You know. Love you.'

'Howcome?'

'It aint you, Luther. I reckon if I was to love anybody, it would be you. But I don't think I can. Not since . . . you know.'

'Since that night.'

'I don't think I know how,' Stella said. 'I'm scared. I don't deserve you, good as you are in your heart . . .'

'You got to let me, to find out,' he said. 'How else could you know?'

'But you'll just run off to your stupid old war, and you'll die . . . or you'll love me awhile and then make up your mind all a sudden you don't. And I'll come in one day and I'll find just a note sayin how sorry you were.'

'No.'

'Yes,' she said. 'That's the way folks do. The minute you start in to loving em, they go away. You aint different. You don't know. It aint happened to you. But it's the only thing ever happened to me, my whole life.' She stood up. She was no longer crying.

His arm hugged her knees. 'Stella, listen . . .'

'What?'

'I think you just got to quit with your grievin and bury em.'

'They're already buried,' she said. 'All except Jacko.'

'They're dead, but they're not gone from you. You got to let em all go.'

'Oh it's bad, Luther. I feel so bad sometimes. I loved em all so much more when they died,' she said. 'That's just how bad I am.'

He said, 'That all happened way back.'

'Not to me,' Stella said. 'It seems like tonight, every day.'

'You always gone be by yourself?'

'I got Jacko,' she said.

'But you look after him. Who's gone look after you?'

'Honey, if you marry me, you got Jacko. You think about that just a minute. Much trouble as that boy can make, and not even your kin.'

'He will be, if you'll just say yes. He'll be my own boy.'

'No,' Stella said. 'He's not like any boy. He's got some kind of somethin else workin inside him.'

'I aint marryin Jacko,' he said. 'I was talkin to you.'

'Oh, but still . . .' Stella stopped. She felt his eyes touching her, soft as his hands. 'Luther. You got to promise me. Promise you won't ever run off or die.'

'Runnin off aint what I do,' he said. 'And if we're lucky, there's plenty of time before the other.'

'I aint never been lucky, Luther.'

Luther said, 'I think you're fixing to start.' His hand found hers, and she knew: This is what it is. I see his sweet face in the light from the moon. 'Sweetheart . . .'

He brought her down beside him. Leaves rustled under his coat. He spoke so close the words blurred, but she knew what they meant.

His mouth found the soft of her shoulder. What sweetness: a touch in the dark. Oh, a shiver. Oh don't please a hand, and a shiver but warm. She tried oh she tried but oh Lord, in the dark she was glad to be burning, to be holding him hard, to be feeling him holding her harder.

A sweet kind of fire.

FORTY-FOUR

It was only April, but it was plenty warm. Jacko's legs loved to float in the creek. Munner promised to take him. And now she would not. He could go. He could go in his wagon. Jacko wheedled and whined, beat the floor with his fist, cried, and swore he would be good, but Munner did not give in. She peered impassively down from the swing, while Luther just grinned and propelled their slow arc with his toe. Jacko could get his way with just Luther, and sometimes with Munner alone, but not when they sat in the swing together. They rocked, sharing a moony look, holding hands and ignoring Jacko.

'But you promised!' he cried. 'Luther, you heard her promise! She said she would, yesterday!'

Luther said something into Stella's ear. She smiled. 'Luther says you look like a newborn babe, red as your face is.' She whispered something, and Luther laughed.

Luther was her friend now. Nobody but Luther. Jacko felt swatted away like a gnat. He abandoned the fit. He would show them. He would get his way.

'Where you goin, Jacko?' Stella cried. 'Don't run off angry like that. Come on back.'

He propped the screen door on his head, forced the scooter wheels over the doorsill, and let the door slap shut behind him. He waited to hear if she was really sorry, but her laughter came in on a current of air.

Jacko's fists thumped the floor, past the doors, down the hall in quick rhythm. He could harness his goat by himself. He could get in the wagon himself. He could drive all the way to the creek. He pushed into the kitchen. The dishes were draining. Aurelia would sleep for an hour, at least. He went back to his little room, gathered his things in the big red bandanna, raised the loose board on his hiding place. Footsteps came down the hall. Jacko fished fast and tucked it in his bundle, just in time.

Everne Dannelly came to the door. 'I thought I heard some-one.'

'Nome,' Jacko said. 'It's just me.'

'Aurelia give you some dinner?'

'Yessum.'

'That's nice.' She ran a finger through her silvery hair. 'Yall going swimming today?'

'Munner won't take me,' Jacko said. 'She's kissin on Luther. She says it aint hot enough yet.'

'Isn't, dear, isn't.' Everne squeezed her hands. 'I suppose you might catch cold. It's just April. And Luther won't be here much longer. You run let them be. Just go play in the yard.'

'But I don't want to,' he said.

'I think I ought to lie down for a while,' Everne said, almost to herself. 'It's a good thing to get plenty of rest.' She wandered away up the hall. Her door closed softly behind her.

Jacko waited the time it would take her to stretch out with one hand over her eyes, the way she did. Then he retrieved his bundle, tied its corners, and rolled to the screen door. He squinted out. Four scary steps to the yard. At last he found nerve, and a plan. He placed the scooter on the incline, and slid down into the soft dust.

He heard a crack! and a tinkle – Cleo shooting at bottles in the gully. No one in the yard. A long long way across. He heaved, dragging the scooter behind him. It might come in handy. He pulled out to the woodshed. His eyes took a moment to see. He crawled to the nail with the harness, then on to the wagon, yanking its tongs into place behind Woof. 'Good boy,' he whispered, 'be still. You be a sweet goat. We goin swimmin.'

With a long stick, he lifted the harness into place, straining up to tie the knots. He had watched Cleo do it a hundred times. Woof stood quietly.

Hoisting over the edge and into the wagon, Jacko was glad of strong arms. He lay for a moment, to hear, but no one was coming. No one would know he was gone till he was. He had his goat and his treasure, and that was enough. He snapped the reins once. Woof nudged the door, waited for Jacko to pull the scooter in, and emerged clinking into the warm sun of noon.

He drove past the garden, past Aurelia's cabin and the little well, through the tomato rows without disturbing the seedlings. Woof hesitated at the yard's edge, but Jacko convinced him past. He knew where the small road went – straight to the creek, and down through, and on past it forever. If he stayed on the road he would not be lost.

He settled against the backboard. He let Woof stop to nibble the sweeter weeds. There was time. No one was coming. No one loved him any, at all. No one scolded or preached or told stories, or even called him a witchy boy. Munner and Luther just talked to each other about some old war someplace Luther planned to go, or the fine white house they were planning to build in some orchard, when Luther came home.

Jacko was not scared of being alone. He was proud, like the morning Little Brown Mary left him by himself, and he found the green crystal treasure.

The day of the night Munner never would ever remember out loud. The night Jacko learned fire.

A bluefly landed on his hand and prickled the hairs. He snatched it, held it up between fingers to pull off its legs, one by one.

The bundle in his lap jiggled open. Everything he would need, ever: a biscuit from breakfast, the hairbrush from Munner, and the green magic whistly thing.

The red liquid swirls at its heart grew more brilliant the longer Jacko stared at it. The dazzling sun made his eyes heavy. He heard a whistle sing out from the glass: hooooooo!

It called out to Jacko.

It told him the way.

He stared hard. He thought fire in his head. Fire shot from its heart to the yellow blooms of a bush. Foosh! The flowers ignited. That was a good trick to do. Jacko clapped his hands, laughing.

WILLIAM McILVANNEY

THE BIG MAN

Dan Scouler is The Big Man, a working-class legend of physical prowess, fighting for his heritage – a decaying community in a small Ayrshire town – fighting to keep it afloat and intact.

'Inspiring and harshly funny. As in Orwell at his fiercest best, McIlvanney's outrage is all the more potent for being tranquil. Grand fiction that reads as truly as fact, (which says), "this is where we've been and this is where we really are"'
David Hughes, in the Mail on Sunday

'Confirms his reputation as the most incisive observer of working-class Scottish life'
Rob Brown, in the Guardian

'A novel of great power and microscopic observations . . . ambitious material, handled with sharpness and poignancy and full of memorable moments and images'
Isabel Quigley, in the Financial Times

'A prose of growing assurance, with vivid and memorable results'
Douglas Dunn, Whitbread Book of the Year winner, in the Glasgow Herald

sceptre